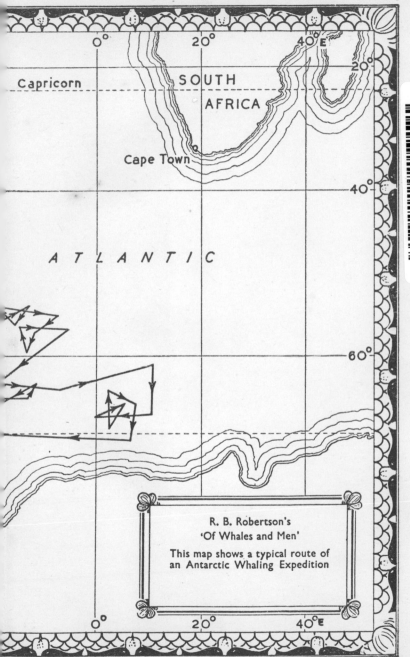

R. B. Robertson's
'Of Whales and Men'

This map shows a typical route of
an Antarctic Whaling Expedition

OF WHALES AND MEN

OF WHALES
AND MEN

BY

R. B. ROBERTSON

THE REPRINT SOCIETY
LONDON

THIS EDITION PUBLISHED BY THE REPRINT SOCIETY LTD
BY ARRANGEMENT WITH MACMILLAN AND CO. LTD., 1958

PRINTED IN GREAT BRITAIN BY
RICHARD CLAY AND COMPANY LTD, BUNGAY, SUFFOLK

TO
KATHARINE TWEED
AND ALL WOMEN WHO
WAIT FOR WHALEMEN

The quotation on page 67 is from 'The Waste Land', in *Collected Poems*, 1909-1935, by T. S. Eliot. (*Faber & Faber Ltd.*)

PREFACE

'IF you're writing a book about whaling,' I was advised by an experienced Whaling Inspector, 'don't tell the *exact* truth. If you do, nobody ashore will believe you, and nobody in the whaling world will recognize you as a whaleman; for no whaleman author ever *has* told the exact truth since Herman Melville set the standard of whaling mendacity.'

I accepted the advice — not because of the literary value the inspector placed on mendacity in whaling tales (obvious though that has been since Jonah), nor yet because I fully concur with the Steinbeck character who said that 'a thing isn't necessarily a lie even if it didn't necessarily happen.' I followed the advice because a strictly factual account of the whaling expedition I accompanied (or any other modern whaling expedition) *could* not, for various reasons, be written. And only one of these reasons is that a doctor cannot talk of his patients, a ship's officer cannot discuss his shipmates, with the candour and veracity he would sometimes like to employ.

Names, characters, timing, and incident must all be changed; and one can only try to change them in such a way that the resultant account gives a truer total picture of a modern whaling expedition than would be the case if one were tied to the sparsity of first-hand fact which can or should be told of one's patients and shipmates, and which one dares to tell of others.

Much of what I have to tell is, of course, based on my actual experiences during a whaling expedition. But much also is based on what I heard and learned during prolonged (incessant would be a better word!) conversation with several hundred whalemen over many months. Every one of those men, whose lives had been spent whaling with many different companies, had a yarn to tell; and if I have thought it worth retelling, it is included in this book in some form or another. My reader is as good a judge of the truth of some of the yarns as I am.

Similarly, the whalemen in my book are only in part — and very small part — the men with whom I sailed and worked. I have not gone so far as to man my *Acushnet* with the crew of a *Pequod*, but any individual connected with the whaling industry who appears in my book is real only in the sense that he is compounded of a bit of this one I knew on my own or other expeditions, and of that one I heard of — only the whales are reported just as they were.

In revising the text, I have, in places, been forced to veer even further towards fiction than I originally intended, because there are those who thought that they found characterizations of themselves, and objected to 'inaccuracies' in my picture of them; and others, paradoxically, who objected to the strict truth when it did peep through. No vessel ever had to steer so tricky a course as I have navigated — at the behest of those who cried, 'That didn't happen exactly as you tell it, so you must change it!', and those others who cried, 'That happened exactly as you tell it, so you must change it!' — unless it was the helmsman of a whaling ship scouring the Antarctic or being scoured for off the coast of Peru!

The photographs illustrating the book were all taken by myself on the expedition I accompanied. But *I* am not the real photographer. The camera with which they were taken, the ideas of what to take, and the instructions on how to take them all came from Katharine Tweed. She — who will be one of the first women to sail on modern whaling expeditions when the whaleship-owners again realize that women are worth more than their weight in ambergris on long whaling voyages — will some day present a true and complete record of such an expedition. But meanwhile she had to make the best she could of the thousand or so ill-composed negatives I brought back from the Antarctic to her dark-room. I am myself astonished at the technical and artistic skill that has enabled her to make the pictures she has from my ignorant and amateurish snaps.

R. B. ROBERTSON

October 1955.
OVER MENZION,
PEEBLESSHIRE, SCOTLAND

CONTENTS

CONTENTS

I

MEN OUTSIDE THE COMMON HERD

Any serious student of abnormal psychology will find 'the whalemen' markedly interesting; it is my own conviction, reached after reading hundreds of log books and sea journals, that the old whaling vessels had more than their arithmetical proportion of madmen.

—CAPT. C. B. HAWES

SOME twelve thousand men go down to the Southern Ocean each year to hunt the whale. They are men of whom the world knows nothing, and of whom I knew nothing until I joined them. I knew vaguely that there was a modern whaling industry, but I thought, as do most, that modern whaling was a poor mechanical remnant of the glorious whaling days of the last century — of the days when Nantucket, New Bedford, Dundee, Aberdeen, and the other whaling ports were names known to everyone and the adventures of the whalers from these ports were followed eagerly by all readers of the newspapers and by businessmen the world over whose markets were dependent on the annual slaughter of the whale. I knew with equal vagueness that modern whaling was carried out largely in the far-south Antarctic seas; that the whales today were chased by high-speed craft and shot by means of harpoon guns; and that they were processed at sea on large floating factories. But what manner of men chase the whales today, where and how the whalemen are recruited, and what sort of life they lead and jobs they do, was as big a blank in my mind as it is in that of the average European whose diet, cleanliness, health, and appearance all, in devious ways, are dependent upon commodities provided by the whale and the men who hunt it.

I had never met a modern whaleman, but I had read much about the old whaling and could, like most who read English, have described in detail life aboard a New Bedford whaling bark, or taken my place as oarsman on a whaleboat without appearing too green or ignorant of the drill. But the modern whaleship and life aboard her was as mysterious to me as life aboard a quinquereme — and, I thought, much less interesting.

However, strange men in peculiar jobs have always been a fascination to me, and in my medical and psychiatric practice I have met and got to know many rare specimens. So, when I saw the opportunity of living and working with the modern whalemen a while and getting to know them, I eagerly accepted. I considered that — though they would not, of course, be comparable to their heroic predecessors in the profession of whaling — the men manning the whaleships of the twentieth century might, for a while, be a more interesting study than the frustrated women and inadequate men who make up the bulk of psychiatric practice in the cities.

And so it was that, one day in the early autumn of 1950, when some good advertising psychologist belonging to a whaling company put an advertisement in the employment columns of a medical journal headed with the last remaining word of pure romance in geography — ANTARCTIC — he found me not only willing but eager to join the whalemen a while to study them in their own environment. The advertisement required, not a psychiatrist, but an 'experienced physician' to undertake the duties of senior medical officer to a pelagic whaling expedition sailing for the Southern Ocean for the 1950–51 whaling season. I reckoned I was eligible, so I did two things: I got on the telephone and found that the average duration of the Antarctic trips is about eight months (which suited my personal plans very well); and I looked up the word *pelagic* in the dictionary and found it meant *sea-borne*. With that, I decided the job was mine, and two days later in the whaling office of a northern port I found myself committed to the responsibility for the health and medical welfare of some six hundred and fifty Scottish and Norwegian whalemen, and with a glorious opportunity to study a different type of man, in an environment which probably no psychiatrist or industrial psychologist has ever visited, and which few would realize is of huge importance to the modern civilized world. I must confess that, when I took this job, I had some half-formed intention of writing up the whalemen for the benefit of my professional colleagues as little-known psychopathic specimens engaged in the most peculiar of all modern jobs. I had not known the whalemen long when I realized that the importance of describing this unknown breed to my fellow psychiatrists as specimens was as nothing to the importance of revealing them to the whole world as *men*.

Now let me say at the start, and then be done with it, that it is difficult for any literate person who has been a-whaling to write of his experiences without constantly quoting and referring to the masterpiece of whaling literature, *Moby Dick*. For even in these mechanized days, when one is with the whalers, one finds that daily, even hourly, the thoughts turn to some phrase or incident in Melville's classic; and, while there is much that is different from the whaling of a hundred years ago, much is still the same, and little is so greatly changed that constant comparisons cannot be made between modern whaling and whalemen, and the events and men that Melville described. I will tell of the first of the Melville characters I sought and found in the modern whaling industry, and then leave those who can to note what further resemblance there may be between the men I met and the experiences I encountered on the whaling ships, and those described by the master pen of whaling.

Inevitably I was Ishmael when I left the whaling office, having signed on for the duration of the southern whaling season as a 'Whaler Group Spec. S.M.O.' (senior medical officer), and I knew that my next move must be to seek the whalemen's inn, and there find Queequeg, Melville's gentle savage, who would be my friend and shipmate for the whole voyage.

The inn was easy enough to find. It was a little pub just round the corner from the whaling office, the bar of which was crowded with pale-faced, black-coated men, very obviously shipping clerks; and ruddy-faced, blue-coated men, very obviously seamen.

Queequeg I could not see at all. There was no hideously tattooed savage in the group, brandishing a harpoon or worshipping a heathen idol before the fire. There was nothing more romantic than a crowd of shipping-office birds and sailormen drinking whisky in a second-rate dockside tavern. So ordinary were they that the dominant figure among them was a tallish man whom, by his black Anthony Eden hat and expensive Bond Street overcoat, I took to be a prosperous businessman, perhaps the president or at least the managing director of the firm that had just employed me. I took my place beside him at the bar, not because I wanted to speak to him — I had had enough of his breed in the past few years — but to await the modern Queequeg I felt was bound to appear before long. However, Mr. Businessman addressed me, and in politeness I had to reply.

'Going whaling?' he asked me, and I noted that he pronounced the *wh* so carefully that his tongue was probably instinctively shaping a *v*. I admitted that I was; that it was my first trip, and that I was doctor to the expedition.

He immediately reacted in a most un-businessman-like way. 'Two large very double whiskies!' he yelled to the barman in a tone and manner quite unsuited to that particular pub, where barroom etiquette demands that one speak almost in whispers and plead quietly for one's drinks as though asking a favour. But I saw that the barman was in no way distressed by this indecorous behaviour, and the clerks and seamen did not even look up from their drinks at the outburst, so I deduced that the businessman and his outlandish manners were known and accepted in the pub.

When the drinks arrived, the businessman turned to me, cleared his throat like a minister beginning a sermon, then thrust out a beringed, well-manicured hand, and, in a shout as loud as that he had used to the barman, announced: 'I am Mansell!' We shook hands, and he continued: 'And you, new whaling doctor, have heard of me!'

I had not, and I said so. But I was immediately sorry for my tactlessness, for his disappointment was piteous. In a moment he was cast down, and no longer the self-confident businessman condescending to drink with the common sailors in their pub and patronizing the new whaling doctor, but like a little boy who had been showing off too much and been reproved in public by an inconsiderate parent. I was glad when a quiet sailor-like man who had been standing by the bar listening to our encounter came to our rescue.

'If you're coming whaling with us, doctor, you'll soon get to know Mansell,' he told me. 'Everybody in the Southern Ocean knows Mansell.'

Mansell, the apparent businessman, brightened up straight away. His recovery was as sudden as had been his casting down. 'Yes! That is true.' He was shouting again. 'Everybody in Zuther Notion know Mansell! You send me postcard, just say, "Mansell — Antarctic," I get it all right. And Mansell know everybody, too. I know all twelve thousand whalemen on south fishing grounds, and most in Labrador and Peru and other grounds, too. This man, now' — he turned to introduce the quiet Scottish seaman who had saved the situation — 'he is MacDonald, junior chief engineer of our expedition. He is good engineer. He make more oil from average whale on our factory ship than any engineer in whaling industry. I teach him when he was young, green boy.'

'And who are you, then?' I asked. 'One of the owners? Or our captain perhaps?'

'No! I am a broduction officer!' he shouted. 'Worst-paid people on the expedition. These men' — he indicated the group of seamen by the bar with a contemptuous wave of his well-tailored arm — 'Whaler Group VIII, you call them, which is firm's name for non-specialist whalemen. Scum of the ocean! They make more money than I do. But they not know about whales. Only me, Mansell, that knows about whales and broduction of whale oil. I been whaling thirty years. I am seaman, chemist, biologist, engineer, and administrator. Yes! I been gunner, too. Once I was mate on a catcher, and gunner take sick, so Mansell shoot whales. Shoot three ninety-foot blue whales in one hour! And I been everywhere where man find whales — Zuther Notion, Arctic Ocean, Australia, South America coast, Japan Sea. Whaling is my life; and I know all whales in world by name, same as I know all whalemen.'

He paused to draw breath, and MacDonald, the quiet-spoken engineer, put in a word. 'There's a grain of truth in all that, doctor,' he told me. 'But don't mistake the crop of talk that Mansell grows out of it for the grain itself. It's probably true that he knows more about whaling than any man alive or dead, and you can take as gospel anything he tells you on that subject, drunk or sober. But don't ever believe a ruddy word he tells you about Mansell!'

At this I was glad to note that Mansell grinned. And I saw that there was probably quite a lot beneath his bombastic veneer. And I suddenly saw something else: I saw that here was Queequeg! A civilized and disguised Queequeg, it is true, brandishing no weapon more dangerous than a fountain pen and worshipping no idol other than the whisky bottle before him; but, beneath his opulent clothes and absurd manner, the same landless, unfathomable Queequeg whom Melville had described a hundred years before, whose life, having failed in its main venture, was now dedicated to the whaling industry. And my psychiatric harpoon plunged silently into him up to the hitches, to make fast his personality for future study and dissection.

Mansell and MacDonald would have kept me in that tavern all day, and I would willingly have stayed listening to their talk of whaling and of whalemen, for I began to see as they talked that this modern whaling was as wide and interesting a field as the much-romanticized old sperm-whale fisheries. But I had work to do. The whaling company had wisely decided that I should myself examine the crews of the expedition and decide which of the men were and which were not fit to face eight months of tough isolation in the Antarctic, and that afternoon I was to begin my examinations. So I returned to the whaling office.

I was impressed by my first sight of the medical arrangements

18

provided by the company for its whalemen. A small consulting-room had been fixed up in the offices, adjacent to the whaling laboratory. Although the room was only in use three or four days in the year, furniture and equipment were all that the most exacting doctor could demand in his workroom. And I was casually told that, if I wanted anything else, I was just to buy it and charge it to the company. 'This firm,' I thought, 'seems to have some regard for the welfare of its employees.' But how much of the firm's apparent generosity in matters of health and welfare was aided by the whalemen themselves, the Norwegian government, and His Majesty's Income Tax Commissioners, I was later to discover in the far south. However, I settled down comfortably and in efficient surroundings to examine my crews.

I could be as tough or as easy-going as I liked in the examinations, but any errors of judgment would come back on myself, for, if any crocks went along with us, the worry and responsibility of caring for them thousands of miles from the nearest hospital would be mine. So I decided to set a fairly high standard of both physical and mental health for my shipmates and be quite merciless in rejecting any with whom I was not completely satisfied. My standards broke down after the first few patients, as we shall see.

Before I tackled my work, I called on my neighbours in the laboratory, partly out of curiosity — I had never been in a whaling laboratory before — and partly to enlist some help should there be any idle young scientists around. Here I found yet another new facet of the whaling world, of the existence of which I had known nothing before, though it had been there for years in the heart of my native country. There were three of the scientific whalemen present, one visitor from the Government Fisheries laboratory, and a pretty little secretary. All were idle, and they were gossiping. Idleness, I came to find, is the natural state of whaling scientists, and gossip is their vice, but they somehow do (or get somebody else to do) a vast amount of work during their apparent idleness, and their gossip is always interesting.

The head of the laboratory, who was that most delightful type of being, the Gabby Scientist, introduced himself and immediately, like everyone else connected with the industry, began to talk of whaling. But the whaling gossip of the Gabby Scientist and his colleagues was quite different from that of Mansell and MacDonald to which I had listened in the pub that morning. They had talked of ships and men and mighty catches of whales. The scientists gossiped of the whale after he was dead, and of the men who had done and were still doing astonishing things with his carcase. Some of their talk I understood. They spoke of vitamins and insulin and ACTH and enzymes and much other materia medica that the whale supplies to the pharmacies of the world in greater concentrations than any other animal contributor to man's welfare. They spoke of current researches into the phsyiology and anatomy of the whale which may in time have far-reaching results in human medicine, and they gossiped mercilessly of their acquaintances and colleagues who were conducting these researches. All this talk I could follow. But when they switched to the nitrogen content of fertilizers made from whalebone meal, and the ideal poultry feed, and the best lubricants for delicate instruments at high altitudes, and the wearing properties of ivory, and the fluctuations of prices on the French perfume market, and a hundred other things that seemed to be connected with the dead whales they studied, I was lost, and I had to cry for quarter. I wanted to get on with my work.

The Gabby Scientist was all apologies when I interrupted him. 'I know what you want, doctor,' he told me. 'The doctor comes in here wanting the same thing every year at the beginning of the season — six hundred and fifty glass receptacles to hold urine specimens, and somebody who can read and write to test the urines for you. Yes? O.K., the glasses are all ready for you, and this is young Evans, another first-tripper, who's sailing on the same expedition as you as junior chemist. He can give you a hand.'

I asked if I might come back and talk to these cheerful savants some more before we sailed; for I saw that, under all their humorous, flighty, scientific back-chat, these men were following a deadly serious purpose — the extraction by any means possible of more food from the sea for a world that cannot grow sufficient on land to feed itself.

'You come in any time you like, doctor,' the Gabby Scientist told me, 'though you'll be sorry you ever got to know us. And, by the way, we want some whales' eye-muscles for the Nuffield Foundation in Oxford. No one's ever examined them yet. You probably know what an eye-muscle is, so you can get some dissected out and packed in formalin? And I'll give you a tip about co-operation between the medical and scientific departments of your expedition to which young Evans had better listen too: there'll be fifty gallons of pure ethyl alcohol in the laboratory stores on the factory ship, but they've got nothing to flavour it with at the end of the season. Now you have in your dispensary all the flavourings and oils needed to make good gin. . . . But you can work all that out with young Evans. Goodbye, doctor.'

I liked the look of young Evans. He was a type I knew well, and I already had several specimens of his personality pattern pasted in my psychiatric scrapbook. A young Welshman, he had an accent that could only have been given him by one of the best English universities; but the huge handle-bar moustache he wore told the world that on graduation he had not gone straight into a laboratory, but had served his time and earned his right to wear the moustache as a fighter pilot in the R.A.F. He asked what help I required of him.

'Find our customers,' I told him. 'Get a specimen of urine off each one — that's always the hold-up in mass medical exams, but you can use what persuasion you like. Make sure it's the man's own, and not borrowed for the occasion. Then wheel them in to me one at a time in the semi-nude, and, while I give them the works, you test their urine.'

'O.K!' said young Evans. 'There's been a crowd of peculiar-looking thugs hanging round the laboratory door all morning. Shall we start with them?'

We did, and the first of them came in. Evans was as new to the whaling industry as I was, so we examined our first 'Whaler

Group VIII' with considerable interest. Physically, he was the alert chimpanzee rather than the heavy gorilla type. If we were a bit self-conscious, this whaleman was not. Though it was new to us, he had been through this procedure many times before, probably each time as drunk as he was this time.

'Name — Gordon, Hamish. Age — thirty-two. Next of kin — wife, Annie Gordon,' he began, giving me the information required on the firm's medical document before I could ask for it, and in the correct order. 'Born — Peterhead. Father drowned at sea. Mother alive and well, age eighty. Been whaling sixteen years. Thirteen seasons in the south, and three in Labrador. Go fishing with the North Sea trawlers during the northern summer. No serious illnesses. One accident three years ago in South Georgia. Shackle parted when we were turning the whale over, an' I was standing where I shouldn't have been — my own ruddy fault. Fractured skull. No after-effects, except I canna' haud my drink the way I used to. Forgot to give you my religion — it goes in that space up at the top — Wee Free Kirk o' Scotland. I'm no damn heathen like these Shelties — they're a' Plymouth Brethern — nor yet like these Lutheran Scowegians we got to work with. . . . Now, you'll not be wanting to sound me or any damn nonsense like that, doc, so I'll get back round the corner to Eagle's Bar, where my friends are waiting. Anything else you want?'

I decided to take a risk with my first whaleman patient and find out what manner of man he was.

'Two things I want,' I told him. 'First, I want to examine you thoroughly, but I'm not going to do it today——'

'Why the hell not?' he interrupted aggressively. 'Now I'm here, you can do any damn silly test you like, but hurry up about it.'

'— and secondly, I'm going to examine you when you're sober, so you can get to hell out of here and come back to-morrow before you've been to Eagle's Bar.'

For a moment he looked more like the truculent gorilla than the impudent chimpanzee, and I prepared myself for a deluge of

22

drunken abuse. I saw young Evans edging toward us with the fighter-pilot look in his eye, and it seemed inevitable that my first interview with a whaleman as a patient was going to end in an inglorious scene. But suddenly the gorilla smiled and was a chimpanzee again. (This sudden transformation I later came to know well with the whalemen.)

'Aye, aye, sir!' he said. And, picking up his clothes, he began to make his exit with the exaggerated care of the well-intoxicated.

'And look, Gordon,' I asked him, 'if there are any of your friends waiting outside in the same condition, do you mind taking them back with you to Eagle's Bar and bringing them along tomorrow before the pubs open?'

He grinned and nodded, and, before the door shut behind him, we heard him say to the crowd waiting outside: 'C'mon, lads. It's no use waiting. He's a good chap, that. He's really going to examine us, and we've tae come back the morn before we start drinking.' And about half a dozen got up from the benches and weaved their way down the corridor with him.

'Well! We'll try again,' commented young Evans. 'The urine was eighty per cent Scotch Ale, and the remainder Black and White or John Haig, I'm not sure which. But we won't record it today. Want the next one in?'

The next was a very different type. A thin, sensitive-looking man, he sat down only when asked, and then gave the information I required through slow question and answer, volunteering nothing. As he spoke, he stuttered slightly, fingered his collar, and showed all the outer manifestations of a shy, tender soul within. His name was Dornoch. He came from the small port of Dunbar, which has supplied a small clique of families to the merciless whaling industry since the first Scottish harpoon was thrown. He apologized for being the second steward of the factory ship, and confessed, as though it were a crime, that he 'had only been whaling for eight seasons.' I was attracted rather than repelled by this man's awkwardness, following on the jovial insolence of Gordon, and I determined to break down his shyness and get to know him.

'What took you to the Antarctic in the first place?' I asked, and (as I found the whalemen often did when asked this question) he gave an explanation most commercial and unromantic.

'I was with Cunard White Star for some years. I made good money there, but I was in port almost two days a week, and spent the money as quickly as I earned it. Then I got married and had to save something, especially when the kiddie came, so I tried the whaling one year because there are no ways of spending money in the south, and I saved all my pay. I liked it, and I've been going back ever since, every year.'

'Must be some other attraction than the money,' I prompted him. 'What do you do with your spare time on the whale-ships?'

'Oh! I read a lot. And there's always something interesting to watch in the birds and animals down there. I do a bit of photography, too — although I'm no good as a photographer, mind you.'

I saw my opening there, through which I could get to know this shy little man (for it is well known to any doctor, never mind one who is supposed to be a psychologist, that, if only he can get his shy patient's walletful of photographs out on the table, he and that patient are friends for life; and much that is clinically useful will emerge with the wallet).

'Got any of your pictures on you?' I asked casually. 'I do a bit myself.' And within a moment the wallet was on the table.

Apologizing for each picture as he showed it to me, and pointing out its defects, as is the way of bashful photographers who are proud of their work, he showed me an assortment of bird pictures — of penguins and skuas and petrels and cape pigeons and other Antarctic fowl — which was far above the capabilities of the average amateur.

I made no comment, but deviated slightly into the psychological channel I wished to explore. 'Do you keep a picture of your wife in the wallet?' I asked. 'Or only the birds?'

'Of course I don't keep her picture here just now,' he said, surprised at my question. 'I see her every day when I'm home, so what would be the point?'

'And when you're down in the Antarctic?'

'Then I carry her picture, and the kiddie's, too.'

'But not the birds?' I asked.

'Of course not.' But now the shy man was getting the better of the photographic enthusiast, and I saw coming into his eye that suspicious look to which one becomes accustomed in psychiatric work when one is following an obscure line of thought impossible to explain to the patient. 'Do you think it's queer of me to carry these bird pictures about with me, doctor?'

'Of course not,' I rapidly assured him. 'I'm hoping to get some pictures half as good as these when we're in the south, and maybe you'll help me. . . . Got any trouble at home?' (One learns to spring such intimate questions rudely and abruptly, for the facial expression in surprise will reveal more than a long explanation.)

'Good God! None at all!' Dornoch exclaimed. I believe he spoke the truth, though I have wondered often since I heard Mark, standing on the bridge of the whaleship, grunting: 'Not a ruddy chance! He's a gone gosling! . . . Turn to starboard. Ring for full ahead and resume your course.'

As each patient left the room, young Evans made his comment, and a good many of his spot diagnoses hit the mark. When Dornoch left, he remarked: 'Nice fellow, that! I wonder what it really is that takes a quiet little home bird like him down to the ice year after year. Maybe his grandmother went astray with an eagle. Anyway, his urine's all clear. Let's get another one in.'

A book could be written about each of our next few patients. There came in Davison, bosun to the factory ship, a giant Shetlander, as gentle as he was gigantic. He, who was later to become my mentor in the anatomy of the whale and my adviser in the art of dealing with drink-crazed whalemen, was the typical textbook bosun. Well over six feet tall, dressed in the traditional blue jersey and monkey jacket of the sailor ashore, he had the prescribed steady blue eyes, rolling gait, and fists like hams that every good

bosun should have. Someday Hollywood will find him when it
seeks an Erik the Red. He had the quiet courtesy that most men
bred on islands seem to develop, and, when his medical examination was finished, he sat at ease with me a while, smoking and
answering my many questions about his fellow islanders and their
participation in the whaling.

He told me that in the old days all the Scottish and English
whaling ships, and many foreign ships too, would sail from their
home ports with only scratch crews, and would recruit the bulk
of their seamen in the Shetland Islands as they rounded the north
of Scotland to push up into the Arctic whaling grounds. 'We
were never whalemen, really, but the whalemen from Dundee
and Hull, and those from over the Atlantic, too, were always a
mixed lot of "get rich quick" fellows who went for one or two
voyages only, and, though they maybe knew a lot about whales,
they were notorious bad seamen. So they came to the islands and
picked up men who could handle small ships, splice a rope, and
not panic in a gale as the mixed bunch in the whaleship forecastles
used often to do. They're still coming for us, and, as we can't
make a living all the year round on the islands, where there's only
the fishing and a few sheep, they still find a few hundred of us
who are willing to go.'

He told me of the term of contempt used by the brassbound
sailors of the world's most snobbish merchant navy for his
countrymen: 'North Sea Chinamen, they call us, because they
reckon we take on jobs at sea, such as running the whaleships
which no self-respecting white seaman would undertake. But I
wouldn't use the expression when there's a Shetlander listening,
if I were you, doctor.' I looked at his magnificent physique again,
and at the size of his hands, and decided I wouldn't. Of Davison I
will tell much anon. The expedition centred around him, as
many whaling expeditions for centuries have centred around
islanders of his breed, be they from Shetland or Nantucket or
Cape Verde.

There came next Davison's two sons, able-bodied young seamen who were to sail with us. And his grandson (official age

stated to be sixteen; medical age I reckoned to be just over fourteen), junior mess-boy to the factory ship. There came a procession of quiet, slow-spoken Shelties, seamen all, and with that old-fashioned but unmistakable trait — reliability — obvious in each of them. There came a group of engineers from Glasgow and Dundee, Kipling's McAndrews every one of them, who knew their mathematics and their Bibles and the best brands of whisky, and who could scarcely disguise their pity — almost contempt — for any man who was not a marine engineer. There came technicians — electricians, repairers, and radiomen — from the lowlands of Scotland, many of them from far inland.

'How in God's name did you get tied up with the whaling industry?' I asked a young wireless-operator from an unromantic town many miles from the sea in the vilest industrial part of Scotland.

'Damn it all, man, my grandfather was chief harpooner of the *Arctic*, the first whaleship that went through the Davis Strait. When he got back, he put the oar on his shoulder, Odysseus fashion, and marched inland. I reckoned it was time the oar was wetted again.'

'You've read your Homer, then?' I asked him, veiling as best I could the astonishment these whalemen were beginning to produce in me.

'Of course!' He was as astonished as I was. 'Haven't you?'

There came Micky, the chief plumber of the expedition. (Having examined the expedition's butcher, the baker, and the lamp-trimmer — whom young Evans, of course, immediately named the 'candlestick-maker' — I was not surprised to find men of any trade who were going to accompany us, but an Antarctic plumber seemed something of an incongruity.) Micky informed me that, not only was he 'the best bluidy plumber south of Cape Horn,' but he was the only Irishman connected with the modern whaling industry. I know now that there must somewhere be a better plumber south of Cape Horn, but certainly I did not meet, and know no others who have met, any other Irishman in the whaling business.

There came an official of a whaling company, who was flying down to Montevideo, where a whalecatcher, one of his firm's small ships, was standing by to take him to the Antarctic island of South Georgia. (He made the island sound as easily accessible as the Isle of Wight, although I was yet to learn how inaccessible it could suddenly become if whalecatchers and aeroplanes were requested to stand by to transport sick and injured instead of business men.) This character slammed a paper written in Spanish on my desk, with the order, 'Sign that there, doc!'

I was very sorry, but would like to know what I was signing.

'Only some damn certificate required by the Uruguayan government to say whether or not I've had syphilis.'

'Well, have you?' I asked. 'Take down your trousers, and lie up there on the couch.'

I think my unpopularity with the business men of whaling began at that moment.

There came in then to be examined the two chief officers of the expedition, Andra and Mark. The first a lovable old Norwegian, a man who had been a-whaling with Larsen, the first whaleman to use steam whalecatchers in the Southern Ocean; who had sailed on the fantastic expedition that was aiming to populate with silver foxes, and make economically productive Norway's only southern colony, the tiny dot called Bouvet Island in the Antarctic seas; who always got sober when other men were getting hilariously drunk; and whose hobby, absurd as it may sound until one meets the whalemen, was the collection of English rustic folk songs.

And Mark — junior chief officer by designation on the firm's books, but the only holder of a British Master's Certificate who was to sail with us. Another quiet Shelty, who regarded navigation and seamanship as two ordinary civilized attributes that every rational human should acquire, just like table manners or the ability to write. Young Evans said, as Mark left us: 'Pity that chap never went into the R.A.F.,' and, this being a high compliment when passed by the Evanses of this world, I knew that his opinion of Mark, on first impression, agreed with my own. We never altered it.

And then came Mansell!

We heard him five minutes before he appeared. Shouting as loudly as he had in the pub, he greeted each and every whaleman outside the door by name and took his place, late though he was, at the head of the queue of waiting examinees. No one objected, and there was much laughter outside our door. No one in the whaling world ever objects to Mansell. His place is — though nobody knows why — at the head of the whaling queue.

He charged through the door without knocking before I was properly finished with my previous patient, and I did not object.

'Hello, Rubbersen! Hello, Rubbersen's assistant!' he shouted as he entered. 'This is very nice office you got. Cost plenty money, uh? Never mind. All whaling companies got plenty money. I make it all for them. Mostly small private companies — very few shareholders — but mostly pay income tax on millions every year. And where the money go, uh? Some companies got old lady shareholders who give it all to church, pay ministers to stand in pulpits saying whalemen very bad men, and to cats' homes. That what we work for! Thirty years I go down to Zuther Notion hunting whale — what for? Keep ministers and old cats in comfort up here! But I talk too much, Rubbersen. You examine me now.'

I recalled my professional gravity and made noises signifying that I agreed with the ultimate suggestion. In half a minute Mansell had stripped and was prancing around the room, naked but still talking.

'No need to examine me. I been examined thirty times by whaling doctor, and each time doctor shake his head, very sorry, and say: "Goodbye, Mansell! I never see you again! You very sick man and you not come home from Zuther Notion next year!" I got heart like dickey, asthma, too much alcohol, varicose veins, stomach ulcers, and maybe this trip I get syphilis from black girl in Aruba. Only trouble I not have is impotence. But look, Rubbersen! I got certificate! Get it today from best

29

doctor in town. Much better doctor than you — only damn fool doctor go whaling. This big doctor, he certify Mansell fit go down south another year, so you not need to examine me.'

I knew the name on the certificate he waved in my face; it was one of the biggest medical names in the city. But, as the eminent doctor who had certified Mansell fit for all duties afloat would not have the medical responsibility for Mansell when he was afloat, I decided to have a look myself. I found the dickey heart, the asthma, the alcoholic stigmata, the varicose veins, and evidence of the ulcers. I found much more besides that might be mortal in rigorous conditions, and I was wondering how I could tactfully, and without breaking his heart, end the whaling career of this modern Queequeg.

Mansell saw what was coming. 'Look, Rubbersen,' he began quietly, and he was more nearly serious than I had yet seen him. 'I see you have got conscience, and you think you leave this old medical museum called Mansell ashore this season. All right, if you say so, I got to stay. But look — last twenty years I been as sick as I am today . . . but I never give trouble to doctor in Zuther Notion. I bet you, except I need plenty aspirin in mornings, I not take any treatment from you all season. Old whalemen all like me — all sick. All go: "Wheeze! Wheeze " all over Antarctic, but not go: "Yelp! Yelp!" same like young fellows. You take my advice: be very strict with young fellows. If have got ingrowing toenail, don't take them to Zuther Notion. Send back to mothers. Tell them get job in office and play golf on Saturdays. Go fishing in Scottish burns, not in Antarctic. But with old fellows — not the same. If man go whaling ten years and he still alive, he probably immortal. You pass him for go whaling for ever — and he not let you down, same like young hothouse athlete will do.'

He talked some more in this strain, and, because it agreed with what I had found during my medical career — that for a tough job one chooses not the carefully nurtured athlete to whom disease is but a name, but the man who has encountered every one of man's morbidities and has survived — I eventually gave in.

30

'O.K., Mansell. You win. But may the shade of Hippocrates forgive me!' And I signed his medical form.

'Thanks, Rubbersen,' said Mansell, still serious. 'Now I want explain. I go to big doctor, get certificate, not to cheat you, but to cover you in case maybe I do hand in my dinner pail this trip and Andra, the mate, read sailor's burial service over me. . . . Now we all go to Café Royal and have dinner. Mansell pay. I have big win at greyhound race-track yesterday — make more money in two hours than I make all last whaling season.'

We declined just then to share his winnings, but, from the shouting outside the door when he departed, we judged that the Whalers Group VIII, scum of the ocean, who were still waiting, had been included in the invitation, and we would have few if any more clients that day.

'Well, well!' I exclaimed to young Evans as we packed up our equipment and closed the office for the day. 'What's your general impression of whalemen in the mass?'

'They'd do to take along as night fighters,' said the R.A.F., paying its highest compliment. 'And if a layman can presume to judge your methods, doc, I've noticed that you used intuition almost as much as your stethoscope in passing or rejecting them — perhaps that's as good a way as any.'

II

THE SHIP WAS CHEERED, THE HARBOUR
CLEARED

O'er the sea from the north there sails a ship
With the people of Hel, at the helm stands Loki;
After the wolf do wild men follow. . . .

THE POETIC EDDA

IT would be wrong to say that Norway is dependent on the modern whaling industry for her existence as a nation (nations like Norway will always continue to exist, though they starve!), but it would not be wrong to say that the rapid recovery of Norway after her wartime occupation has been in part — and large part — due to her present supremacy in that industry. Taking the Southern Ocean whale-fisheries alone, of the twenty-odd pelagic whaling expeditions that annually proceed there, ten are Norwegian. And when one reckons that a single average whaling expedition sails with a capital value of some £3,000,000 and returns after eight months with a gross profit (so far as one can estimate the undisclosed profits of the private whaling companies) often well over £2,000,000, one can see that ten whaling expeditions are of no small importance to this little country, which has arable land of acreage only slightly greater than that of the State of Rhode Island and one five-hundredth part of the farmland of Texas.

Nor would it be wrong to say that the modern whaling industry is at present dependent for its existence on Norway. Other countries participate. Scotland has two pelagic expeditions annually going south, and England one; Japan has two; South Africa, Holland, and Russia have one apiece. There is one expedition, manned largely by Germans, whose offices are registered in New York and its ships in Panama. Italy and Argentina are reported to be building and equipping fleets to join the annual Antarctic hunt. But the Norwegians have a finger in every pelagic whaling pie, except perhaps the Japanese. Even the Russians have had to admit that they are amateurs at the business of Antarctic whaling, and have reluctantly sought help from the old whaling cliques of Norway to find men bred to the whale hunt and at home in the Antarctic ice.

And, as well as a large proportion of the manpower of international whaling originating from Norway, many of the tools and techniques of the job have come (well protected by patent rights) out of Norway.

Thomas Alva Edison is usually regarded as the man who, when he turned on the switch of the Pearl Street power station in New York in 1882, blew out the sperm-oil lanterns and candles for ever and so ended the old whaling industry of New Bedford and Dundee. But at about the same time that Edison was working, another inventor — Sven Foyn, a Norwegian — produced the harpoon gun and made possible for the first time the capture of the fast and non-buoyant whales that (unlike the sperm whales, which are inedible) man can use for food as well as for lubricant and illuminant, and the whaling industry, despite Edison, was assured of resurrection, though in a different form. Practically all the twenty-thousand-odd whales shot in the Antarctic every year are shot with Sven Foyn guns.

Similarly, the grab or *hval kla*, the ingenious device that hauls whale after mighty, slippery whale up onto the decks of the factory ships, the device that ended the dangerous practice of outboard flensing and made possible the utilization of the entire whale carcass and not just the blubber, is a Norwegian invention. Again, the naval architecture of the little whale-catching ship came from Norway, as did the design of the steam-press boiler, which replaced the old try-works on the decks of the whaleships in which the oil was boiled out of the blubber.

Scottish engineers have taken over these and many other whaling contrivances, and have made changes and improvements (and perhaps if America, with its genius for gadgets, ever re-enters the whaling industry, the whole technology will be changed), but at present the tooling of the industry, like the greater part of its manning, is Norwegian.

The industry is controlled from Norway by an international board, which sits in Sandefiord. It is interesting to note that as far back as 1817 there were men like William Scoresby (the 'Mansell' of whaling of those days) and Hamilton, the Scottish biological authority on the whale, who worried about the preservation of the whole species. Scoresby talked of the 'appalling slaughter' of forty-four whales by one ship during an Arctic season, and Hamilton wrote: 'So keenly has the fishery been prosecuted, and so great has been the number of whales taken, that it has been feared that, unless some restriction be imposed, the race will be extinguished, and the trade destroyed.' That was some fifty years before the first harpoon gun banged, and a hundred and thirty years before an American journalist, reporting the increasing popularity of an electric harpoon only a few months ago, wrote: 'The goose that lays the golden eggs has her marine counterpart; for the habitual killing of immature whales that happen to fall within the terms of the international agreement is bound to end in extermination unless stricter regulations are framed.'

But the poor old whale lives on, and, though some of his species are seldom seen today, there were still enough of the larger, faster types left for the Southern Ocean fleets to find and kill sixteen thousand (the year's quota in 1950–51) a month before the season was scheduled to end. So perhaps the fears of Dr. Hamilton and the journalist are groundless, or at least exaggerated; if so, the thanks must go to Sandefiord in Norway.

Back about 1905 the whaling companies themselves began co-operating to preserve their industry, the Norwegians being the instigators of this co-operation. But it was not until 1930 that the various governments became interested to the extent of agreeing among themselves on how to preserve, and if possible increase, the stocks of whales. They met in Sandefiord and signed the first International Whaling Convention, which constituted the International Whaling Board, arranged the 'rules' for the annual whale hunt, designated certain vast stretches of ocean as whale sanctuaries, placed some species and sizes of whales under total and some under partial protection, and — perhaps most important of all — arranged a system of inspection and enforcement of its edicts by a group of incorruptible and (in the business sense) disinterested men.

(America was a signatory of that convention, along with some twenty other nations, including even the Soviet. I once heard a whale owner — Scottish, alas! — say testily of the American representative on the whaling board: 'He's not interested in helping the whaling industry to make more money while the going's good! He's filled with a lot of cranky ideas about preserving the species of whale!' Long may he sit on the board, though his country does little whaling today! And there are others like him, even from the U.K. and from Norway, the two countries most concerned with modern whaling.)

But more about the whaling laws and their enforcement later, when we meet Commander Gyle, the senior whaling inspector of our expedition, and see how he enforced the edicts of Sandefiord. Let us sail into Tönsberg, oldest inhabited town in Norway and second city of the modern whaling industry, where we have to pick up our Norwegian contingent for this Scottish whaling expedition.

Tönsberg has no dock and no wharf where a ship of any size can go alongside, so our great hulking factory ship, after a pleasant trip across the North Sea, anchored off in the fiord. From the ship we could see a small (twelve thousand population) town of wooden houses built on hills, as pleasant a habitation amid greenery and sunshine and blue water as man could devise. The chief engineer of our expedition, Old Burnett, was leaning over the rail with me as we dropped anchor. I was being thoroughly romantic about the beauty and history of the place, and extolling the virtues of the Scandinavian peoples, but Old Burnett, who sees no romance outside his smoothly turning engines and hates all nations, including his own, most bitterly cut my eulogy short.

'D'you know what the word *viking* means, Robertson?' he asked. 'It means a pirate lurking up a creek; and there are more pirates lurking up this creek than in the whole of Norway. Look how well painted their town is. It's painted with *my* paint, or at least with paint stolen from all the British whaling ships that have been calling in here for the past twenty years. Same with most other things in the town. You'll find even the toilets in the houses ashore here have the badge of a British whaling company on them, and have been filched off one of our ships when the mate and the chief engineer weren't looking. I reckon we lose stores and equipment at the rate of about a hundred pounds an hour all the time we're anchored here. Better lock up your medical stores tight, but, even so, they'll get half of them, the bastards!'

I already knew the prejudiced old grumbler well enough to discount some of what he said, though I learned later that there was more than a substratum of truth in this particular grumble. But he had been whaling many years, and his opinion on any whaling matter was usually worth listening to, so I asked him how it came about that the Norwegians have such a hold on international whaling today, to the extent that it is almost a Norwegian closed shop. This was his explanation, which is probably at least partly true:

'They invented the grenade harpoon and the harpoon gun in the late nineteenth century. At that time there were probably ten British and American whalemen to every Norwegian engaged in the industry. But our people and the Americans, like damned fools, thought it was unsporting to blow the guts out of a whale, and likely to exterminate the whale in no time if they adopted this method, so they tried to keep the old-style whaling going, and did so, in fact, right up to about 1912. They were fishing the Southern Ocean much more extensively than the Norwegians — look at the names on the map of the Antarctic seas and islands, and you'll see that's true — but they were killing sperm and humpbacks, the slowest and most easily captured of the whales, by old-fashioned methods, whilst the Norwegians were developing shore stations on South Georgia and the Falklands, from which they operated fast steam catchers with Sven Foyn guns and went after the more valuable blue and fin whales. In 1903 the Norwegians sent the first sea-borne expedition with factory ship and accompanying catcher fleet to the Southern Ocean, but still our people and the Americans played around with small boats and hand irons — you'll find many more old men in Dundee or in the Shetlands who have thrown a hand harpoon than you'll find in the whole of Norway. Then, just when we were beginning to wake up and discover that Norwegian whaling was twenty years ahead of us, the Great War came along, and all our whaling packed up for several years.

'Neutral Norway didn't pack up. After the war, around 1924, we tried to get back in the game, but now we had to send to Norway for men who could fire a grenade gun and knew something about the fast blue and fin whales. They came — but on their own conditions, and one of them was that they trained only other Norwegians — mainly lads from their own families around here in Tönsberg and Sandefiord — to handle steam catcher and gun and chase the blue whale. I don't think there's been a British whale-gunner trained since then, though the whole industry's ultimately financed by the British margarine consumer. There was one American, a former New York taxi-driver whom you'll meet down in the south. He got into the racket when his rum-running days were over in 1933. He passed himself off as a Norwegian and after the war as a trained gunner, and in one year he destroyed the myth that only men from Tönsberg and Sandefiord can shoot whales, for no one has touched his record since, but wait until you see how the Norwegians loathe him and boycott him! But look — here they come, the bloody pirates!'

With venom in his voice, the old chief engineer finished his harangue and pointed out to me a small fleet of motor-boats approaching the ship, bringing the Norwegian quota (about 50 per cent) of the crews of our expedition.

For the sake of international accord, I must repeat that Old Burnett criticized and abused his own countrymen, and all men of all nations, with a virulence equalling that with which he expressed his dislike of Norwegians; and I must admit that, despite his disapproval of the Norwegian whalemen, I found no fault in my first view with the crowd of husky vikings who swarmed up the gangways from the motor-boats.

Physically they were identical with the Shelties, for they share a common ancestry. (Although the Shelties say: 'We and the Icelanders were the vikings of history who sailed out into the sunset. The Norwegians and the Danes are the ones who stayed at home.') They were noticeably well scrubbed and well dressed, but all wore their clothes with that vague discomfort which bespeaks the soldier out of uniform or the sailor in his shore-going suit. I got talking to them as soon as I could. Most of them spoke English, but if there was language trouble, an early question in nearly every conversation was: 'Where is Mansell? He sail with us this trip?' and that character (who is not Norwegian, but speaks Norwegian well) would soon be brought along and would interpret when Scot and Scandinavian could not make themselves understood.

I began, with the help of Mansell, to sort them out into their various trades and shipboard occupations. I met my Norwegian assistant, a young, dark, most un-Scandinavian-looking man from northern Norway. He had no whaling connections; in fact, his early professional life, I was told, had been spent mainly as a lecturer and propagandist for birth-control. But I rapidly realized, as we worked together on our first few medical jobs, that the tough whaling men from Tönsberg and Sandefiord had a more than ordinary respect for this slim, dark man who thought and even spoke differently from them. It was late in the voyage when I discovered the reason. The slender, almost fragile Sigrid had come down to Oslo during the war, and, working under cover of a job in a mental hospital where many of Hitler's worst enemies were sheltered as patients during the occupation, he had become a figure to be reckoned with in the underground movement. He knew which of the Thors and Eriks and Hanses and other tough guys from around Tönsberg, now working for a

British company, had worked with him during the war, and which had traded their country and their seamanship to Quisling and Hitler in return for their skins.

I met the gunners, the modern harpooners. They are the princes of Tönsberg, and the man who has killed the most whales in the Antarctic the previous season is their king. They live (and, at £7:10s. for every whale they kill in addition to their princely salaries, they can well afford to live) in the best houses in the district. I went ashore and called upon their emperor, now abdicated, the man who has probably been the most destructive enemy of the whale of all time. I wanted to talk Antarctic whaling and whalemen to him, but he would only talk about the flowers he had grown that summer. His daughter gave me tea, and talked of modern English poetry, of which she knew much more than I did. His wife (perhaps Old Burnett was right!) was interested only in what she could scrounge off our ship in the way of medical stores, linen, and comforts, and tried to enlist me as an ally. But talk of whaling there was none.

And then there arrived two of the gunners who were joining our expedition, and in a moment the scene and the atmosphere were changed. The old emperor of gunners and the two aspiring princelings were very quickly in a huddle together, and I was left aside with the poetical daughter. The three harpooners used English in politeness to me for a minute or two, and they talked of naught but gunners and harpoons and Thar She Blows! I sat mum, with one ear on T. S. Eliot and the other in the Antarctic. But very soon an argument began among the three, the gist of it being, so far as I could make out, that Knut would or would not have killed more big blues than Lars in 1931 if his harpoon gun hadn't jammed half-way through the season. English was no longer able to contain their vehement thoughts, and they burst into Norwegian. An hour or two later, when I took my leave of daughter with a forcedly loaned book of poetry under my arm and an admonition from mother to be sure and let the boatman have some penicillin ointment for daughter's acne, I could still hear above the shouts of the three the only Norwegian words I had yet learned: '*Skytter*,' '*Harpun*,' and '*Hvalblast!*' I went back to the ship realizing that whale-gunnery, like flying, photography, gardening, and a few other more widely known professions, is an occupation that absorbs its practitioners to the exclusion of all else, even their own personalities and reactions, and an occupation where the outsider will always be far outside.

Back on the ship, I was in time to watch come aboard the flensers, lemmers, the blubber boys, and others who deal with the whale on the deck of the factory ship; and the cookers, separators, and oilmen, who deal with the whale in the bowels of the ship and turn him into useful products. I noted that what the Shelty bosun had told me was true: that these men from Norway were all specialists in some branch of whaling, and perhaps knew some job that only a handful of other men afloat could tackle, but there was not a single general able-bodied seaman among them. The navigation, handling, and manning of the ship was a closed shop for the Shelties, as much as whale-gunnery was for the Norwegians.

I watched with interest the baggage of the Norwegian whalemen as it was piled on the deck. One can tell much of a man from his luggage. I remarked the high proportion of musical instruments, including — surprisingly in the most un-Latin men of Europe other than the Scots — many guitars and mandolins. I noted that nearly every man, whatever his rank or station on the ship, and regardless of whether he slept on the lower deck or had a stateroom with private bath, carried a bucket or a washbasin, either of canvas or made from the lower end of a barrel. Although I cross-questioned them on this point, I never got an adequate explanation. Even the manager of the expedition, who occupied a palatial three-room suite with bathroom, brought aboard his canvas bucket. Perhaps in his case it was because — all honour to him — he had climbed to his present rank from that of mess-boy, and still regarded the utensil in which to wash himself and his gear as the most essential item of any seaman's kit.

I could not help noticing that every pile of luggage was decorated somewhere with a Norwegian flag, and I prepared to meet in these men an aggressive pride of nation. I saw that there was a high proportion of canvas bags that rattled as only canvas bags filled with bottles can rattle. I was pleased to mark an occasional flenser (like the harpooneers of old who made fetish objects of their harping-irons) carefully carrying his own flensing-knife — a long, hockey-stick-shaped object wrapped in sacking — as the principal and most carefully tended item in his gear.

One flenser, a tall, angular, solitary fellow of somewhere beyond middle age, caught my attention. None of the others spoke to him, yet he seemed at ease and in familiar surroundings as he stood on deck clutching a flensing-knife that was dark and battered by many hard knocks. He had no flag or bottles or musical instrument in the very small pile of personal property by which he stood.

Commander Gyle, who had become my friend on the brief voyage across the North Sea, came over beside me as I watched the Norwegians join the ship. A retired naval officer, unable to keep away from the sea and the small ships he loved, he was now senior whaling inspector, and, being a deeply read and intelligent man, as are many former fighting-sailors, and also being the only 'outside observer' accompanying the expedition who was not entangled with the company and the economic side of whaling, he was usually sound in his opinion on the whalemen.

He nodded in the direction of the lone flenser. 'You know your *Moby Dick*, doctor. "Know ye not Bulkington?"' he quoted.

I caught the point and smiled. 'Tell me more about him,' I said.

'You won't see him again until the whaling starts,' Gyle told me. 'He will disappear into his cabin, wherever that is, and will next be seen in a month or so when we take the first whale. Then he will leap on top its carcass as though he had done the same thing the day before, instead of last season, and he will slice the blubber as neatly and as accurately as any man in the

Antarctic will do — or better, for in his own estimation, and in mine, too, he's the greatest flenser of all time. But master flensers are as touchy and as professionally proud as master gunners — they're artists by temperament — so our friend here will take no part in the running of the ship or its social life. He is a chief flenser, and he will not lower himself by doing anything except flense.'

'What's his name?' I asked.

'I don't think anybody knows,' Gyle said in all seriousness, 'although it must be on the ship's articles somewhere. I've sailed with him several times, and first trip I met him I gave him the nickname of the "Gaunt Stranger," because I never saw him — bar once — except on the back of a dead whale, bending over at the same angle as his flensing-knife and looking like a vulture. No one knows where he eats or drinks or even lives on the ship.'

'When was the once you saw him other than on the back of a dead whale?' I wanted to know.

'That was the queerest appearance he ever made. It was late one night down in the ice when the factory ship was hove to, waiting for the catchers to bring in some whales. I've got to inspect and measure every whale that comes aboard, so I was sitting in the mate's office down aft on the flensing-deck playing cut-throat bridge with Mark, the chief officer, and Victor, the deck storeman. Mark's a bridge-player well above average; Victor, who wasn't always a deck storeman, once played regularly for his college; and I was once reckoned the best player in the Home Fleet. Well, the whales were a long time a-coming, so we were remarking how we wished we had a fourth of our own calibre to join us, when the Gaunt Stranger came in the door unannounced and said: "You play breedge? I take a hand, uugh?" Anything to pass the time, so we tried not to laugh and said O.K., sit down. He did. And, believe me, within half an hour the three of us realized that we had with us a bridge-player of a standard we had never met before, or hoped to meet. We changed partners and tried again. It was the same thing. That fellow was in a bridge-playing class we couldn't ever hope to touch. The whales were about five hours a-coming, and in that time, no matter how we changed partners or how the cards ran, the Gaunt Stranger couldn't be beaten. When we heard the first catcher coming alongside, we packed up, and we were full of congratulations and questions for the Stranger, so we asked him to have a drink and talk a while. But: "I thank you, no!" — the only words he had spoken all night, except to call his hands in perfect bridge English — and off he went. We next saw him atop the whale, and, in all the trips I've done with him since, I've never seen him anywhere else.'

'I'll get to know this character,' I rashly boasted to Gyle.

'A bottle of whisky that you don't!' he replied. 'Though you'll be living within five hundred feet of him for the next eight months.'

I paid Gyle his bottle of whisky at the end of the voyage.

But enough of the examination of these various interesting characters. I am as anxious to get this ship to sea as no doubt is my reader, and we shall see them all again, and see them differently, for no sailor's personality — no man's personality, for that matter — is the same ashore as it is afloat.

The factory ship set sail from Tönsberg amid as noisy and demonstrative a send-off as any old bark ever had from New Bedford. 'Where is this alleged Nordic reserve and Scandinavian control of emotion?' I wondered as sirens hooted, every motor horn screamed madly, boatloads of desperate women chased the ship down the fiord as though to retrieve their men before it was too late, and the men themselves hung over the ship's side weeping openly and making as though to dive over and swim back to their women. I remembered the curt nods the Scots women had given their men before walking off down the wharf without looking back, and the single toot of recognition from a fellow whaleship which had been our only send-off from the U.K. But the Norwegians' favourite sentimental songs are all about a motherly woman, while Scotland's saddest songs are written round the figure of one man who failed to return. Maybe that gives the clue to the different reactions to parting shown by Gael and Viking.

Our immediate destination was Aruba, a West Indian island belonging ostensibly to the Dutch, but factually to that great colonial power, the Standard Oil Company. There, ridiculous as it sounds, we were to load twenty thousand tons (our ship's total capacity) of oil, in order that we might sail to the ice at the other end of the world to seek a full cargo of — oil! 'Wouldn't it be easier to dig for it?' the woman *I* was leaving behind asked in her letter to me in Aruba, when I had explained this situation; but we neither of us at that time realized the value and importance of whale oil to this half-starved modern world.

On the voyage to Aruba, the ship and the ship's company settled down — as much, that is, as a whaleship and whalemen ever settle down. I, along with young Evans and the other first-trippers, was happy exploring the great factory ship, the like of which we had never seen or imagined on the high seas. There were at that time only nineteen such vessels in the world, and, because they spend most of their time in waters where no other ship ever ventures, few — even among old sailors — have ever seen one. (In fact, Mark told me that the signal he commonly received from passing vessels as we crossed the transatlantic shipping routes was not the usual courteous query: 'What ship? Where bound?' but more often: 'What in God's name are *you*?') And we greenhorns, although we rapidly became as proud of our ship as any yachtsman, realized, when we examined her, that she was in fact the ugliest thing afloat.

This was young Evans's comment: 'You know, there are men who spend their lives designing beautiful things — beautiful gardens, beautiful houses, even beautiful cities. Specialists in beauty. Well, in the same way, I've often thought there must be big brains at work somewhere designing ugly things. Take the river front at South Shields, where we joined this ship; no accident or chance could have produced so much ugliness and squalor. There must have been a designer — a specialist in ugliness — who vetoed anything that might have alleviated the hor-

44

rible view and suggested various gas tanks and garbage heaps which would improve the ugliness.'

Evans's 'Specialist in Ugliness' became one of our shipmates of fantasy — every whaleship carries many amusing crew members who are not on the articles. We appreciated the genius of the Specialist even more when we saw Aruba, and were overwhelmed with admiration at his work on the whaling station in South Georgia, but at his birth we saw him as a naval architect who had designed our ship.

'Look at her!' said Evans, shuddering, as we wandered over the factory ship. 'You couldn't change any line or spar of her anywhere without improving her appearance!'

And he was right. For seamen who have not seen a factory ship, I would describe her thus: Imagine two large oil tankers stuck together beam to beam, so that their funnels are abeam, and not fore and aft. Place the two in an immense blunt-bowed hull, with a wide, shallow draft and a freeboard of prodigious height. Then cut off the stern of this Siamese ship, carve a great obscene-looking hole where the sternpost was, and run a tunnel that could accommodate two railway trains from the waterline between the two screws at a gently sloping angle up to the main deck, just forward of the funnels. . . . Or, in landsmen's language: a great hulking lummox of a ship not much smaller than the *Queen Mary*, blunt at the front, and with a big hole at the back where the bump should be; and with funnels side by side instead of one in front of the other: and with sticks and chimneys and all sorts of gadgets sticking up everywhere except in the places they do on a proper ship.

In her superstructure, a factory ship is divided in two — the reason being that two vast areas of deck space, each capable of accommodating two or more ninety-foot whale carcasses, must be left clear in the middle of the ship; below this clear space is the factory, a maze of machinery, occupying three decks and a floor space measurable in acres; and below that again are the tanks, capable of accommodating twenty thousand tons or more of oil, and reaching down to the bilges. The engines that drive

45

the ship are abaft — behind, that is — the factory space; and the bridge, stores, offices, and administrative part of the ship are forward of the factory space.

The places where the seven hundred men (who, with reinforcements for South Georgia, make up the ship's normal complement on her way south) live and have their home for eight months are divided, some being forward of the factory below the bridge, and some aft of the factory above the engines. The social consequences of this division of the ship's company by several hundred feet are complex and at times distressing; but in our early explorations of the ship we were more concerned with finding out who lived where than with the problem of who associated with whom and why. For, when it is realized that a factory ship heading south to the whaling grounds carries the numerical equivalent of a regiment of soldiers packed into two tiny four-storey apartment houses, the intricacy of our original explorations may be understood.

'We'd better employ a guide,' said Evans as we started off. 'We'll crash first time if we're flying blind.'

So, of course, we went to find Mansell, who, in his eternally obliging way, was only too pleased to throw up his work a while to show two green hands over the ship. I will not try to reproduce his running commentary and libellous asides on owners, officers, and crews of the expedition, which he shouted continually in a voice audible from truck to keelson as he conducted us over the inhabited parts of our grotesque vessel, but will describe some of the visits we made and what he showed us. We began on the flying bridge, the highest part of the ship, away up on the 'roof' of the forward apartment house.

Here we encountered the first of those strange anachronisms that never fail to fascinate one who is constantly comparing the modern whaling with the old. The flying bridge, a sizable platform, was deserted, for, other than greenhorns like ourselves who came to gape, no one but Davison the bosun — who mounted once a day to perform a duty as old as the whaling industry — ever came near the place. The platform contained

46

four objects of interest — two representing the electronic age, and the other two as ancient as the art of navigation itself. There was the mighty 'eye' of our main radar set, circling continuously, scrutinizing the sea to the horizon and beyond, and reporting on the screen in the wheelhouse below every floating object within thirty miles of us which might be large enough to damage the factory. On a clear day on the edge of the Sargasso Sea, with nothing for hundreds of miles around more harmful than the gulf-weed, this miraculous eye was of little value, but Mansell did not need to explain to us how we would bless this apparatus when we would be crawling through Antarctic gales or fogs with often a hundred or more lethal masses of ice floating in the murk around us where only radar could see them. Below the radar eye was the antenna of our direction-finding apparatus, another electronic device — of little value in the clear tropical Atlantic — which would earn its cost many thousandfold in the south when our seventeen little ships, many commanded by gunners whose navigational knowledge was elementary, sought to come home to their mother ship.

But the other two objects on the flying bridge interested me more than the modern wonders. The first of these was an old-fashioned magnetic mariner's compass — eight bars of magnetized iron, fixed to a card and swung on gimbals in a battered old brass binnacle, identical with the compasses of the earliest whaling barks and not very different from the suspended lodestone of the earliest Chinese navigators. Below, in wheelhouse and chartroom, we had duplicate gyrocompasses with dials that read accurately, not to a degree, but to the thousandth of a minute; but the Board of Trade requires that every British ship shall carry a mariner's compass, and there it stood as it has stood for six hundred years or more.

The second anachronism was a rack of wood, painted white, on which stood six bright-red iron buckets with plaited-rope handles. This was our ship's fire-fighting equipment, again in accordance with the standards laid down by the Board of Trade. We had below an electronic warning system, which gave

47

immediate notice to the bridge of any disparity of temperature in any compartment of the ship, and the most modern apparatus for piping foam and other anti-conflagrants to any place aboard at the press of a button. Our anti-fire service was as efficient as that of any ship afloat, for, if our oil-filled ship took fire in the Southern Ocean, we would not one of us survive long enough to know what had happened. But the B.O.T. said that every ship shall carry on the flying bridge a rack with six red buckets of water, and, again, there they were, as they had been on the deck of Drake's galleon, and every morning Davison, the bosun, climbed up to inspect and fill them as Drake's bosun had done.

On the storey of the forward apartment house below the flying bridge, we found the main bridge, wheelhouse, chartroom, and radio room, forming compositely the brain of the expedition. Here — as seemed to be the case any time by day or night when we subsequently visited the bridge — we found Mark in control, and with this friendly and enthusiastic Sheltie we spent the next hour or two, learning not only the marvels of his intricate equipment, which varied from an Asdic sounding-gear — accurate to a tenth of a fathom and sufficiently sensitive to be disturbed by a shoal of herring — to a tortoise, the ship's mascot and the only tortoise that has crossed the Antarctic Circle twice. We also learned how a modern whaling expedition, as complicated an organization as a naval force in battle, is administered and controlled.

Mark was in a curious position aboard our ship, as are many other men who take employment in whaling ships flying the British flag. For most of these ships were commanded by Norwegians. In fact, I believe I am right in saying that during the 1950–51 season not a single one of the many British registered ships actively engaged in the whale hunt was commanded by a Britisher. No doubt the law permits this, as it appears at times to have permitted British whaling ships to sail without a single Britisher aboard, and as other countries such as Panama allow whole expeditions manned by foreigners to use their flag. But sometimes, apparently, British law demands that a ship flying the Red Ensign shall at least carry on board some person who holds a British Master's Certificate, even though that person is not factually the Master of the ship. Mark, although the holder of a British Master's Certificate, was signed on our ship as 'Junior Chief Officer,' serving under a Norwegian Manager and a Norwegian Chief Officer.

The excuse I have heard given for this strange but usual set-up in British whaling vessels is that if Britishers were put in command, the Norwegians would go on strike — as they have done in the past — and the only sufferer would be the British housewife, whose protein supply would fall considerably. This may be so. And there may be other reasons why the whaling companies consistently place British seamen with British qualifications under foreign command; but the interesting thing is why the authorities, and the trade unions, and the British seamen themselves accept the situation.

Anyway, there was nothing of the 'North Sea Chinaman' about Mark, and whatever his reasons may have been for serving in an inferior position despite his superior qualifications, his quiet efficiency on the bridge and his obvious knowledge of all aspects of his job, gave confidence to the seamen aboard, and convinced the landsmen like Evans and myself that our expedition would be as safe as modern science and inborn seamanship could make it.

Leaving Mark, Mansell took us into the radio room, where sat — or, rather, lay — Tom Archibald, our senior Marconi man. I never saw a less alert-looking watch-keeper, and it occurred to me that Tom's whaling ancestors might have been ashamed of him lying there semi-somnolent on a settee while a clamour of peeps and buzzes in Morse too fast for me to understand came from receivers in every corner of the room, perhaps with somewhere amid it a message of importance to our ship, or the radiogram I was awaiting from my girl in America, or even a cry for help from someone in distress in mid-Atlantic. But Tom dozed on. Mansell, however, explained. Any cry for help, any SOS from a radius of a thousand miles, would set off automatic alarm bells all over the radio room and in the wheel-

49

house and by the bunk of every radio-operator we carried. As for important messages for the ship or for me personally, it only needed one far-distant transmitter in Rugby or Capetown or Boston to add our ship's call sign to the discordant jangle coming in over the receivers, and Tom would be awake, as surely and as rapidly as if we were to speak his name into his soporific consciousness.

Mansell put it to the test by whistling softly: '— — · — · — — · .' Instantly Tom was awake and reaching for his transmitting-key.

On the storey below the ship's brain, our visits were social, though still instructive. First we called on the manager in his palatial quarters. We sat down in his comfortable chairs, and Mansell rang the bell and informed the steward who answered that the manager wanted two bottles out of the ship's bond and four glasses. They came, and we settled down a while to get to know this boss of ours. We liked him. One of the pleasantest types of modern young viking, he was much more conscious and diffident about his anomalous position of superiority in this British expedition than was Mark in his complementary position of inferiority. The manager welcomed us and, of course, began to talk whaling straight away. When he saw we were really interested in the trade that had been his whole life since he joined the company as a mess-boy twenty years before, he hauled out the plans of the expedition and gave us a comprehensive picture of how it was organized and the strategy we would adopt in our attack on the whale this year.

The manager's lecture on the strategy and tactics of whaling was clear and explicit, and, when we left his room, we felt that we were now really whalemen, coming to understand something of the industry we had joined.

On the deck below the manager's quarters we found the rooms and offices of the administrative staff of the ship. There was Mansell's own room and office; there were the cabins of the mates, four in all; there were the secretary and his assistants (a whale-factory ship needs an office staff as large as any other industrial plant employing over six hundred men); and also on this floor were those key men of any ship, the stewards.

Stewards — by nature or professional training, I know not which — look with grave and very obvious suspicion upon anybody who tries to be nice to them, and ours were no exception. Acting on the assumption that we had come to scrounge something, one of these fellows, who later in the voyage was given the name of the Intolerable Ho by the Bramah fans aboard, quickly antagonized young Evans and myself. He tried his best to antagonize Mansell, but that was impossible; the boyish old whaleman did not even notice that this was the first frigid reception we had encountered in our tour of the ship. But stewards the world over, be they catering-managers on huge liners or cook-'n'-cabin boys on fishing trawlers, are of that kidney. I know not why.

The remainder of the ship's company, visited in their floating apartment houses, were pleasant to a man. Some were shy. The twenty-odd little mess-boys, who lived in a dormitory in the 'basement' of the forward apartment house, were overcome with confusion when they received a visit in their humble abode from great personages like the doctor and the junior chemist and Mansell! But as their ages ranged, in my medical opinion, from thirteen to sixteen — although on the ship's articles all were listed as in their seventeenth year — their schoolboy embarrassment was understandable. The two cadets, future whaleship officers, who lived in a cabin that would have made an excellent small closet, were very adult and composed in comparison. The senior cadet, two years at sea and nearing his seventeenth birthday, behaved like some veritable admiral entertaining on his flagship, and hoped we would 'call again some time at the cocktail hour.' On such silly occasions I always watch the wrong person. I watched Mansell. He behaved as though he were indeed taking leave of an admiral.

Then we began the long trek aft to the other small four-storey apartment house. At this early stage on the way south, the main deck of a whale-factory ship is like the yard of a large and busy contracting firm. First we wound our way between vast coils of brand-new six-inch hemp rope. This was the whale line, later to be divided and issued to our catcher fleet. I forget its fantastic length: I remember its price — £20,000 worth of rope was what we carried, Mansell told me. 'But what the hell! Twelve whales — one day's work during the season — pay for all of that!'

Next we passed between stack after stack of new timber. I do not know the size or the value of a stand or a cord or any other woody measure (Mansell, of course, did), but it seemed to me there was enough good white pine on that deck to build a city. Then a pile of machinery. Spare parts are not readily available in the Antarctic, so the engineers had had to anticipate break-down of or damage to every moving part of a fleet of seventeen ships, and here were all the spares that might possibly be needed to get the small ships or ourselves going again. 'It has never happened yet,' said Mansell, 'but I think, if it become necessary, we can build a small ship down in ice as good as any built in Glasgow.'

Then, in the space beyond that cluttered up with machinery, we came to the deck cargo of oil. Not fuel oil — we had twenty thousand tons of that below decks — but lubricating oil. And not a few drums of it; not a few tons of it; but enough lubricant to keep high-speed engines collectively amounting to millions of horse power turning smoothly for the next eight months. Al-though it is not in my nature to be overawed by material — and especially commercial — wonders, I began to make comparisons with the old whaleships that went to sea with 'forty barrels of salt provisions . . . six hundred fathoms of tow line . . . one lantern . . . one boathook . . . one hand saw . . . one parge hammer' and other tools and stores in like proportion. I com-pared the mighty preparations that modern whaling entails, and, while I could clearly see the romance of the 'one boathook,' I also began to see something fascinating in the idea of maintaining the most modern and complicated machinery, and keeping an intricate industrial plant running, in that part of the earth farthest from all human habitation and in the most inclement conditions nature can offer to man.

But right at the after end of the main deck we came upon a throwback to the past — the pigpen, containing some thirty young porkers; the only fresh meat other than whale meat we could expect to eat until we returned the following year. What ship other than a whaleship today carries its provisions 'on the hoof'?

And leaning over the pigpen in the 'basement' of the after apartment house we can dismiss Mansell as our guide, for this part of the ship was our own home. Here, above the engine room, young Evans and I lived for the next eight months. Our neighbours were the other scientists, the engineers, Davison, the bosun, and Victor, the storeman, and two or three hundred others ranging in social position from Whaler Group VIII ('scum of the ocean') to Old Burnett, the chief engineer and self-appointed backbone of the expedition. We were a happy bunch down aft — happier and more friendly, we thought, than the bunch who lived in that strange, foreign, far-off place, the other end of the ship; but we were not happy all the time.

When we left Aruba in the West Indies, our last civilized port of call, and began our long journey south, a deep depression settled over the seven hundred men aboard our ship. In the U.K., in Norway, and as we were bunkering at Aruba, they had been gay, reckless, and jovial in manner and conversation. But after we turned southward, despite various attempts at organized fun on the ship in the way of parties, concerts, high jinks at the equator, and the like, we all tended to become solitary and avoid the society of the friends we had made. We began to be irritated by one another, and especially by the buffoons, the lives-and-souls-of-the-party who had formerly amused us so much.

I felt some responsibility for the morale of the expedition, so I consulted the old hands about its obvious deterioration. They all agreed that it was a usual geographical phenomenon during the long trip south, and they assured me that it would partly disappear when we reached the island of South Georgia, our Antarctic base, and would vanish altogether when the first whale was killed. But they did not agree on the causes of the depression. Some said it was delayed homesickness, and a sudden realization by the men that they were going to waste another year of their lives away not only from their families, but from all civilization.

'Look how they're all beginning to grow daffodils and listen to music; look how Old Burnett has brought out a tea-set of delicate china and is delighting in asking his cabin guests whether they take milk and sugar; we're all trying to bluff ourselves that we are not outcasts of civilization, but are engaged in as ordinary an occupation as catching the nine-thirty train to town.' That was Mark's explanation.

Davison said it was simply boredom, and the same reaction would be found on any ship engaged on a very long voyage. 'And the man who said the world's a small place never sailed from Aruba to South Georgia at twelve knots,' he added.

Gyle explained the depression at a deeper philosophical level, which may have applied to him as an admirer of Abner Dean, but I think was too flattering to the intellect of the average whaleman: 'We've all got the what-am-I-doing-here's,' he put it. 'Of all human pursuits which illustrate the utter futility of human life and civilization, that in which we are engaged is the most absurd. We are on a journey of many thousands of miles, at the end of which it is our intention to disrupt the peace and happiness of a harmless species which knows nothing of man's existence, and will know nothing until the harpoons start exploding in their innocent guts. And why are we engaged in committing this crime worse than genocide? Because civilized man is such a damned fool he can't use the land except as a battlefield where he squabbles about his futile little ideas. And we have all suddenly realized that we are doing this at considerable discomfort to ourselves for the benefit of the colonies of pitiful little termites in the northern hemisphere, who are all busily engaged in going nowhere and need fats and proteins to feed them on their journey there.'

Mansell's explanation of the ship's gloom was simpler and

perhaps more accurate, psychiatrically speaking: 'Women!' he shouted. 'We got no women, so we are gloomy. You put one good-looking girl working in ship's laboratory, or nurse in sick bay, or even serving at saloon table instead of that gargoyle of a steward who puts me off my breakfast, and we all fight like tom-cats to get smile from her, but we all be very happy!'

Whoever was right, it was true that, when we sighted the jagged white peaks of South Georgia breaking above the mist ahead, we all began to lift our heads up from between our knees, where they had been for the past few weeks, and, when the mist was suddenly sucked away, as Antarctic mists often are, leaving South Georgia's frightening but exhilarating coastline like a gigantic high-contrast photograph set down in front of our bows, then our gloom was likewise expunged. The whole effect was like that well known to photographers in the dark-room when the main light is switched on, making every object and every picture sharper and more vivid than it had appeared under the murky safe-light. There was singing heard again on the ship, and the chief engineer was heard to bid a cheerful 'Good morning!' to the mate — a most unlikely occurrence on any ship, and a miracle on ours.

'And I will tell you, Rubbersen,' said Mansell, when I re-marked that, if his theory was true, South Georgia seemed to have had the effect of a Ziegfeld chorus on the crew. 'Some very great men who come here love this place and very happy here; not only ignorant whalemen. Ernest Shackleton, greatest explorer who ever go to Antarctic, he was always very gloomy shipmate on way south. Never laugh all the time, until he arrive at South Georgia. Then he was always very happy man. Like he leave the world and enter different happier world. . . .'

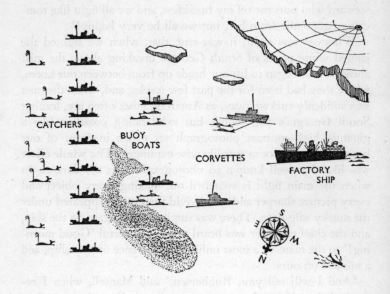

CATCHERS

BUOY
BOATS

CORVETTES

FACTORY
SHIP

PELAGIC WHALING FLEET

III

SOUTH ATLANTIC SANCTUARY

A small speck near the bottom of an unfamiliar map may be all that
South Georgia means to most.
— ROBERT CUSHMAN MURPHY

SOUTH Georgia is a two-faced island, in every meaning of that
term. It is two-faced geographically, climatically, scenically,
and in all natural ways; and this intrinsic duplicity seems to have
been emulated and added to by the deeds and works of men
upon the island.

Geographically it is a crescent-shaped island, presenting a
wrinkled, sometimes smiling, Northern face, indented by many
fine natural harbours, with glens around which are habitable
by man and beast and hardy growing things. But Southwards,
facing the Pole, it presents as grim a lip of sterile sneering cliff,
with the ice-enamelled fangs of a hideous mountain range snarling above it, as one could find in the physiognomy of the whole
world.

Its climate is as ambivalent as its geography. A ship may approach the island in visibility so distinct that the officer of the
watch dulls his view with sun-glasses and the eager photographer
beside him prepares to take his first picture of the island through
an aperture of f.32. And then, within minutes, and without ever
passing through the B.B.C. stages of 'moderate, becoming poor,'
the visibility will become zero; and the officer of the watch will
dash to the lanyard of his siren while the photographer fumbles
his way down the bridge ladder to fetch an infra-red film.

And the wind is as treacherous as the visibility. A shore whaling station on the island may be flushing in a midsummer sunshine as strong as ever was felt by the Scots and Norwegian
whalemen in their own countries, and the smoke from the factory

chimneys may be rising perpendicularly toward a placid sky. Then one of the many glaciers cleaving through the mountain range high above the whaling station will give an angry growl, and will seem to puff out a blast of snow which fills the glen. And within a minute the station will be the centre of a snarling blizzard, corrugated iron will be flying about, men will be dashing for shelter, and the ships anchored in a harbour that seemed only moments before to be the gentlest of sea-lochs, will be snapping and tearing at their anchor chains, like tethered dogs with the wolf-pack upon them.

Regarding the scenery and æsthetic appearance of the island, suffice it for me to say, in travel lingo, that I have seen the Himalayan sky-lines, the Rocky Mountain gorges, the fiords of Norway, and the lochs of Scotland; but the little island of South Georgia had something to show me to rival the grandeur of all of these — and something more. And then, with its inevitable perversity, South Georgia had some sickening sights to show, although in defence of the lovely island, it must be admitted that these were, or resulted from, man's contribution to the scenery. But they were as foul and unsightly as anything I have ever seen, although I am no stranger to such hideous works of man as the slums of Glasgow, Cairo, or Calcutta, and though I have dwelt in the most squalid African and Asiatic villages which each year raise themselves a few inches higher on their own excreta.

A narrative of modern whaling would not be complete if it did not include some account of both aspects of Britain's greatest whaling base in the South — the sordid, ugly, and disgraceful, as well as the spectacular fascinating things the visitor sees on the island. But our whaling fleet pays two visits to the 'small speck near the bottom of an unfamiliar map,' one visit at the beginning and the other at the end of the whaling season. And so, let me leave until later in this book and the end of the season any attempt to describe the man-made unpleasantnesses one encounters on the island, which might at this stage distract my reader from the whales and men of my story, and might blind him (as it nearly did me) to the allure of the strange place.

And let me pretend that I went ashore on my first visit (accompanied, of course, by Gyle and Mansell) without seeing the premier British whaling station where we landed, and that we walked inland, with the intention of cutting across country to visit some friends in a near-by and rather less revolting settlement.

'Near by' is a term which needs some explanation anent South Georgia, although the area of the whole island is only about that of Sussex.

The engineering works which we proposed to visit were only, as the albatross flies, some three miles from the whaling station —twenty minutes by motor-boat along the coast of the bay. But to cross those three miles by land was a strenuous three-hour scramble for fit active men; for it was necessary to cross two wicked shoulders of the mountains which jut into the sea between the two main British settlements, and although South Georgia is an old-established British colony, no government agency has yet seen fit to mark a track, never mind build a road, anywhere on the island.

There was nothing venturesome about the journey, though whalemen who set out alone to walk across had occasionally got lost and been found frozen far up one of the confusing South Georgia glens when the fog or blizzard that benighted them had subsided. There are no perils in the way of wild animals, if one excepts the huge bull sea elephants, which lie about, even far inland from Stromness Bay, during their rutting season, but only attack if provoked or accidentally trodden upon. There are minor crevasses, a few deep tarns with a treacherous covering of soft snow, and some loose screes, which may start sliding and precipitate major landslides; but to make this two-hour walk out to be an adventurous journey would be an absurdity. It does, however, give one an inkling of the difficulties of overland travel on the island, and explains why the island is still only very sketchily explored.

We struck inland, and immediately — as often happens on South Georgia, and is often enough true — we had the feeling that we were walking where no man had walked before; and where no man had any right, for the island belonged to its fauna and flora.

The flora was uninspiring. Tussock grass, growing round the sea fringe of the island, could not exist above a few hundred feet. Higher, there was nothing but occasional lichen growing on the rock. The snowfields, though the Antarctic spring was well advanced, reached in places right down to the shore, but were generally encountered at about five hundred feet, and above their level nothing grew. I asked about trees, of which there are none on the island. They told me that many attempts had been made by amateur whaleman arboriculturists to find trees in Scotland or Norway which would survive, but all attempts had failed. Comparing the country with other places I had seen, ignorant though I am about trees, I thought the only one that might survive would be the mountain ash, or rowan, of my own country, which survives gale and hard weather like no other tree. My guides told me they thought nothing but conifers had yet been tried, so I decided to take some rowan with me when next I visited the island.

The fauna was astounding. The sea elephants, largest of the southern seals, lay all around the beaches and occasionally, far inland, each gigantic slug of a bull surrounded by his fifteen or twenty smaller but equally repulsive cows. We intentionally aggravated some of the bulls to see what they would do. They reared up, when we threw stones at them, blew out the little trunk-like proboscis that gives them their name, then began lumbering toward us, meaning murder. Their awkward progression on land was so slow that they could easily be avoided, and one was perfectly safe unless one slipped and fell in their track; but the interesting thing was that, if you walked round behind them, they immediately forgot your existence, and lay down to sleep or make love in a sluggish but apparently satiating way: it took another stone to raise them again in surprised realization of one's existence. I think it unlikely that any animal psychologist studying memory has ever experimented with these beasts, but, when he does, I can promise him an all-time low level of retentiveness.

The penguins were everywhere. They obligingly collect in rookeries handy to the whaling stations and lay their eggs just when the whaling season is beginning, so that any expedition like ours calling at the island can lay in a huge store of delicious fresh gourmand-sized eggs. The rookeries and the quaint, seemingly human behaviour of the penguins have been described so often, I shall not attempt it again. And, in any case, I was more interested in the lonely penguins that one found wandering in the most unlikely places on the island, far from the noisy rookeries. Standing in the goal-mouth of a little soccer pitch laid out by the whalemen on a patch of level ground near the whaling station was a black and yellow King penguin, keeping goal on a deserted pitch and thinking in his penguin way, perhaps, of the absurd antics of the interloping humans he had often witnessed on that spot. In the gun embrasure was a little black-and-white Adelie (named, though it seems not too complimentary, by the Russian explorer Bellingshausen after his French wife). This little chap was demonstrative and Gallic in his conversation and gestures when we disputed his possession of Sergeant Mansell's fortress. Away up the glens, where no food or companionship or anything of worth in the penguin scale of values could possibly be found, were other lonely but apparently contented little fellows. One of these, seen at a distance, looked enormous — twice the size even of the Emperor penguin, which is never seen except on the continent of Antarctica. Full of zoological enthusiasm, we scrambled half a mile up the glen to make it captive, and Gyle and Mansell were disputing hotly who saw it first and whether the name Gylonica or Manselli should be given to the species, when the huge penguin came round a rock and spoke to us. It was our second steward, pottering about by himself with his camera. He was polite to us, and passed the time of day for a few minutes, but he refused our invitation to walk with us over to the other settlement. Like the lonely penguins that preferred the silence and detachment of the glens to the companionship and chatter of the rookeries, Dornoch had things to do which satisfied him more than our proffered conviviality.

As we scrambled on over the rocks and snow, we talked of penguins. Or, rather, Gyle and Mansell talked about them, for the only interesting contribution I could make to the discussion was a fact I had learned shortly before, talking to an official in Edinburgh Zoo. This was that penguins are an international form of currency, between zoos. If a zoo somewhere has, say, more lions than it needs, it will offer them to other zoos — but not for money. They will be valued and paid for at so many penguins a time. And so, since frequently the Scottish whalemen take penguins back to their national zoo, it is, in terms of zoo finance, one of the wealthiest in the world.

Gyle was a supporter of the classic and most generally recognized theory of the penguin: that it is a bird which, to its eternal disgrace, has traded its demi-godlike power of flight for a full belly of fish, and lives in the Antarctic today because that is the only place in the world where there are no four-footed land marauders which would rapidly destroy a species of flightless birds. Mansell upheld the more recent but usually ridiculed evolutionary hypothesis of this species: that it is not a degenerate bird, but an amphibious reptile which was hardy enough to survive climes and conditions which no other species could endure, and, as its reward, has been given the chance of, and is even now developing, the power of flight.

'Come on!' said Gyle, picking up a lump of snow and heaving it at an unfortunate ring penguin that crossed our path. 'I hate these brutes. Let's climb up a bit and talk to the albatrosses and the petrels and the other real birds which may be hungry, but are worthy of a sailor's respect.'

'U-u-u-gh!' protested Mansell, with the unreproducible Scandinavian grunt. 'Your wonderful albatrosses! You watch them round the whale carcases in the bay — they gorge so much, they cannot rise from water, never mind fly thousand miles. After ten million years, albatrosses be sitting on ice floes flapping useless flipper, and penguins be soaring above masts of ships.'

During our walk we saw no land animals. We expected this, for, apart from the imported reindeer — that have flourished on the island now for nearly fifty years, providing sport and food for the whalemen — and the rats, for which ill-kept whaling stations make a paradise, there are no land mammals on South Georgia. 'Only dangerous animal on this island is Whaler Group VIII' was Mansell's prejudiced comment. 'We see plenty of him over in shipyard, where he stink even more than in whaling station.'

The place we were going to did no active whaling, but was the repair depot and engineering shop for the British whaling companies. It did not, therefore, sit in a mire of stinking *grax* as did Leith Harbour, but the same unhygienic, unsalubrious conditions prevailed, with no apparent effort on the part of anybody to relieve them. Arriving in the station, we called — for whaling is a democratic, classless world — on a friend of Mansell in the bosun's mess. There we found our own bosun, Davison, who had sailed round by motor-boat while we walked over the hills. He and the Norwegian bosun of the station (the whaling stations are staffed by seamen, who keep their shipboard ranks) were sitting in the first really comfortable room I had yet seen in South Georgia. It had been made and decorated entirely by the petty officers of the station, and had decent furniture, curtains, flowers, clean linen, and much that seemed incongruous when one looked through the clean window at the unsanitary filth outside.

Davison had brought his Norwegian friend a bottle, it being an unwritten whaleman's law that anyone coming off a ship from home is given food, but supplies the drink. Gyle and Mansell knew the law, and, having anticipated that we might go a-visiting, each had a fat flask, which they added to the general pool on the bosun's table. I, the green hand, not knowing the law, had brought nothing, and I made my apologies, which started us discussing the liquor problems of the island.

South Georgia is not dry by law. The Falkland Island administration imposes no restrictions, other than the usual customs dues, on the importation of liquor to the island: but the whaling companies, which have a virtual monopoly of transport to the island and seem to hold an immutable belief that all whalemen are mental defectives and incorrigible drunks, not only made no provision to meet a reasonable demand for drink, but have been known to take active steps to prevent it reaching the whalemen. The result is that men isolated on the island — most of them fairly healthy drinkers, though by no means drunks — are deprived of all alcohol during their eighteen-month segregation.

Or so it is thought by whoever has the impertinence to decide these things! In actual fact, I learned, probably as much drink is consumed on South Georgia as in any other similar land area of similar population in the world. Every whaleman on the island is an expert brewer, and can produce palatable drinks from raisins, rice, oatmeal, or any other vinous or cereal substance supplied to him in his rations. They are expert distillers, too, and most have some ingenious home-made apparatus under their bunks designed to distil and concentrate strong liquor from their various brews. The work and ingenuity that go into this island industry exceed even that put into the whaling, and a South Georgian's brains and ability are estimated by his fellows according to the quality of liquor he can manufacture.

I asked for samples, and found most of them good. 'Plonk' is the generic term used for all whalemen's home-made liquor, and there are as many and varied recognized brands of plonk as there are reputable liquors in a well-stocked bar. The best variety, or at least the one most to my taste, was that made from raisins and laced, to increase its strength, with compass fluid. (The few old-fashioned magnetic compasses on the small craft attached to the island consume, the Norwegian bosun told me, around fifty gallons of pure alcohol per year, and the two thermometers at the meteorological station are almost equally thirsty.) Another popular brand of plonk is distilled from a well-known hair-cream. This I found invigorating, but not too palatable. The only home-distilled product I could not stomach — though the old whalemen prized it highly and drank it with relish — was a black liqueur that, I afterwards ascertained, was manufactured by heating a tin of boot-polish (the brand is a whaleman's secret, and it is imported to South Georgia in vast quantities, though it is unlikely that any pair of shoes has ever been cleaned on the island). When melted, the boot-polish is strained through a loaf of bread, after which, to get the best results, it should be fermented for three days, then bottled and placed in the cellar for four months: but in emergency it may be collected and drunk as soon as it drips through the bread.

As may be guessed, when my introduction to the alcoholic life of the Southern Ocean whalemen was completed, the motor-boat that had brought Davison round from the other station had long since departed, so we had no option but to spend the night with our hosts or walk back again across the trackless hill. We elected the latter, for there is a time during a night of good-fellowship when the risk of a broken leg or a pitch down a hundred-foot rock seems a minor thing. We set off in the darkness — the Norwegian bosun of course accompanying us 'to show us the way.'

I am glad we made this stupid and rather reckless decision, because half-way back to our harbour, none of us being very sure of our direction, we stopped to rest and finish the remainder of Gyle's flask; and I shall remember that halt for the span of my life. We sat down on the tussock grass on a high promontory sticking into a ghostly bay. There was a faint light, I know not whether from moon or star or 'ice-blink,' but sufficient for us to see the narrow entrance of the bay, which a huge tabular iceberg was threatening to block, and to see the towering unnamed mountains all round us. We were a Scottish doctor, recently a psychiatrist; an English naval officer; a Shetland seaman, the finest seaman I had yet met; a Norwegian whaleman who had spent more than half his life in the Polar seas; and Mansell.

We sat silent for a time, while the flask passed round twice. Then began a conversation which changed many of the bitter, angry thoughts which that day had begun to form in my mind regarding this island.

It was Gyle who opened the conversation (and do not think, from the way I reproduce his words as I remember them, that he was talking over the heads of the seamen who listened — for old whalemen are not as other seamen).

'It's a strange thing,' he began. 'There's a huge literature of whaling in prose; but there's little or no poetry about us or our job. I wonder why. Think what Byron might have written if he'd gone a-whaling instead of to Greece; or if Coleridge's wedding guest had been stopped by an ancient harpooneer instead of by a retired merchant-navy man. Think what William Blake might have written of the whale, had he known it; or think what wonderful doggerel Kipling's unwritten "Master Flenser" would have been!'

Davison was tickled by this idea. 'Aye!' he said. 'Or Robert Service's (maybe Bret Harte's) unwritten poem called "Blue Whale Mansell"; or "The Voice of the Antarctic."'

Mansell had a suggestion — probably, alas, a vain one: 'Maybe we persuade John Masefield, if he be not too old, sign on whalecatcher for one trip and write great whaling poem before long trick's over!'

'It is strange,' I mused. 'There's no whaling poetry I know, except one stanza of Kipling's which *is* actually about a master flenser from Dundee . . . but there's some mighty prose. Same with the Antarctic sea and continent — there's been some fine prose written about them, mainly by seamen with no literary education or pretension; but not a word of verse that I know.'

'Nor music neither,' added the Norwegian bosun. 'Except one piece written last year — a symphony called *The Albatross* written by an Italian who had read *Moby Dick*, but never been in Southern Ocean. It wass no good!'

Then I remembered the only part of the poetical lecture given me by the old gunner's daughter in Tönsberg which had interested me: 'But there have been a few lines of poetry written about this island, though the man who wrote them didn't realize that it was about a place a few miles from here that he was writing. . . .'

I was very cross when Gyle stole my effect and quoted the lines entire:

> Who is the third who walks always beside you?
> When I count there are only you and I together
> But when I look ahead up the white road
> There is always another one walking beside you
> Gliding wrapt in a brown mantle, hooded. . . .

'Who wrote that?' asked Davison. 'And why d'you say it's about South Georgia?'

'T. S. Eliot wrote it,' Gyle told him, 'in a poem called "The Waste Land." And he wrote a footnote to explain it.'

(Gyle could not, of course, quote Mr. Eliot's footnote accurately, but I do so for him now:

The lines were stimulated by the account of one of the Antarctic expeditions—I forget which, but I think one of Shackleton's; it was related that the party of explorers, at the extremity of their strength, had the constant delusion that there was *one more member* than could actually be counted.)

Mansell took up, at this point, this strange conversation between half-inebriated whaling men sitting on a frozen headland at night on the fringe of the Antarctic seas. 'I am not very well-read man,' he confessed. 'I never read anything except about whaling and the sea, so I not know this Mr. Eliot. But I knew Ernest Shackleton, explorer about who this Mr. Eliot write. I know about this other man, too — this strange, queer one more member who accompany Shackleton and his two men when they march across South Georgia. I was here — so was Davison — the day Shackleton walk into whaling station over the mountains, when we and all the world think he and his men lost down in ice. Shackleton dead twenty years now — I go to his funeral when he die down here, and his wife, who know her man well and where he want to lie, say: "Bury him in South Georgia, not in Westminster Abbey like government want" — and maybe most people in north forget even his name, but we not forget him down here. I tell the story of Shackleton to Rubbersen here, u-u-u-gh?'

Gyle, Davison, and the Norwegian bosun had heard the story at source, and a thousand times since, and I had been reading and re-reading it since this most inspiring of Antarctic explorers had started on his last quest into the white south when I was nine years old. But we all nodded, and, sitting there on the lonely cliff, Mansell told the story again. I wish I could convey the drama and feeling with which the old whaleman retold South Georgia's most inspiring tale, and I wish I could reproduce the atmosphere in which Shackleton, hero of the Southern Ocean whalemen, though a forgotten man in England and America today, was brought to life again on that lonely foreland of the island he loved so well.

The tale that Mansell told was this:

The year was 1915. The South Pole had been reached by Amundsen and Scott three years before, but the continent of Antarctica was still almost entirely unknown, and Shackleton was aiming to lead some scientific men across the continent from Weddell Sea to Ross Sea to get a general picture of its formation. The Antarctic continent is bigger than the U.S.A., and most of it is lying beneath hundreds — often thousands — of feet of solid ice, so this journey was no light undertaking.

Shackleton had sailed from Britain the very day the First World War was declared on Germany, and from their first port of call, he and his men had offered to abandon their projected expedition and place themselves and their ship at the disposal of their country. In answer Shackleton received a cable from a statesman who, even in the fury of war, could see the value and overriding if not immediate importance of a venture such as they proposed to make. The cable was a single word: 'PROCEED'; and it was signed by the First Lord of the Admiralty — Winston Churchill.

So Shackleton sailed into the ice of the Weddell Sea; but, before his transcontinental journey could start, he met disaster. His ship was crushed and totally lost in the pack ice, and he and twenty-seven of his men found themselves sitting with three tiny whaleboats in the middle of the most remote frozen sea on earth, with no radio and no means of telling the world of their disaster.

'So what they do?' Mansell asked, pausing in his story. 'They sit down and pray to God? Or start writing dramatic diaries about all is lost, same like Captain Scott? Na-a-a-w! Shackleton just say: "O.K., boys! We go home!" — and he bring 'em all home, safe and well. And how he do it, u-u-gh?'

The way he did it was to trek, part sledding, part sailing, with his three boats to the nearest point of solid land — the fearful and hitherto unvisited rock called Elephant Island at the mouth of the Weddell Sea. There he left twenty-two of his men to support life precariously on seal and penguin meat, with upturned boats as shelter, until he could return with aid. With five companions Shackleton set out on as fantastic a journey as has been undertaken through the ages by any leader to save his crew: a journey in an open twenty-foot whaleboat across nearly a thousand miles of Antarctic Ocean, on the remote chance of reaching that tiny inhabited speck in the far South Atlantic, the whaling island of South Georgia.

'And you know what his men and everybody in Zuther Notion call Shackleton?' Mansell went on. 'They call him "Cautious Jack" — "Canny Jack," the Scots boys say — because he never took unnecessary risk. Now you think, Rubbersen! When we leave the island, we sail down to mouth of Weddell Sea in twenty-five-thousand-ton ship — and maybe that is difficult and dangerous at times. You think what a risk Canny Jack and his five men take crossing same ocean in tiny whaleboat!'

But against all the currents and terrifying gales of the Southern Ocean, and against all the laws of chance as mathematicians work them out, the tiny cockleshell hit South Georgia — but on the wrong side. They landed on the southern coast of the island where no man had ever attempted to land, never mind support life, before, and there was not a hope under the prevailing weather conditions of sailing round the island. So Shackleton made another cautious move. 'Right!' he said. 'We'll walk across the island to Stromness whaling station.'

'You think that not a very exciting thing?' Mansell asked me, and I could see his eyes gleaming in the dim light as he talked. 'Maybe you scoff and say it is only few miles across island from where Shackleton land to here, u-u-gh? But I tell you, no man — not even all the crazy British, American, and Norwegian men who come to this island before and since Shackleton — ever try to climb to top of the ridge, never mind walk across island. You look up there behind you. . . . You see what I mean!'

But Cautious Jack Shackleton, with Worsley and Crean (these names are not remembered anywhere in the world today except on South Georgia Island), fixed screwnails into the soles of their boots, and, seamen as they were, with not a mountaineer among them, began a climb and a descent across a nine-thousand-foot unexplored range. They had no map, for such a thing does not exist for the interior of the island even today, and they had only a schoolboy's pocket compass to guide them as they pushed into the mountains, hoping to find a pass of some sort through the range before one of the South Georgia blizzards, the most fiendish known on earth, should destroy them.

They reached the top of the ridge — to find themselves trapped. There was no way down the other side. They began painfully cutting steps in the ice slopes, but soon realized that this offered no hope, for night was on them, along with it the certainty of freezing to death, and no man would hear of them again, or of their twenty-two shipmates a thousand miles behind them down in the Weddell Sea.

So: 'We'll slide!' That was Cautious Jack's suggestion in this predicament! And the three of them coiled up their rope, sat down upon it, and grasped one another round the waist. Cautious Jack kicked off.

This is what Worsley, the man in the middle position on the rope, wrote about it afterwards:

Slide down what was practically a precipice, in the darkness, to meet — what? . . . It seemed to me a most impossible project. The slope was well nigh precipitous, and a rock in our path — we

70

could never have seen it in the darkness in time to avoid it — would mean certain disaster. . . .

But Canny Jack, their leader, said: 'We'll slide!' and the other two did not demur, so whe-e-e-e! Off they went.

'It's not good to do that kind of thing too often' was Shackleton's comment when they found themselves at the bottom and, to their astonishment, safe. And next morning they heard in the distance the steam whistle at Stromness whaling station calling the men to work.

Mansell concluded his yarn: 'I was in manager's office at Stromness that day. Everybody at Stromness knew Shackleton well, and we very sorry he is lost in ice with all hands. But we not know three terrible-looking bearded men who walk into the office off the mountainside that morning. Manager say: "Who the *hell* are you?" and terrible bearded man in the centre of the three say very quietly: "My name is Shackleton." Me — I turn away and weep. I think manager weep, too.'

We sat a while in silence when the old whaleman had finished the often-told yarn; but each of us occasionally turned round and looked up at the awful mass of jagged black rock and immense glaciers towering away behind us into the gloom toward the interior of the island, and we did silent homage to South Georgia's greatest spirit.

'Tomorrow, Rubbersen,' Mansell whispered to me, ashamed of his sentiment, 'I take you round to Grytviken visit Canny Jack's grave. Maybe Old Burnett give us some of his daffodils to lay there. Every year we leave some.' (As, in fact, the whalemen do; and they tend that grave as well as it would be tended in Westminster Abbey, or better, though they come out of their stinking, *grax*-polluted dwellings to do so.)

We made a move back to the ship, and during the next hour or so, as we stumbled over rock and snow slope and worked our way slowly round the headland, we talked of Antarctic explorers, and the motives that take men down to that terrifying white desert, not once, but time and time again, to dedicate a large part of their lives to its ghastly wastes, often to die there.

71

'The motives of some of them are only too painfully obvious,' Gyle said. 'Personal glory, kudos, or even material gain. Most of the big expeditions which go today with prefabricated, centrally heated palaces, airplanes — and, of course, accompanying journalists and radio commentators — come into this category. Even some of the heroes of the past, such as Amundsen, brave men though they undoubtedly were, had motives which were suspect. Some others are real scientists who reckon that the knowledge they gain of the last unknown part of the earth is worth the agony of getting it. But, besides those two types, there's always a handful of men like Shackleton who keep coming down here as it were for the fun of it. My explanation of them is that they find something down here which is an absolute necessity here if men are to survive, but is rarely met with in other places and conditions — namely, real comradeship. That's a human relationship second only to sexual love, and a thousand times rarer. You find it in war, but war's a filthy business and the comradeships of war are tainted as a result. But down here, where it's not man against man, but man backed by his comrades against the worst that elemental nature can do — against God, if you like — then you find a real comradeship such as you will find nowhere else on earth, and men like Shackleton keep coming back again and again to experience it.'

Davison was not satisfied with this explanation. 'Aye! But there's more to it than that,' he said. 'It's the old urge to see what's over the next hill; and Antarctica's the only part of the world left where it's still possible to look over a hill without knowing for a certainty what you're going to find on the other side. Of course, it will probably be more ice and snow; but it *might* not be — and it's that "might" that brings the Shackletons down here time after time.'

The Norwegian bosun had another theory: 'It is not because they want to come down here — it is because they want get away from up there. Some like us whalemen — they not fit up there in your country and mine, and people up there not want queer folk around like Shackleton and whalemen. And we no can write poetry or paint pictures or get away from silly world which want no part of us, same like artists do. So we come here because we not at home — *and* we no damn use — anywhere else.'

Mansell stopped and gestured complete disagreement with the other three. 'I think you all talk nonsense, and you know it. Shackletons, and best kind of explorers, and maybe old whalemen, too, come here because they know there is *something* else, that man can feel but not quite understand in this world. And they get closer to that thing — that fourth man who march with Shackleton across South Georgia — when they are down here than anywhere else in world. This island, Zuther Notion, Antarctic continent — all haunted places. Not many haunted places left in modern world, and, when man like Shackleton find one, he keep coming back to discover — haunted by *what*? C'mon! Time we get back to ship!'

For the remainder of that walk through the night I speculated on these things. I saw the world divided into two types of men: on the one side, the pitiful little men wasting their lives in their armchairs, or grabbing goods and gear and meaningless money from one another; and, as the epitome of this type, I saw the businessmen responsible for the squalor and sordidness I had passed by that morning. And, on the other side, I saw the old whalemen, the misfits of this world, and the men who are engaged in an endless quest for they know not quite what, but who — like their magnificent prototype, Ernest Shackleton — are above and perhaps do not even notice the discomforts and difficulties they encounter in that quest, whether these be laid by nature or by other, lesser men.

And I wondered if some deep, unexpressed, and inexpressible religious urge was in fact, as Mansell suggested, the motivating force that urged such men — sneered at by their civilized fellows as 'psychopaths' and misfits — on their endless, useless, unproductive quest.

When we got back to the ship I was tired, more tired than I had been since I took up whaling — but not so tired that I did not

73

get out Ernest Shackleton's book and read his own comment about the mysterious 'fourth man' who accompanied him on the adventure which Mansell had so vividly described. Shackleton wrote:

When I look back at those days, I have no doubt that Providence guided us, not only across those snow fields, but across the storm-white sea that separated Elephant Island from our landing place on South Georgia. I know that during that long and racking march of thirty-six hours over the unnamed mountains and glaciers of South Georgia, it seemed to me often that we were four, not three. I said nothing to my companions on the point, but afterwards Worsley said to me, 'Boss, I had a curious feeling on the march that there was another person with us.' Crean confessed to the same idea. One feels the 'dearth of human words, the roughness of mortal speech' in trying to describe things intangible, but a record of our journey would not be complete without a reference to a subject very near to our hearts.

After that night on the lonely coast with the old whalemen, and with the spirit of Shackleton as the 'other man' among us, I looked on South Georgia in a very different way. It was no longer merely the 'slum of the Southern Ocean,' but had become, as it is to Mansell and many others who choose to make their home there, a mystical and inspiring isle.

IV

THE SOUTHERN OCEAN

The mariner should exercise great care when navigating in these waters.
—The Antarctic Pilot

LEAVING South Georgia and heading due south, with the last human habitation astern of us and no living man ahead, was a bracing experience. It was so at least for me, and for young Evans and the other greenhorns on the ship, and I suspect it was also even for the old whalemen like Mansell and Burnett who had done it twenty or thirty times before. For we knew when we cast off the last rope from the filthy little wharf of Leith Harbour and saw the South Georgia mountains fading over the northern horizon that for the next few months we and our six-hundred-and-fifty-strong team were utterly dependent on ourselves and the resources we carried with us; that the world of men could bring us no aid if anything went wrong; and that we had turned our backs on man's last outpost and were entering that part of the earth from which the glacial period has not yet retreated, and where there is nothing but the fiercest of seas, surrounded by even fiercer ice, and sterile rock.

'Well! We're off — for better or for worse!' said Old Burnett in the saloon the night we sailed, presumably in a heavy-handed effort to cheer up the greenhorns. 'And God alone knows what will happen to us before we tie up anywhere again.'

'You keep your engineers sober and your engines running, old man,' was Mansell's riposte. 'Then we be all right. Mark sail the ship safely if you give him plenty steam; I make plenty whale oil and earn big bonus for you; and doctor try to keep you alive until you get home; so you no need to worry.'

Whether Old Burnett and the other departmental heads of the

expedition really did worry about the huge and unalleviated responsibility they would have to carry for the next few months, I do not know. I can speak only for myself. I tried not to over-dramatize the situation, and repeatedly reminded myself that our well-equipped expedition of seventeen ships and six hundred and fifty men moving into the fringe of the Polar seas was a minor venture compared with the enterprises of the explorers like Shackleton who took small parties of men and single wooden ships hundreds of miles farther into the ice than we proposed to go. Nevertheless, I saw the departure from our last land station through the eyes of the doctor responsible for whatever might happen to my shipmates in the way of accident or injury or disease in the next five months. My exhilaration was tinged by some anxiety about the grave accidents that are bound to happen when modern industry is pursued at the uttermost and most dangerous end of the earth, and the illness that would undoubtedly occur among my hundreds of shipmates. No doctor is medically and surgically omniscient, and a whaling trip into the Southern Ocean is the only situation in the modern world where he is expected so to be, both by his employers and by his patients.

But worries fade rapidly if one goes into the company of another whose worries are much greater, so the first few days out of South Georgia I spent much of my time on the bridge with Mark, who carried a heavy responsibility for our ship and our men and everything that would happen to us until we dropped anchor again. He was always ready to talk to the ignorant and was an unending and never repetitive source of nautical and polar information. From him I learned the lore of ice and frigid sea, and of the birds and beasts and monstrosities and men that frequent the ocean — Mark's major study during an intelligent and keenly observant life.

I was with him on the bridge the day we sighted our first large iceberg. Needless to say I dashed down aft to get my camera, and met the other greenhorns on the same errand as I did so.

Mark smiled when he saw our enthusiasm. 'You'll see plenty

of them before the trip's finished,' he told me, 'and I wouldn't waste any film on that little half-mile-long one if I were you. We'll get in among the big ones when we get farther south, and, anyway, they're very unsatisfactory objects to photograph.'

He advised me — rightly, as I know today — that, if I wanted to take good pictures of the Antarctic bergs, the best way to do so was to float ice cubes in my bath and take close-ups of them, for all the southern bergs had the same flat-topped sugar-cake shape. To find the fairy-castle and cathedral-shaped icebergs that artists love to draw, it is necessary to go to the other end of the earth, to the Arctic, where the bergs are formed in a completely different way.

Mark's course of instruction to me on icebergs lasted for days, and I can reproduce only the highlights of it. The biggest Antarctic berg he had seen, he told me, was about thirty-five miles by ten, and a hundred feet high, but much bigger ones have been reported. But, rather than in the size, he was interested — and he got me to share his interest — in the extreme age and apparently (from the human point of view) futile life history of the Antarctic icebergs.

All of them are formed of glacier ice. Snow falls through the centuries on the Antarctic continent, perhaps many hundreds of miles inland. Further falls of snow, assisted by a sloping of the land from the plateau around the Pole to the periphery of the continent, push the older snow, now squeezed by unbelievable pressures into hard crystalline ice, in mighty glacial streams down toward the sea. The outcrops of these glaciers form huge ice shelves jutting into the sea, afloat but still attached to the continent — 'many of them bigger than the whole of Scotland,' as Mark put it. Then chunks start breaking off and become floating islands of ice, which drift northward and in general eastward in the Antarctic currents, away from the Polar seas up to the warmer waters. 'The whole process,' to quote Mark again, 'takes, not hundreds, but thousands of years. The snow which went to make that small berg out there fell on Antarctica maybe six thousand years ago — long before Tutankhamen was king of

Egypt. And no man's ever seen it during those six thousand years. And, once it breaks away from the ice shelf, what's its fate? To drift up here and be seen once by you and me before it melts; for it's very unlikely any other ship will ever sight it. At most, it will drift nor'east and become a menace to shipping on the Cape-to-New-Zealand run for a week or two, then dissolve into the sea. It all seems kind of pointless, doesn't it? Or it makes you wonder whether we're the all-important things on this planet we imagine we are.'

Mark, who was by no means a bigot, but, like most Shelties, held strong religious views, was inclined to lead such discussions into theological arguments, so I headed him off and brought the conversation round to the dangers of navigation in the Polar seas in modern times.

Big bergs are no longer a danger to whaleships. Radar has eliminated their menace. As we went farther south, it was nothing unusual to have twenty or thirty large bergs in sight around the ship at the same moment, and, though fog or heavy weather might obscure them in a few minutes, every piece of ice sizable enough to sink our ship for thirty miles around remained clearly visible on the radar screen, and the bearing and distance of each could be read off in a moment. International sea law still demands that, when a ship is fog-bound, it shall drop to half-speed and sound a siren or other warning device every two minutes. When Mark was on the bridge, this regulation was still complied with, even on occasions when the radar showed no catcher within thirty miles and showed the large ice so clearly that we could have steamed full-speed with complete safety among it. Some of the other whalemen, more concerned with the catch of whales and the size of their bonus than with the safety of the ship, would razz Mark for being over-cautious, and would compare his retention of the old precautions of pre-radar days with the six buckets of water on the flying bridge for fire-fighting. But their criticism did not perturb him, for he knew that, in not trusting entirely to one gadget or means of navigation, he had the approval of all the really experienced old sailors on the ship, such as

Gyle and Davison. And to those who advocated a blind faith in radar under ice conditions Mark would argue: 'When you've used radar as much as I have, you'll often have seen large bergs on the radar screen that weren't there in the sea when you looked with your glasses; so maybe some day, if I wait long enough, I'll see a berg in the fog dead ahead which doesn't show any existence on the radar screen. But I'll be going half-speed the day I do, and I'll have heard the echo of the siren off it long before I come near hitting it.'

Icebergs, Mark maintained, are objects that any real seaman respects and fears, even when he has the latest ice-detecting and navigating equipment to help him. But, he told me, expeditions paradoxically will often find the ice their best friend. If a gale is blowing — and a Southern Ocean gale is something very different from a gale in any other sea in the world — there is always a big berg somewhere handy for the whalecatchers and other small craft of a whaling expedition to run to for shelter in its lee. I was told, and later experienced it, that even a huge ship like ours, if it has whales on deck and on tow, may have to seek the shelter of an iceberg when the weather gets up.

I asked Mark if many ships were lost down in the ice nowadays.

'The whaling companies don't talk, and their policy is to avoid publicity of anything to do with modern whaling,' he told me, 'so it's difficult to get accurate information. I know there have been factory ships lost since steam whaling started, and there's a catcher or two lost by some company nearly every year — we lost one the year before last, and another the year before that — but it never gets into the papers. Many of the companies carry their own insurance, or sail their ships under peculiar foreign flags, and their relations with the shipping authorities of their respective countries are usually a bit strained at the best of times, so the less the public knows and the fewer questions people ask about whaling, the better the companies like it.'

I often discussed with Mark and other old hands the comparative dangers of modern whaling and whaling in the heroic old days of the small boat and the hand harpoon. They were all agreed that, though a great many dangers have been eliminated from the industry, at least as many have been added. There are perils associated with modern whaling which would daunt the most daring harpooneer of old, just as killing whale from small boats is not a job any modern gunner would care to tackle.

'But always remember,' Mark warned me as we talked on the bridge one day, 'when you're seeking information about the dangers of whaling, new or old, remember that whalemen are and always have been mighty fine liars. Since the first Phoenician threw the first harpoon, every whaleman has considered it his right and one of the prerogatives of his trade to tell the landsmen, or even other seamen, the biggest whoppers he could get them to believe. Read any whaling yarn written in the English language, or listen to the whalemen, old or new, talking, and you can safely discount all but about ten per cent of what you hear. My people have been in whaling for five generations, so I've been reading and listening to nothing but whaling stories since I was a wean. There's always some truth in every whaling tale — unless it's a gunner that's telling it — but there's a good deal of exaggeration when it comes to the heroism of the job.'

Mark used to refer to the great days of the sperm-whale fisheries from New Bedford and Dundee as the 'Maybe Dick' days, and was always inclined to cry down the exploits of the whalemen of the last century — exploits in which his own ancestors had participated — but some of the comparisons he made between the dangers of old and new whaling were just.

Take the ships. The huge tub in which we were sailing south seemed the safest thing afloat; but she was not by any means, and all our ship's officers were agreed that they would rather weather out an Antarctic gale in a Nantucket bark than on top of twenty thousand tons of industrial machinery in a blunt iron box. On the other hand, we had radar, echo-sounding gear, electric logs, and a thousand other safety devices that would make the old whaling skippers laugh us to scorn, and, best of all, we had double specially plated and reinforced bows, which could crash into and brush aside pieces of ice that would cause to founder the largest and strongest whaling ship of the last century.

But with our catchers and small craft it was different. They had no double bows or watertight bulkheads. They were about half the size of a whaling bark, and were little more than single-plated, over-engined steel speedboats that could not withstand a single squeeze from the pack ice or a hefty blow from a small growler. Yet they were ready and eager to go much deeper into the ice than the old barks normally ventured.

And, though no modern expedition would dream of lowering small boats to chase the whale, to counterbalance this the modern whalers go after mainly the blue and the fin whales. The old hands never attempted to catch these two species because, in the first place, they lacked a fourteen-knot engine and could never catch up with blues and fins, the fastest in the ocean. In the second place, these whales sink when they die, and a powerful modern winch or other mechanical means is needed to raise them and keep them afloat. Finally, the old-timers would never have dared to attack blue and fin whales even if they came up alongside, for these two species fight in a way no monster sperm ever did.

Again, though the size of the craft that hunt the whale has increased, everything else has increased in proportion, and often enough the danger increases with the size. Take the ropes. The three-quarter-inch hemp line that the old whalemen used was dangerous enough as it smoked past the loggerhead and burned the hand of any man who grasped it. There are on record at least three authentic cases of men being hauled out of the whaleboat and lost through being entangled in the line. But compare the modern eight-inch Manila whale line, and the damage that results when anything goes wrong with that. As Mark said to me: 'Jesus! I'd like to see my grandfather try to handle some modern cordage, and I'd like to see his face and hear the stories he'd tell afterwards if ever he were present when a three-inch nylon rope with a strain of a thousand tons on it and stretched to half its length again fouls and is cut by a catcher's propeller!'

Not all my time on the bridge with Mark as we headed south was spent in the discussion of Polar navigation and whaling, for the Southern Ocean had much other diversion to offer us. I began to find that my instructor was a well-informed authority on most of the things we saw as we yarned together, leaning over the dodger. The birds were always the most obvious diversion, and on these he would talk for hours. I carried in my pocket all the time a little handbook of ocean birds which supplied the scientific data, but Mark would back this up with innumerable whalemen's legends and much accurate information based on his own observation of the birds of the Southern Ocean.

As with all who are new to the southern seas, it was the albatrosses that interested me most. There was invariably one of these great birds, and often enough twenty or more, gliding over and round our ship as we steamed toward the ice pack. The first sight of them had been disappointing. They looked no bigger and no more inspiring than large sea-gulls, and the colour of most of them was not the evil white so often described, but a patchy, mundane brown.

But occasionally, as we stood motionless on the wing of the bridge, one of them would glide down to skim the water far below us. There it would coast along, undulating its flight to fit exactly the shape of the ocean swell and seeming as though it would hit the crest of every wave that swept from our bows, but never quite doing so. Then, when it had kept up this surface-skimming for minutes or even hours, a bigger and steeper swell would come along, and the bird would rise without effort. It would veer toward the highest part of the swell, approaching the advancing wall of water so closely as to give the impression that its intention was to burst through and come out the other side. Then, at the last moment, an imperceptible muscular twitch would change its direction, and the pressure ridge of air caused by the advancing swell would do the rest. Without the flicker of a wing-tip the bird would rise steeply from the water, and in a moment would be gliding right alongside us by the bridge, fifty feet high. And there, where we could have leaned out and touched it, we saw this bird greater than the eagle, in its true dimension and grandeur.

Then we could see — and, had we wished, could have bent over to measure — its astounding wing span: eight to ten feet in the small ones, eleven to thirteen feet in the greater. And we could bear witness to its apparent utter immobility in the air — except for the eyes. My guidebook did not tell me, but Mark pointed out, that the eyes of the albatross are never still and fixed, as are the eyes of most birds in flight, but are continually flickering up, sideways, down, then ahead.

'They're seamen's eyes,' Mark said, and I saw what he meant. For I had noted during our long hours on the bridge together that, though he would remain motionless except for a slight movement to compensate for the rolling of the ship, Mark's eyes were never still. Although he might be talking to me of birds or whales or ice, his eyes would never be on me, but would be moving up to the sky, then sweeping the horizon, then the bows of the ship below us, then straight ahead for their steadiest and most prolonged gaze.

'Would you kill an albatross?' I asked Mark suddenly one day as we were watching the great birds.

'Christ! No! . . . And don't you do so either, or I'll heave you over the side!' was his violent rejoinder. 'I'm a religious man,' he added, 'though you might not think so at times by my language; and I believe in heaven and hell, and my church doesn't approve of superstitions — like the superstition that the souls of dead seamen enter into albatrosses. But if I were God' (a not uncommon and by no means intentionally blasphemous phrase on the lips of a Scot) 'I wouldn't take seamen up to strum harps with their horny hands. But I *would* put their souls into albatrosses; and, you see, doctor, it's possible that God does have enough sense to do that. So don't you go killing any albatrosses around here!'

Partly from my bird book and partly from Mark I learned the explanation of the absence of the classical pure-white albatross from the vicinity of our ship. The book told me that in this part of the ocean we could expect to encounter mainly the sooty albatross, which breeds on South Georgia and will be found seeking its food hundreds of miles from its breeding-place. This species, as the name implies, is a smutty-looking bird. Only the great wandering albatross is pure white all over, except for his primaries (which are the feathers forming the tips of his wings). But it is only the adult that is pure white, and all birds under about two years in this species retain their dirty-brown fledgling feathers. Although we saw many hundreds of the young birds we saw no adult white wandering albatrosses around our ship. This the book did not explain, but Mark took up the story from there:

'There are various theories,' he said, 'to explain why no whaling ship ever sights a pure-white adult wandering albatross. One is that the older members of the species are too delicate to stand the cold of the Southern Ocean and always head north from their nesting-grounds. The other is that, when they have turned pure white, they are old and wise enough to know that they'll find damned little grub thrown overboard from a British whaleship with a Norwegian chief steward, so they fly up astern of us, take one look at our port of registration, smell the Norwegian cooking, and sheer off in a panic to find an American ship with an Argentine chief steward.'

One particular albatross that we met about a week out of South Georgia I shall never forget. We were still steaming due south, and loose pack ice was beginning to appear around us. From up on the bridge we first saw this bird as a tiny speck flying on a course northward, exactly opposite to ours. The wind was from the north, and he was gliding on it, mast-high, in the effortless way of his species. We assumed with unconscious vanity that he was coming out of the ice to meet us, and would turn and join the dozen or so of his brethren which were already in our convoy. But, as we watched him approach, he showed no sign of turning, but maintained a steady course. Our courses crossed with about ten yards between us, and he sailed serenely over our right shoulders and past our rigging without the slightest deviation and without even, it seemed, a glance sideways, and continued on astern of us. When he had finally disappeared away into the evening haze behind us, Mark exploded. 'Would you bloody well believe it!' he swore. 'He didn't even notice us!'

When Mark was busy, I used to seek out Dornoch, the second steward, who was also an endless source of ornithological information, perhaps not as amusing but certainly as accurate as that of Mark. Dornoch introduced me to the smaller birds of the Antarctic, and many hours we spent hanging over the side of the ship with our cameras, he augmenting his already wonderful series of sea-bird photographs, and I taking a succession of pictures invariably the same, and invariably on development turning out to resemble the child photographer's first blurred and disappointing effort to catch a sea-gull on the wing from the beach. However, I learned much about the little birds during these sessions. Two species in particular fascinated Dornoch, and he communicated his fascination to me.

The first was a little brownish fellow which fluttered low near the water below us. Like the albatrosses, this small bird and his kind stayed with us for weeks on end, though they seemed to lack all the advantages that enabled the albatrosses to do so. They could not glide like the great birds, and they never settled on the water, so that they were never at rest, but continued to flutter — flutter — flutter — day and night for weeks on end, occasionally darting down to the surface of the water to pick up a morsel of grub, but never alighting on the sea. It seemed, in fact, that they could not swim, though the bird book did not mention this. Their expenditure of energy in proportion to their size and the food they ate must have been tremendous, and we felt sorry for them as we watched, for it made one tired by empathy to look at them. Dornoch told me the whalemen's legend concerning them. It appears that, while the albatross is the seaman's soul in a state of bliss, the Wilson's petrel is the damned soul of a landsman, condemned for ever to find his livelihood on the ocean, and denied any sea-going attributes to aid him. The myth was appropriate to the tormented little bird, and was rather frightening. It occurred to me that this was something Dante might have used, had he known about it, in his diabolic prescriptions for the disposal of damned souls.

Dornoch's other Southern Ocean pet was the prion, a small, graceful, slender bird that skims the wave tops and descends deep into the troughs seeking air currents, albatross fashion, but differing from its mighty cousin in that it occasionally dives deep below the surface seeking live fish. This sharp-winged alert little bird has many aliases among seamen. Some call it the 'ice bird' because the men of the old sailing ships believed that it indicated the presence of ice. This might be so, for certainly we never saw it except when there was ice about. And the old whalemen called it the 'whalebird,' for they reckoned it led them to the whales. This Dornoch disputed, and my own subsequent observation made me agree with him, for, when we were among the whales, we never saw a prion. The real 'whalebird' is the Cape pigeon, a plump black-and-white bird sitting high and serene on the water, looking just like a pigeon, as its name implies. It seldom rises in flight for more than a yard or two. This bird, which has a most attractive appearance but a most unattractive personality, we never saw in passage anywhere, and it ignored our ship completely if we were whale-less. But, if whales were about, it would begin to appear, and, let one whale be killed, and the Cape pigeons would be on the sea all round us, literally by the thousands, waiting to share our spoils with us. They are surface feeders, preferring whale guts to any other diet, and neither Mark nor Dornoch nor the bird book could tell me what they could find to eat on the surface of the icebound Southern Ocean when no whalers were around. We could only speculate that they followed the schools of live whales, hungry but hopeful, anticipating their early death at our hands, and a good feed to follow.

'They're like the whaleship-owners,' Dornoch put it, expressing the whaleman's age-old cynical opinion of his employers. 'They only take an interest in us when there's some profits to be disbursed. Maybe we should call them the "whale-owner birds"!'

I was again with Dornoch one evening when I had an unforgettable ornithological experience. The long twilight of high latitudes, when objects are still fairly clear but photography is impossible, had descended, and we were up in the bows. Dornoch was gazing hypnotically at the cleavage made by our ship through the icy water, and I was trying in a desultory way to find some subject of conversation which would make this interesting little character open up a bit more and reveal his philosophy.

Suddenly there came a loud 'Ca-a-a-k! Ca-a-a-k!' from the sea, seemingly from about fifty yards out. It was a most unmarine and farmyard-like noise, and, when I looked quickly, I saw nothing but empty water. Dornoch noticed my astonishment, and explained. This was the noise made by the penguin when he is in his real home, the sea. I watched closely for a while, and soon I saw them: four flashing black shapes suddenly shot out of the water to a height of about a foot, projected themselves through the air in a graceful streamlined curve, and re-entered the water without causing a ripple. A few seconds later, and a hundred feet ahead, they repeated the action. The glide and dive were smoother, faster, and more graceful than the surfacing of any dolphin, and my first glimpse of it changed immediately my opinion of the penguin as an awkward and ridiculous or frustrated and unnatural creature. For there was nothing ridiculous or unnatural in this astonishing progression through and over the water. I have seen it aptly described since as 'flying in water' instead of in the air, and seeing it the first time produces the same effect as that moment in circus routine when the incredibly awkward and ludicrous clown who has been rolling in the sawdust, amusing the children, suddenly seizes the trapeze and swings gracefully to the top of the tent with a skill even greater than that of the beautiful lady and sleek, well-polished gentleman who earn their living by daring acrobatic feats. I had glimpsed the other side of the life of the sad little comic of the Antarctic, and, as the four glossy black shapes drew ahead at twice the speed of our ship, I saluted them. Maybe they had, as Gyle averred in South Georgia, earned our contempt for giving up their heritage of flight for a full belly of fish, but, if they had left the kingdom of the air, it was to claim regal dignity in the ocean. And, if Mansell was correct (and I began to hope he was) in theorizing that they would in some dim future age rise right out of the sea to return no more, then they fully deserved their elevation in the evolutionary scheme.

It might be thought, from my description, that a whaling expedition sailing south to the ice from its last port of call is tranquil and idle, the hands having nothing to do but hang over the side looking at the birds. Certainly the whalemen do spend much of their spare time examining and, according to their individual psychic states, communing with the other beings that make the Southern Ocean their home and hunting ground. But there is in fact little idle time for anyone as the whaling ground is approached. Even the senior medical officer, who, next to the chief engineer, is reckoned by the average unappreciative whaleman to have the softest job on the expedition, was very busy for the week or so after our expedition left South Georgia. Although he spent as much time as he could bird-watching, he spent rather more time during that period in the sick bay.

For an epidemic of 'influenza,' as we called it, had broken out on our ships, and the men were going down like the traditional flies, with three-day fevers, coughs, and occasionally a threatened pneumonia. I had been forewarned by predecessors in my job of this peculiar outbreak, which attacks nearly every whaling expedition leaving South Georgia. It had scared the wits out of many a whaling doctor in the old days of Dover's Powders, and had killed many a whaleman and explorer who had left the island (including the toughest of them — Shackleton), but in these days of penicillin and various -mycins, it was a troublesome but not frightening outbreak. It would take an epidemiologist to explain properly the South Georgia 'flu' that was affecting us all at this time. I can only say vaguely that it seems to be connected with the fact that the resistance to all respiratory infections among the island inhabitants drops sharply during the winter, when they are cut off from all the coughs and sneezes of the rest of the world. The whaling ships bring the bugs back to the ill-prepared islanders in the southern spring, and the whole immunity-starved island is knocked flat by germs that have been browbeaten and rendered harmless in the crowded northern hemisphere. Then, by what the bacteriologists call 'serial passage' through a succession of highly susceptible subjects, the germs resume their virulence — get back their self-confidence, as it were, in their malevolent attack on the human race — and, by the time the whaleships leave the island, are malignant enough to make another assault on the men who brought them to the island. So even I was busy as we headed south.

But again, if I felt inclined to complain about my job, I had only to go up to the bridge, where others, Mark chief among them, were ten times busier than I was and had responsibilities exceeding mine, and my complaints would be silenced. For the whaling was about to start, and, though Mark and the other bridge officers all had the flu, they were on their toes sixteen hours a day, with only occasional intermissions to talk to the doctor and watch the birds.

Mark took time off to show me what was going on (probably, I think, because I had remembered Mansell's advice to take special care of the health of this man, and had given him particular and discriminative treatment to keep him on his feet when the fever did hit him), and he took me into the chartroom often to explain the expedition's plans.

The general plan of attack on the cetacean world was this: One of our little whale-catching ships, commanded by Thor, that phenomenon among gunners, the former New York taxi-driver, had gone ahead of us by several days to 'look for the whales.' Thor had headed due south to the edge of the pack ice, which he was now skirting in an easterly direction, somewhere south of the South Sandwich Islands. Every few hours he reported back to the factory ship. Accompanying us were the other sixteen small vessels that made up our fleet: catchers, corvettes, and buoy-boats. They were ahead, astern, and all round us. 'Like a hen and her chickens' is the conventional metaphor for such occasions, but, though our huge ship may have behaved like a lumbering old hen, these vicious little hawklets around us were no chickens. In a day or two they would be biting, and biting hard and fatally, at the greatest of the mammals.

When we reached the whales in any quantity, the thirteen catchers, assisted by their superior speed of fifteen knots, would draw ahead of us and fan out over an arc of ocean that in the beginning would be about fifty miles across. Within this arc, between us and the catchers, would steam the two buoy-boats, vessels almost identical with the catchers and armed like them. Their job would be to buoy and collect such whales as the catchers killed, and do a bit of hunting themselves if circumstances permitted. Also in the arc would be the two unarmed corvettes, which would form a fast connecting shuttle service between us and the fleet of small ships, and would tow in to us the dead whales. Communication within the fleet would be by a continuous day-and-night radio-telephone service.

'I'd better show you how that works, doc,' Mark said. 'They'll be wanting to talk to you oftener than they talk to me, to yarn about their aches and pains and how to deal with their hangovers. All whaling gunners have stomach ulcers — have you found that out yet? And most of them will have the d.t.'s some time during the trip, and the mates of the catchers will be calling you on the blower to ask what to do.'

He took me over to a complicated gadget of the wire-and-dial-and-glowing-bulb type that always terrifies me. It turned out to be very simple, however, and in a few minutes I had got the hang of the one-way conversations and the 'over to you.'

'Now, the first thing to remember,' Mark warned me, 'is that the whole fleet will be listening to every word you say, and they'll be specially interested in any secrets you have to give away. There's a duplicate set in the wireless room, another in the manager's cabin, and speakers in the wheelhouse and the secretary's office; and every one of the small ships has a set which they leave on all the time to pick up what gossip they can. . . . Now let's talk to Thor on Number One catcher — he's about a hundred and fifty miles away, which is the extreme effective range of this machine — and see what he's got to say.' He twisted the necessary knobs and buttons, the machine came to humming life, and he spoke into the handset:

'Hello, Number One! Hello, Number One! Factory calling! Factory calling: Is the gunner there? Is the gunner there? Is the gunner there? Good morning, Thor! Good morning, Thor! Over!'

He put in the 'Over' switch, and the low, whining hum the machine was making changed into a mighty roar, in which I was eventually able to distinguish human words and syllables through the speakers. It bellowed through the chartroom, outside on the bridge, and from half a dozen points in the distance.

'U-u-u-rgh. 'Ullo! Fagdory! 'Ullo! Fagdory! Number One here! Number One here! Gutt mornig, Mark! Gutt mornig, Mark! You want to know about whales — u-u-u-rgh? You call at right time! We chasing sperm now — plenty sperm around here. Maybe we be "fast-fish" in a few minutes. You send up other catchers now. We have gutt day's fishing tomorrow. . . . You talk to mate now. I go forrard and kill first whale of season!'

A few minutes later the radio-telephone began to roar and crackle again, and we heard the voice of the catcher's mate: 'Hello! Factory! Hello! Factory! Number One here! Number One here! "Fast-fish." Large sperm. Lots of others around; weather good. Lots of ice. We'll stick around here and wait for the corvettes to come up. Gunner reckons he'll get three or four sperm anyway. Get the other catchers up quickly. G'bye!'

'Bloody fool might have told us where he is!' was Mark's unexcited comment. 'Only he probably doesn't know himself. However, we should pick them up about midnight. Then you'll see your first whale close up, doc, and neither of us will have much time for watching the birds. I'll leave you to amuse yourself now, if you don't mind. I've got work to do.'

He glanced at the chart, looked up at the gyrocompass over

91

the table, turned the radar on a moment and gazed at the screen, read the speed from the electric log, shouted a word to the cadet out on the bridge, then picked up the telephone and informed the engineer of the watch profanely and dogmatically that it would be entirely his fault if we did not have a whale on the deck by nightfall.

V

HVALBLAST!

> 'Fish,' he said, 'I love you and respect you very much. But I will kill
> you dead before this day ends.'
>
> —Ernest Hemingway

I should like to be able to say that I dashed straight off on the catchers to see the first of the whales being killed, but it was not so. The first few hundred whales I saw were dead ones, for I was tied to the factory ship at the beginning of the season, and, as soon as I planned a catcher trip, some ignorant Whaler Group VIII would thrust his foot into a piece of machinery where no man had ever thrust a foot before, and it would take all night to extricate him and a week to get his foot looking like a foot again. Or the manager would inconsiderately go down with the South Georgia flu when I had just told him the expedition was clear of infection; or old Alec MacDougall, the boilermaker, would come along apologetically just as I was about to go off on one of the catchers, with yet another non-magnetic brass splinter embedded deeply in his eye, and it would be several days before we could assure him that his sight would be all right.

So it was only later — considerably later — in the season that I did manage to slip away for a few days' holiday on the small ships and see this whaling butchery in its initial phases. When I could get away, naturally I chose to go with Thor, not only because he was the best gunner in the Antarctic, but also because I found him better company and easier to get along with than the heavy, suspicious Norwegian-fisherman type to which most of our other gunners belonged.

Some time after November 9, when the baleen whaling season opened, I found myself standing on the tiny bridge of Thor's catcher, with him beside me. We were agreed that the farther we could get away from the factory ship for a few days, the better both for them and us. So he laid his course due south through the drift ice and ordered the highest speed compatible with safety.

The bridge of the little ship was uncovered and open all round — very different from the comfortable bridge of the factory, with its double-glass electrically heated wheelhouse, windproof doors, and de-icing equipment. The catchermen faced the Antarctic weather without any protection other than their thick clothing. At first sight it seemed like masochism, but they have good reason for forgoing all protection from wind and snow and spray. In the whale-hunt it is necessary to have a clear, uninterrupted view all round, and the distant feathery spouting of many a whale would be missed if the keen-eyed men searching for it were behind glass. Thor grasped the dodger of the little bridge in front of him like a steering-wheel, and, though the helmsman was three paces behind him following his directions, it seemed to be he who was pulling the small ship this way and that with his large, ungloved hands as we wound in and out between the ice floes.

'Anyone who can drive a taxi in New York City can handle a whalecatcher in the Southern Ocean,' he said in his Swedish-American accent. 'Start; stop; go astern; no right turn; mind that iceberg; don't swerve suddenly on a greasy road; keep an eye on the cop or the whaling inspector; and all the time watch out for a fare spluttering on the sidewalk or a whale spouting on the horizon.'

'You talk as though you knew both jobs,' I prompted him.

'I do. I drove a taxi in New York for several years,' he told me. Such incongruities were not uncommon when the whalemen gave one brief glimpses into their pre-whaling lives, but this sounded a more than usually interesting one, so I eased Thor's life history out of him piece by piece. A Swede, but born in Norway and brought up to speak Norwegian as well as the Norskis, he had emigrated to America, where he became trilingual and worked as a taximan for several years. This occupation, as he probably rightly maintained, had given him the alerted instincts, the quickness of decision in emergencies, and the ability to synchronize and synthesize several dissociated activities, which had taken him rapidly to the top of the profession of whale-gunnery. But driving a taxi had not been adventurous enough for him, and, when he saw a chance of going to sea, he took it.

'I served my apprenticeship on small, fast vessels trading between Bermuda and some lesser-known ports on the eastern seaboard of the States. I got a very good training in navigation by night. . . .'

He hummed and hawed a bit over this period of his life story, and I remembered something Old Burnett had told me. 'You were a rum-runner,' I accused.

'Well, it was a good preparatory education for whaling,' he replied indirectly. 'The Long Island coast-guard men are not always as quick-witted as whales, never mind whaling inspectors, but dodging them taught me a lot about the handling of small, fast ships.'

He admitted that the repeal of the Eighteenth Amendment had been one of the greatest set-backs in his career. Finding himself idle, he had drifted back across the Atlantic and become involved in the British whaling business. Here he had remained ever since, except for six years of wartime service in command of North Sea minesweepers, in which he had been blown up twice and survived to rise to the rank of lieutenant-commander. The war finished, he returned to whaling, now a gunner, and in his first Antarctic season had made himself the greatest menace the whale species has ever known in its long, hunted history.

'It's a dull job at times, but will do to fill in the time until America or some other big country starts Prohibition again,' he ended sadly.

'Married?' I inquired.

'No-o-o,' he replied a bit wistfully. 'I had a temporary wife during the war — I was put in prison once for keeping her in a restricted naval area for three years without the Admiralty knowing — but after the war she wanted to settle down, and thought I should do so, too, in an apartment in Edinburgh. I tried it for a month or two, but it was no good. She's still there, any time I want her enough to give up this kind of life.'

As we talked, his eyes moved restlessly but systematically round the horizon, and other eyes, too, searched for a 'fare,' as we now began jokingly to call our prey. The ice was becoming thicker the farther south we went, and the little ships now crept along at a gentle seven knots. The mate, a young Canadian seaman, stood beside us, searching through powerful glasses; the man at the wheel behind us, an old Hebridean Islander by name of Angus, had his eyes on the sea more than on the compass before him; and above us, on the crow's nest or 'barrel' at the masthead, the youngest lad on the ship, who by right of his juniority was given the coldest and least attractive job, searched for the elusive and by no means easily spotted puffs of vapour that would disclose our innocent victim.

Thor explained to me what they were all looking for. The baleen season being well advanced, we were after the really big whales. 'I'm sick of sperm and fin and sei and tiddlers like that,' he said. 'I haven't had a really big blue this year yet, and I want to get in among them. They're around here somewhere, I feel certain.'

'How do you know?' I challenged him. 'We haven't seen any for two days.'

'No. But I can smell the bastards,' was his inadequate explanation. 'I'll lay you half my bonus we kill one before the sun goes down.'

I was glad I had not accepted his bet, for a moment or two later there came wild cries from the little Norwegian mess-boy up in the barrel: '*Hvalblast! Hvalblast!* . . .' and a stream of Norwegian in an adolescent and excited tone which caused all hands to peer with glasses and naked eyes away to the starboard bow. I could see nothing (though I did not, of course, admit it) and felt chagrined when old Angus at the wheel, who like myself had no glasses, gazed steadily for a few moments and said: 'Aye! They're blues. Three — four of them at least, maybe more. Headin' sou'-sou'-east. We'll hae a bit to add tae the bonus ere night-time!'

Thor had already rung down to the engine room for full speed, and the catcher swung to starboard as she gathered up her fifteen knots and charged through the water. The stretch between us and the whales was fairly clear of ice. Soon everybody on the ship had forgotten me, the idle passenger, and I stood as far out of the way as is possible on a tiny catcher bridge, and watched. The clang of the telegraph and the increased speed had warned those below of what was afoot, and others began to appear. The Scottish chief engineer heaved himself — he weighed nearly two hundred and fifty pounds — out of the miniature saloon below the bridge and climbed down to the foredeck, where he fiddled with the powerful winch to which the whale line was attached. The second mate and two seamen appeared, dishevelled, from their bunks and went up to the gun platform in the bows to check the gun, clear the lines, and arrange various long bamboo poles and flags and buoys and strange gadgets that stuck up around the foremast aft of the gun platform. The A.B./telegraphist, a sort of seaman-cum-radioman, turned on the blower so that the gunner might inform the factory ship that we were chasing, then went forward to heave some massive chains, the use of which I did not yet understand, through special hawse holes in the ship's bulwarks.

I looked aft. A moderate sea was running, and, with the catcher at full speed, the only part aft of the bridge which was not continually flooded with water and where it was possible to maintain a foothold was the engine-room coping. On this stood the steward and the third engineer, who could have remained below had they wished, and who had seen thousands of whales killed in their time, but could not resist the excitement of yet another chase. And every now and again I saw the white pow and clay pipe of old Julius, second engineer and oldest man in the whaling business, sticking up through a skylight to see how things were going, when he should have been standing by his telegraph and controls in the engine room below. The only missing member of the crew was the fireman/greaser, who presumably was firing or greasing something in the bowels of the little ship.

I looked again toward the whales. This time I did see something, and, had I known what I was looking for, I would have seen it before. I had been searching for a great fountain of water shooting toward the sky, as artists and tale-tellers had taught me to expect, but of course, as we were a mile or so away, all there was to see was a feathery and momentary puff of vapour seeming only a few inches high against the grey sea beyond. I grabbed the mate's glasses when he turned to attend to something else, and through them the spoutings seemed sizable jets, rising straight and slender upwards — a shape and direction that told the experienced men they were blue whales, and not sperm or humpback. Occasionally below the jets I could see a rounded black shape just awash above the water. Angus at the wheel kept up his running commentary (he was talking to himself and not to me, for, like all the others, he had forgotten all but the whales and the chase): 'Aye! There's twa there 'tween eighty an' ninety feet. Thar ones on the port bow's probably a cow and calf. That's a gey wee spout, the yin on the left; but thon's a muckle beggar over there. Are ye wantin' me to steer for that one, gunner?'

Thor did not take his eyes off the school of whales, nor bother to answer Angus, but pushed him away from the wheel and took it himself. 'Tell Julius to give us more speed, for Chrissake!' he told the mate, and from then on there were only he and that huge whale. The rest of the catcher crew stood around trying to anticipate his every need or wish before he expressed it.

There was no pretence of creeping up on the whale — the thrash of our propeller could be heard by every living thing in the sea for miles around. Thor's aim was to get to the spot before the whale realized what was going on and sounded, or else to scare it into a surface dash to windward and, by means of our

98

two or three knots' superiority in speed, to follow it up and come within hitting distance — around fifty to a hundred feet — of the modern harpoon gun.

As we came near shooting range, Thor precipitately left the wheel, which old Angus was ready to grab, and ran down the flying bridge — an elevated walk-way that joins the wheel bridge to the gun platform in the bows. The harpoon gun stood ready. A simple swivel gun, with a pistol grip and a sighting-bar along the top, it was loaded with a six-foot harpoon weighing two hundred pounds. Murderous enough in itself, the harpoon was made more lethal by a grenade attached to its point, fused to explode in three seconds when the harpoon, if the shooting was good, should be lodged in some vital part of the whale's great body.

Standing by the gun, Thor still kept control of the ship. By arm signals, or by shouted commands to his mate on the bridge, he directed her to port or starboard, and a duplicate telegraph beside him on the gun platform carried his commands to old Julius in the engine room. As he closed on the whale, he alone saw the fun. We spectators behind him by the wheel or on the flying bridge (no one but the gunner dare set foot on the gun platform) saw nothing but Thor's bottom bouncing up and down with excitement as he swivelled and sighted his gun. I myself, frustrated as all photographers are bound to be when they try to shoot the actual killing of a whale, photographed that unromantic object several times, then closed my camera against the spray and consoled myself by listening to Thor's language.

The Swedish and Norwegian tongues contain only one swear word between them, and that a not very satisfying one, and Thor had realized that nobody aboard understood the language of the New York taxi-driver, so the language used aboard his ship during the whale-hunt was English, or, rather, broken Scots. In this unlovely tongue Thor swore at the mate. The mate swore back and found time between breaths to curse old Angus at the wheel and the boy in the barrel. The plump engineer down at the winch began to yell profane encouragement to all and sundry. The engine-room telegraph began to yammer as Thor started and stopped his little ship, wheeled it, and sometimes went astern. The cross-talk became even more heated and impious. Thor's bottom bounced up and down even more excitedly. Then, in the middle of it all, there was the clap of a cannon shot, and it seemed obvious to me, the untutored observer, that Thor had accidentally pulled the trigger in a paroxysm of wrath. But no! There was the whale, which everybody seemed to have forgotten, thrashing the water fifty feet off the bows, with the harpoon securely fixed in a wound just forward of its dorsal fin, and blood gushing into the sea. The dull detonation of the grenade inside the whale ended this stage of the shooting.

Sometimes the whale is killed outright, but more often it either races away on the surface or dives deep as though to think over this disconcerting matter of an explosion inside its tummy. This one was a 'sounder,' and the nylon rope whirred out of its locker in the bows of our ship as the whale plunged down.

Then began a battle between whale and catcher which can only be understood properly by one who has played a fighting fish on rod and line. The fish in this case is no salmon measured in pounds, however, but has the size and weight of a large coast-guard cutter. The 'hook' has the weight of a ploughshare and is twice its size. The 'cast' is not a thin strand of gut, but twenty fathoms of three-inch nylon rope that will take a strain of thousands of tons. The 'line' is even stouter hempen rope. The 'rod' is the mast of the catcher, up which the line runs; it bends and takes an even strain as the angler's rod does to the fighting salmon. And the 'reel' at the butt of the rod, taking in line, letting it run, reeling in gently, is a powerful winch. On this winch our fat, cheerful Scottish engineer played the whale, as in his youth he had played the salmon in his native highland rivers. The whale did not stand a chance.

For, unlike a fish, it had to rise to the surface to breathe, and, each time it did so, Thor was waiting, his gun loaded with a 'killer' harpoon, which had another grenade on its tip, but no rope attached. The harpoon gun boomed again; there was a welter of blood under our bows and flowing around the ship, and our whale, which did not oblige us with the traditional spout of blood or 'chimney afire,' as the old whalemen termed it, quietly turned its belly upward and was dead.

Thor ambled back up the flying bridge, wiping his hands on his trousers, and glanced once, casually but a little sadly, at the mighty thing he had fought and killed. Perhaps, like myself at that moment, he was seeing the drama from the whale's point of view. Ten minutes before, this harmless monster had not known that man existed, and now it lay, smashed and upside down, without having known or comprehended why or how it had been attacked. Maybe, had it been less innocent, had it realized that brains can outwit bulk, it would have fought back more intelligently and might have inflicted death and gained its revenge on its tormentors before it surrendered.

Sometimes whales do. I have known cases where the whale has dived below the catcher and by accident — or possibly by cunning — has cut the nylon fore-runner on the blades of the propeller, causing the elastic rope to whirl back inboard, smashing the limbs of whoever is on the deck. And in other more mysterious ways the whale sometimes gets his revenge. Commander Gyle, our whaling inspector, once told the story of the most fantastic case yet of the whale's revenge — the case of the whale that shot the gunner.

It seems this gunner had his harpoon fast in a fin whale, and a killer harpoon without a line loaded in his gun. When the whale was hauled up under the bows of the catcher, the gunner noticed that the harpoon in the beast was not deeply enough embedded to hold it. It still had plenty of life, and another harpoon with a line was needed. He trained his gun inboard, unscrewed the grenade from the killer harpoon, and was about to unload the gun, when the harpoon in the whale tore out. As it did so, the nylon fore-runner flew up with great force, caught under the trigger of the gun, and fired it. The killer harpoon struck the gunner, shattering his right arm, smashing his ribs, and throwing him against the fo'c'sle rail. He lived only long enough to be taken to the factory ship. Next day he was buried at sea, and perhaps the whale he had attacked still lives somewhere in that vast Southern Ocean where the gunner found his grave.

But Thor's whale was indubitably dead, though the battle was not quite over. Had it been a sperm or a right whale or any of the smaller breeds the old whalemen used to hunt, we could have flagged it and left it as we went to kill the others in the school. But this was a hundred-ton blue whale, which sinks after death and must be kept afloat by artificial means. So the engineer was now racing his winch, 'reeling in,' and the A.B./telegraphist was waiting on the foredeck ready to 'gaff' the whale when it was slowly hauled in alongside. A wire rope was passed around its tail, and, when it was securely made fast to the little ship, the A.B./telegraphist leaned over the side with one of the long bamboo poles lying handy beside the foremast. Attached to the end of the pole was a blubber spade, of shape and size identical with those ancient tools that are to be seen in the museum at Mystic, Conn.; with this the seaman made a neat puncture in the side of the whale's belly. Through this an air pipe was inserted, and then the engineer turned a knob or two and thousands of cubic feet of compressed air hissed into the whale's carcass to keep it afloat.

'Now,' said Thor, 'we buoy and flag her.' (The whale, being now belly upward, was indubitably a 'she.') 'Then we leave her for the buoy-boats to pick up, and we go off and kill another. Make another seven pounds ten for me, and another ten shillings for old Angus here. Which way did the others head, Angus?'

'They're two points off the starboard bow, 'bout mile an' a half away,' replied old Angus, who, with the co-operation of the boy in the barrel, had been keeping track of the other whales during all the excitement. 'There's another big bastard amongst them——'

But, thanks to me, that 'big bastard' of a whale probably still lives and roams the Southern Ocean in peace. For, before old Angus had finished his sentence, the 'blower' behind us began to scream and whistle and we gathered that the manager on the factory wanted to speak to the gunner of Number One very urgently.

'You got the doctor with you, Thor?' the manager wanted to know. 'Well, bring him back to the factory as quick as you can. Chippy the carpenter's just pushed his fist into his band saw, and there's blood all over the ruddy ship. Got a whale to use as a fender?'

Thor had to admit that he had a whale, so we were ordered right back. I watched the faces of Thor and the mate and old Angus, and could almost hear them counting up to ten as they struggled to be reasonable and keep their tempers, for they stood to lose a lot of money through their rashness in having the doctor as a passenger the first time they got in among the big blue whales. But, as whalemen generally do, instead of growling, they smiled.

'Get the flukes off her, Nick,' Thor ordered his mate. 'Then set a course for the factory. . . . And as for you, you bloody Jonah' — he turned to me in mock rage — 'come down below and give me what's left of that bottle of rum you brought aboard with you!'

I did not obey his instruction immediately, for I wanted to see the whale-catching process right through and inquire about this amputation of the flukes, or immense tail fins, of the whale. Nick, the Canadian mate, explained to me as the A.B.s hacked them off with blubber spades. 'I don't know whether there's any scientific backing for the idea,' he told me, 'but all whalemen believe that, if a whale is left adrift after death with the flukes still here, it will propel itself or be propelled by some twist or something for miles, and will probably never be picked up again. So we always cut them off, and all the machinery on the factory ship is designed for dealing only with flukeless whales. The "grab" which hauls them aboard the factory is shaped only to fit the stumps and not the flukes, so we cut off a ton or two of pretty valuable whale tissue and dump it in the sea before we go any further.'

Perhaps within the next few years commercial demand and

scientific invention may overcome this whalemen's belief or superstition, as many have been overcome before. For it appears that soon there may be a big demand for whale tendon for use as surgical sutures, because it has certain advantages over the expensive catgut, kangaroo tendon, and plastic sutures that surgeons use today. When the firms that equip operating-theatres seek whale tendon, they find it in greatest length and strength in the now despised and discarded flukes.

And, if there should be any foundation for the whalemen's belief that a dead whale with the flukes on will keep moving through the ocean and never be found again, another scientific invention will overcome that. This is a little device invented, tested, and found adequate about two years ago. It is a tiny radio transmitter that is shot into the whale's carcass, and battery charged, gives out direction-finding signals that enable buoy-boat or corvette to sail straight to the dead whale, no matter where its flukes may mysteriously have propelled it. There is something uncanny about the idea of a dead whale drifting amid the ice of the Southern Ocean, broadcasting its whereabouts as it does so, but many things in modern whaling are as weird as the strange ways and superstitions of the whalemen of old, or weirder.

By the time Nick had finished his explanation, the flukes were off our whale and dumped into the sea. Then I saw a seaman cutting a single notch in the stump of the tail with his blubber spade. The reason for this I was told without having to ask.

'One notch means the whale's been killed by Number One Catcher,' Nick explained. 'Everybody on the factory from the bosun to the whaling inspector knows now that's our whale. We don't want the other catchers claiming our whales and drawing our bonus. Haraldsen's buoy-boat, now, which is Number Fourteen vessel of the fleet, has to put fourteen notches in the tail of any whales it may kill — not that Haraldsen has ever been sober enough to kill a whale!' he added with the usual contempt which the crew of the leading catcher have for everybody else in the expedition.

The point about our having a whale to use as a fender I did not need to have explained to me, for I had seen the necessity for it a hundred times when I had watched catchers coming alongside the factory ship. No fender yet devised by man is big or strong enough to keep a small ship from smashing in the side of a factory ship when it is tied up to it and a high Antarctic sea is running. But the Lord supplies unlimited hundred-ton fenders with the consistency and resilience of rubber for the catchers to use when they want to go alongside. If the factory ship has not got a whale, however, and a catcher wants to tie up to her, then, no matter how urgent the matter is, it just cannot do so until it finds and kills a whale to use as a fender.

Thor and Nick were among the few catcher officers who understood and took advantage of 'new-fangled' gadgets, so, when we were ordered in, we had no difficulty locating the factory ship and laying our course toward her. We did this on the direction-finding beam, a radio signal sent out by the factory every fifteen minutes. I had come to know this device well from the other side, for the automatic gadget that sent it out was located on the deck directly above my cabin on the factory, making radio reception a noisy frustration for me and interrupting conversation in my room regularly every quarter hour. But now I saw it from the other side and appreciated its value. One must return to the well-tried metaphor to describe it: it was as though the old hen was clucking, and her tiny chick, blind though it was, raced directly toward her to seek her protection.

I wanted to stay up on the bridge to watch the whole interesting technique of finding our way home through that desolate sea, but Nick advised me: 'For Christ sake, go below and give Thor enough rum to put him in a good humour. Maybe he was a taxi-driver and an American citizen, but he's as temperamental as any of those Norski gunners when anything keeps him away from fat blue whales.' So Thor and I sat below in his cabin, drinking rum and yarning, while the efficient young Canadian took us in on the radio beam. Within an hour or two he gave us a shout that he had picked up the huge hull of the factory ship in the evening haze, and a few minutes later we were alongside.

The small ships bringing in whales, or tying up to the factory ship, always do so on the starboard side. (The reason for this, nobody, not even Mansell or Mark, could tell me, except that it has always been so since the days of outboard flensing, which was invariably performed on the starboard side of the whaling barks. 'It somehow just seems the right way to do it' was the best explanation I was offered, and I had to agree, though I could not tell you why, that it did.) Wire ropes were made fast between the huge, seemingly immobile hull of the factory ship and our bouncing little craft, but not without difficulty even though the whale between us acted as a fairly adequate cushion, for by now a very high sea was running.

It was then that I had my first experience of transferring from ship to ship in mid-ocean during bad weather. This experience I had many times later when my services were needed on the catchers, but the experience never lost its excitement, nor I my mortal terror of it.

This is the procedure: a basket, not much bigger than, or very different from, a fish basket and fixed to a wire rope by a most insecure-looking shackle, is slung out by a derrick from the factory and dropped onto the deck of the catcher, with plenty of slack rope. The unfortunate victim, with as casual and indifferent an expression on his face as he can muster, steps into the basket and crouches down, either in an Oriental squat or in an appropriate kneeling position. Now the fun begins. The man at the winch cannot see the basket, and must obey the signals of the bosun, who leans over the side of the factory ship far above, with a look of calm unconcern on his face if the contents of the basket are something as unimportant as the doctor, and with more anxiety if it should be a load of valuable harpoons coming aboard. The victim squats or kneels for a while in terror, awaiting 'the moment.' The moment may be a long time a-coming. For, while the factory ship is reeling gently from side to side like a large man carrying too much drink, the catcher is bouncing about in a way the traditional cork never did. And, if the wrong moment is chosen, several uncomfortable things may happen. If the slack of the rope is taken in too soon, the catcher may suddenly descend twenty feet into the trough of a sea, leaving the basket poised in mid-air like a pendulum, to be dashed against the hull of the factory. The inhabitant of the basket feels as the champagne bottle must feel when it leaves the hand of the fair lady performing a launching ceremony. Or, if the bosun or winchman should be a bit slow in taking in the slack, the catcher will descend and the basket will rise smoothly — but it will still be there when the catcher comes up again with a mighty rush on the crest of the wave, and the helpless contents of the basket will be banged on the bottom by five hundred tons of rapidly ascending machinery. I never properly understood Dr. Einstein's major theory until I sat in that basket, a point in space with one motion relative to the catcher and an entirely different motion relative to the factory ship, but I believe I do now, and certainly Davison, our bosun, seemed on most occasions to have a fair grasp of the theory. On this first time when I was the principal actor, he chose the 'moment' well. The basket rose smoothly from the deck of the crazily bouncing catcher, dodged out of the gap between catcher and factory ship about a fiftieth of a second before that gap closed to a few inches, swung gently out of the way as the heavy steel mast of the catcher leaned over at an angle of forty-five degrees to give the basket a twenty-ton tap, and a few seconds later I was on the deck of the factory, saying: 'Thank you, Davy!' to the bosun and trying to make my tone as offhand as the one I would have used to an elevator boy.

Thor had cast off as soon as the basket with its unlucky contents had left the deck of his little ship, and was steaming off into the evening, hoping to catch up with the blues again before the brief Antarctic night descended.

'Well, only Thor would have been crazy enough to come alongside and put you aboard with a sea like this running,' commented Davison unemotionally and, I thought, rather inconsiderately. 'However, you made it!'

I went aft to attend to Chippy, the damaged carpenter, and, as I did so, I pondered on the difficulties and dangers faced by the men who scour the Southern Ocean in small ships; for my brief trip with Thor had convinced me that those difficulties and dangers, though altered, are as great as those that confronted the men of the old romantic whaling days.

VI

BROBDINGNAGIAN BUTCHER'S SHOP

What is your substance, whereof are you made,
That millions of strange shadows on you tend?
SHAKESPEARE

IN talking or writing of whales, especially that greatest of them all, the blue whale or sulphur-bottom, one quickly runs out of adjectives. *Huge, immense, enormous, titanic, mighty, vast, stupendous, monstrous, gigantic, elephantine, mammoth, giant, colossal, Cyclopean, Gargantuan* — these are all the adjectives that Mr. Roget can find to help us. None of them is adequate to convey the bulk of the blue whale to one who has not seen it; some of them, such as *elephantine*, are pygmy adjectives which give only an emaciated impression of this greatest of all monsters of all time, for he has the bulk and weight of fifty elephants.

So, when I ran out of words, I went to Mansell seeking figures, and, as usual, he was able to give them to me — figures more accurate (I believe) than any yet published of the size and weight of a fairly large blue whale. The whale was weighed and measured piece by piece at Stromness Whaling Station, South Georgia, on November 8, 1926, the day after it was killed. Mansell was present at the operation. He believes — and, considering his great knowledge of whaling, he is probably right — that it is the only occasion in whaling history when such an operation has been performed. The weights were computed for commercial reasons, for I do not believe that any whaling firm would have held up production long enough to perform such a task for scientific purposes; if the figures contain some commercial secret which scientists should not know, I can but say that Mansell and I are more interested in the whale than we are in the whale owner.

Here they are ('The whale is what man calls a fat nice whale' was
Mansell's heading to the page of figures):

MEASUREMENTS

Length	27·18 metres	(89 feet approx.)
Height (lying on side)	3·10 ,,	(10 ,,)
Circumference	13·90 ,,	(46 ,,)
Jawbone length	6·95 ,,	(23 ,,)
Flukes ,,	5·90 ,,	(18 ,,)
Fins ,,	3·00 ,,	(9½ ,,)

WEIGHTS

Blubbers	25,651 kilos	(26 tons approx.)
Meat	56,444 ,,	(56 ,,)
Bone	22,280 ,,	(22 ,,)
Tongue	3,158 ,,	(3 ,,)
Lungs	1,226 ,,	(1 ,,)
Heart	631 ,,	(½ ,,)
Kidneys	547 ,,	(½ ,,)
Stomach	416 ,,	(½ ,,)
Intestines	1,600 ,,	(1½ ,,)
Liver	935 ,,	(1 ,,)
Blood	8,000 ,,	(8 ,,)
Jawbone	2,177 ,,	(2 ,,)
Skull	4,508 ,,	(4½ ,,)
Backbone	10,230 ,,	(10 ,,)
Ribs	3,863 ,,	(4 ,,)
Flukes	1,153 ,,	(1 ,,)
Fins	960 ,,	(1 ,,)

The total weight of this 'fat nice' (but not extraordinarily
large) blue whale was 122,004 kilograms — that is to say, about
120 long tons. Reduced to oil (and perhaps this is where the commercial secret, if any, lurks) she made the following:

Blubber Oil	13,604 kilos	(13½ tons approx. or 80 barrels)
Meat Oil	6,880 ,,	(6½ ,, 40 ,,)
Bone Oil	7,224 ,,	(7 ,, 42 ,,)
Total	27,708 ,,	(27 ,, 162 ,,)

In passing, compare with the production of oil from this whale
by modern methods a statement in a book concerning a cruise of

the famous *Charles W. Morgan*, last of the New Bedford whale-ships: 'We continued our cruise for some six weeks longer and took whales enough to make us about two hundred and fifty barrels.' . . . But they did not hunt the 'fat nice' whales in those days.

Now, to make these unique figures I have quoted intelligible to mathematical imbeciles like myself, let us correlate them with better-known things: the length of the beast is that of a railway carriage, and its height and girth are about the same. An elephant could walk under its up-ended jawbone without touching at any point. Its fins are the size and weight of a pretty large dining-table, and its flukes would make an excellent pair of wings for a fighter aircraft. (They are also perfectly streamlined, and, as I am sure their toughness and durability exceed that of duralumin, I commend them to aircraft designers.) Its blubber, Mansell estimates, would keep all the votive candles burning in St. Peter's, Rome, for a century or more; and its meat would supply a hamburger (and a good one, too!) to every person in Liverpool. Its tongue would overload a fair-sized truck, and it would take six very strong men to lift its heart. Its skull is the size and weight of a motor-car, but the brain contained therein is not much bigger than the carburettor. Its blood would fill seven thousand milk bottles, and, if we wish to go into physiological astronomy, it contains by my reckoning some eight million million red blood corpuscles.

A fairly large monster! (Its value, for those who are interested in such things, is today about two thousand pounds.)

One day at the height of the season, when I climbed up onto my favourite place of observation, a perch on the winchdeck, to see how the whaling business was progressing, there were fourteen such monsters made fast by wire ropes to the stern of the factory ship.

'We'll easily stow this lot before morning!' Davison, the bosun, told me in passing as he checked up on his winchmen; so I stayed up all night to watch him do it.

By international law, every whale, except those used for

fenders, must be on the deck of the factory ship within thirty-three hours of his killing. Anyone who has smelled a whale more than thirty hours old and remembers that it is eventually going to be eaten in some form or other by the British people, realizes the wisdom of this law; but the lawyers who devised the law, and laid down a prison sentence of three months for failure to comply with it, should have stood with me in heavy weather on the winchdeck of the factory ship that evening.

The whales floated belly upward in the sea astern of us, looking uncomfortably pathetic and ridiculous as they tossed about with their huge sexual organs or cavities exposed to the glare of the floodlights. A few hours before, they had been the lords and the ladies of the ocean, the mightiest animals that ever knew life on this planet; and now they were so many tons of dead organic matter, waiting their turn to be converted into margarine and poultry-feed!

Davison began the business of getting them aboard, and I witnessed a show of seamanship which even the oldest hands on factory ships never tire of watching.

The great steel 'grab,' or *hval kla*, weighing several tons and cunningly shaped to fit over and clasp the stump of the whale's tail, was raised from the deck by wire ropes attached to five powerful winches and was carried suspended in the air down the skidway, the spacious tunnel from the main deck down to the water-line at the stern of the ship between its two funnels and two screws. Arriving in position over the tail of the first whale, which was lashing about in the seas breaking into the lower end of the tunnel, the grab hovered about in the air for a moment or two, mysteriously following the wild movements of the tail. It crept closer, its jaws wide open. When it was directly over the tail and a few feet above it, it seemed suddenly to pounce, and with a crash of iron which could be heard throughout the huge ship it grabbed just behind the stumps of the flukes, the jaws snapped together, and the hundred-ton whale was secure and ready to be pulled on board.

The first time I had seen the grab in action, it had seemed to me to have a brain and consciousness of its own, enabling it to follow the wildly heaving whale carcass and leap on the tail at the critical moment when sea and ship's movements permitted. But I knew now that the brain and consciousness were those of Davison, the bosun, who was quietly leaning over the rail half-way down the skidway in the only place where he could be seen by all five winch-drivers at once. With slight movements of his hands and head he was starting, stopping, slacking, and controlling the finest movements of the wire ropes attached to the grab, by signs made to the winchmen hundreds of feet away at the after end of the ship. He conducted his winchmen rather like a suave and undemonstrative orchestra conductor. The rhythmic movement of the grab and the grand climax when it secured the whale seemed to demand a musical accompaniment.

Once the grab was securely in position, I saw Davison in the floodlight far below me jerk his right thumb sharply upward once, then disappear. The powerful winches two hundred feet up amidships went into action and the whole mighty whale began to move bodily up the skidway onto the deck of the factory. I felt like applauding, and I half expected Davison to come back and take at least one bow, but he was already gone among the heaving tangle of wire ropes at the stern of the ship, coaxing the next hundred-ton monster to the lower end of the skidway that he might give an encore of his symphony of seamanship.

As the first whale glided smoothly and steadily up the skidway, I found a comparison which seemed fantastic, but which a little mental arithmetic showed me was true and apt. This comparison gives some indication of the vast bulk of the whale and the power of the winches. If a battalion of infantry, eight hundred strong in full battle equipment, were marching up that skidway, it would take them some fifteen minutes to pass through to the top. But this blue whale weighing more than a battalion of infantrymen in battle order was hauled to the top of the skidway in less than a minute.

The Gaunt Stranger, our mysterious chief flenser who appeared only when there was a whale to flense, was waiting at the top of the skidway to receive it. Weighing and balancing his curved knife in its four-foot shaft, he looked much like a surgeon, confident of his skill, about to commence a big operation. He did not wait for his hundred-ton patient to come to rest on the operating-table before he began his dissection; as the whale was drawn out of the tunnel, he stuck in his knife and, letting the winch do the work, made a long, anatomically accurate incision through the six-inch thickness of the blubber as the whale was drawn past him. Then, the whale having come to rest, he neatly carved out steps in its side, as a mountaineer does on an unscalable ice slope, and with their help, climbed and leaped atop the carcass. There he balanced, though the ship was pitching heavily, his spiked boots and his long training enabling him to maintain his position.

He made some more long and, to the uninitiated, apparently haphazard cuts through the blubber, sometimes cutting out a chunk and kicking it off onto the deck, sometimes making a lengthy slash with bends and corners here and there. Then the other flensers leaped at the whale, like a hockey team making a rush at goal. They also sliced and hacked with what seemed to be random fury. But every cut was deliberate, and was the same cut that the same man had been making on the same type of whale during all the years of his experience.

Wire ropes began descending from the derricks overhead. A flenser waited for each rope as it swung down, and, catching it, he fixed it to a toggle through one of the apparently random holes cut in the blubber. Then the winches steamed up, and great slabs of blubber, which would have taken hours to remove by the old methods, were stripped from the whale as easily as peeling an orange — or so it seemed. But the job was one that had taken years of training to master, and there was no room for mistakes among the flensers. One false cut, one loose shackle, or one careless release of the brake of a winch, and there would have been blood other than whale blood sluicing over the pitching, slippery deck.

A flenser who did not fully understand and appreciate the

dangers of his job could not possibly live for a month in the midst of this maelstrom of whirling machinery, straining ropes, and razor-sharp knives. They hurried; they rushed; they appeared to be in a state of complete confusion throughout the blubber-stripping process; but I began to see that every man among them was being extremely methodical and careful. None of the curved hockey-stick blades was ever turned in the direction of a fellow flenser in the mêlée; every wire rope lying on the deck was walked round as carefully as a man will walk round a rattlesnake; and no flenser would signal to his winch to haul away until he had ascertained that his mates were standing clear.

On two occasions during the process everybody on or near the after deck (myself included, for I had been warned) was particularly careful. The first was during the ceremony of the turning of the whale. The blubber having been stripped from one side, the hundred-ton carcass had to be turned over on the heaving deck to allow the flensers to attack the other side. This was done by passing a wire rope through a pulley fixed to the deck by a shackle, then over the top of the whale, and securing it through the base of the fin on the farther side. Then the donkey engine mustered all its power, the wire rope and shackle began to take the strain of a hundred inert tons, and the huge body, the size of a railway carriage, began to turn over. As this happened, every flenser quietly left the deck to stand in the mouths of the alleyways leading off it, and I stood back six paces to place a winch between me and the shackle. The first time I had seen the operation I had leaned far out over the rail of the winchdeck, but Davison, seeing me, had shouted: 'Get back, for Christ sake! You bloody fool!' and I got back quickly, for the blast of profanity came from the quietest-spoken and most courteous old Shelty on the ship, and I knew there must be good reason underlying it.

The rope tightened further, and rope and shackle began to make that groaning, protesting noise which sailors respect when a wire rope is 'bar tight,' for it signifies that the rope and shackle have nearly 'had it.' But the whale gave first, and, with a slithering smack that shook the whole ship, the whale crashed over, with hundreds of gallons of blood pouring from it, and slopped down on its immense belly. The flensers immediately leaped out from their places of shelter and attacked it again, for the first of the two most dangerous moments was past.

Davison had made the danger clear to me on that first occasion, after he had heaved himself up the ladder to the winch-deck to apologize for using bad language to his superior officer. 'That's the most dangerous time of the flensing process, doctor,' he pointed out. 'The whole weight of the whale is taken by that one shackle on the deck, and there never was a shackle of that type made yet which won't give way sometimes with a bar-tight rope running through it. When it does give way — and I've seen it happen several times — it acts like a catapult. The shackle is the shot, and the wire rope is the sling, and anyone who happens to be standing or leaning inside the angle made by the rope will have to be scraped off the deck with a shovel. Sorry if I was rude, but you were right in line with the shackle if it had given way, and there wasn't time to do anything but bawl you out.'

I thanked the old man for his admonishment, and now, later in the season, I needed no bosun's abrupt warning to make me stand well back as the whale was turned over.

The second very dangerous procedure is the removal and dumping overside of the tons of baleen or whalebone which cases the tongue and mouth cavity of the whale. A century ago, in the days of corsets and kepis and before steel and plastics pushed our flesh and the flesh of our women in ways God never intended it to go, whalebone was the most valuable part of the baleen whale; but in this age it is so much junk, not worth its passage home, and is therefore removed from the whale and jettisoned. It is done in this way: a hole is cut through the whale's 'gums' in line with the centre of the 'upper lip.' A wire rope from a derrick overhead is passed through the hole and fixed securely. The winchman takes a heavy strain on this rope, pulling the mass of whalebone upward and outward. As he does so, the head flenser, starting from the 'upper lip,' slices through the base of the gums toward the angle of the jaw. The winchman increases the strain, tears the tons of baleen from the roof of the mouth, and heaves it into the air. The head flenser, just before he makes his last cut, which will sever the huge, cartilaginous mass from the whale, raises the cry of '*Bada!*' (the Norwegian for baleen), which others around take up, and everybody dives for cover. The last cut is made. The winch, synchronized with the flenser's knife, accelerates, and the *bada*, with a wrenching tear, parts from the whale and swings wildly up into the air, and outboard over the ship's side, just grazing the bulwarks. During the half-second when it is outboard the winchman lets go his brake, and the lethal mass, which would smash to pulp anyone or anything in its way, plunges down toward the sea — usually! But occasionally the ship will roll just at the wrong moment, or the flenser will not shout loud enough, or the winchman will be busy lighting his pipe, and the great, jagged lump of bony whale will come crashing inboard again to smash on the spot where the head flenser would be standing. He would not be a head flenser for many days, however, if he had not sense enough to be on the other side of the whale in anticipation of this very thing happening.

'I've seen maybe five or six men killed by the *bada* alone,' Davison told me at the time he warned me of the dangers of flensing, 'and I'd advise you, doctor, if you're on the after plan and you hear the cry of "*bada*," don't wait to look round to see where it is, but just fall down flat on your face in the *grax* and wait until it's safely overboard.' Some time later in the voyage, when a man was brought to me in the sick bay looking as though he had just spent twenty rounds in the ring with Joe Louis and just able to mutter: 'I no hear them shout "*bada*,"' I realized the wisdom of the old bosun's advice.

When the baleen was safely overboard and the whale had been stripped, the blubber was cut into long slivers eighteen inches wide and ten feet long. These strips were seized upon by the 'blubber boys,' a motley collection of ragamuffins of ages ranging from eighteen to eighty who fixed their whale hooks into the strips and hauled them across the deck to heave them into round iron-clad holes, which belched forth steam and fritters of boiling fat. These holes, which exactly resembled the manholes one sees in every street, led down to the press boilers on the factory deck below.

I watched the blubber boys a while as they stowed ton after ton of oily fat into the maws of the huge, modern pressure cookers below. Each wielded his whale hook, a simple piece of iron about two feet long with a sharp hook at one end and a wooden handgrasp at the other. (Identical instruments are to be seen on the walls of the whaling museums of New Bedford and Mystic and Sandefiord and Dundee, for this simple tool has been an essential whaling implement since the first whaleman tried to handle a slippery piece of blubber.) A Whaler Group VIII without his whale hook is a sorry, useless lump of sailordom. With his whale hook in his hand, he is a prestidigitator of the first order who, with his fifth limb, can perform feats of juggling ability which no eye can follow. He is seen at his best in his battles with the flensers. For flensers as a class hate blubber boys and all Whaler Group VIII's nearly as much as Mansell did. It was quite usual for a flenser who had cut out a five-pound triangular chunk of blubber, in order to insert a toggle, to catch up the slobbery mass on the end of his knife and hurl it venomously at the nearest blubber boy. But, without even turning his eyes in the direction of the projectile, the blubber boy would twitch his whale hook and divert the piece of blubber to smack accurately and invariably against the cheek of the head flenser standing some twenty yards away.

There is a legend that blubber boys eat with their whale hooks and darn their socks with them. That is not strictly true, but it is true that they put the hooks to a variety of extraordinary uses for which they were never designed. Let a blubber boy reach for a rope, and he will reach with his hook. Hand him any object — his coat, a wrench, a book — and he will stretch out his hook, not his hand, and flick the object neatly toward him. Or watch him performing any operation such as opening a door, lifting a lid, steadying himself as the ship rolls, and he will always use his dexterous iron third arm in preference to the two God gave him. Hopping round the deck in a ring on the outskirts of the flensing-team, they are like nothing so much as a horde of pantomime Captain Hooks playing outfield in some mysterious nautical game.

When the blubber was all flensed and stowed, the Gaunt Stranger stood back, still solemn, still silent, and surveyed his work. He looked now more like a priest than a surgeon, standing in silent prayer over the remains of his sacrifice. Then he gave a curt nod — it seemed no more than that — and walked quickly off the scene, not to appear again until the next whale was on the deck. His nod was seen by two winchmen away forward on the ship, fully two hundred feet away. Wire ropes tightened, all hands stood clear and formed little groups by the bulwarks, lighting their pipes and sharpening their knives, and the skinned whale, now a pink-and-white smelly mountain of flesh and blood and bone, began to slide slowly through another tunnel amidships. This tunnel, known inevitably as Hell's Gates because of the steam and blood and noise that filled it, led to the forward plan or lemming-deck, where the lemmers, the expert anatomists of the ship, awaited it.

These lemmers, the origin of whose trade name is obscure, used the same type of knives as the flensers, but had in addition heavy steam-driven bone-saws to assist them. With these they began the process of disarticulation of the whole whale carcass and the sorting out into various categories of the huge and ghastly looking dismembered portions.

From my position of safety on the after winchdeck I could see little of this interesting dissection, so — my medical curiosity overcoming my terror of the contorting and straining wire ropes, the belching maws of the press boilers, and the mysterious objects (including the ten-ton iron *hval kla*) swinging in the air overhead and occasionally crashing onto the deck — I ventured forward. And let me explain here, before setting out on this perilous journey during which I may sit down in four inches of blood and *grax* if I slip, that my dress was no longer that of the civilized psychiatrist of city practice, but was identical with that of all whalemen, from the captain to the youngest fourteen-year-old Whaler Group XIII mess-boy: a khaki shirt; old corduroy pants; a Norwegian fisherman's jacket, and underneath it, since it was cold, a Board of Trade fur waistcoat marked 'A Gift of the Fur Industry of the U.S.A. to British Seamen.' But the important items of my attire were those which protected me from hazards from above and below. I hate hats, and I laughed when the old whalemen cautioned me to wear one, but, after I had sewed up one or two four-inch scalp wounds caused by ice falling from the masthead, I saw the point of the warning and quit laughing. And, as I crossed the deck, I made sure my fur bonnet was tight down over my ears. The protection at the other end consisted of sea-boots (I have them yet, and they carry the stink of that flensing-deck around with them to this day) into the heels of which Victor, the deck storeman, had fixed three sawed-off brass screwnails, so that, if I were walking through a morass of slimy spermaceti and blood and *grax* and the deck suddenly tilted twenty degrees, I could dig in my heels and avoid landing in the scuppers with a hundred gallons of whale filth sluicing round about and all over me.

Thus attired, I picked my way cautiously forward. The whale had reached the forward plan before me, and the lemmers had already attacked it. The steam and noise and variety of lethal objects flying about were tenfold greater than on the flensing-deck, and the diabolic tempo at which the lemmers worked made the flensers seem slow and awkward. At this stage of the season I had become well accustomed to moving about the flensing-deck, for my quarters aft looked out onto it and I crossed it several times a day going forrard for my meals, but the lemming-deck was still a place where I could not move with safety, and the lemming process was still one fraught with mystery and fear to me. So I stood a while in dazed uncertainty in the midst of the grotesque phantasmagoria on the forward plan, not sure whether to retreat through the straining ropes which were already hauling the next whale up onto the flensing-deck, or to plunge forward into the steam and blood and noise and take my chance among the demons rushing about therein wielding flashing, blood-stained knife blades. But in the midst of the hellish charade I suddenly saw a cheerful and familiar face, and, though I could not hear the words the mouth was shaping, I could see that the expression was encouraging, and I was being beckoned forward. It was my friend Hamish Gordon, Whaler Group VIII, bone-sawman — the first whaleman patient I had examined in the U.K.

Hamish looked very different now. He had been sober for nearly two months; he had grown a magnificent bristling black beard; and he had the confident bearing of a man who is on a job that he knows and understands as well as or better than any-one else on earth. I dived through the steam toward him and found a place of comparative safety at the rear of his bone-saw.

'You've never been forrard here to see us working yet, doc, have you?' he shouted in my ear. 'Well, wait ere I fix this bluidy backbone, then I'll tell you what's going on.'

'Fixing the bluidy backbone' looked dead easy as Hamish did it, but I could see that it was indeed a miracle of co-operation be-tween a team of many brains and much machinery. The lemmers had sliced the tons of flesh from the back of the whale as neatly as a butcher cuts a rump steak, and down its special hole in the deck had gone this vast quantity of meat. The casing of ribs from each side, every rib bigger than a man, had been dissected off and heaved into the air, and the mighty thoracic walls of the whale swung suspended from the derricks like a giant's feast of pork chops. The 'innards' of the whale had been hauled out, and lay, each anatomical pile in its right place on the deck, awaiting disposal or rejection. And now only the massive backbone re-mained, and it was Hamish's turn.

First a chain was passed under the great ligament, as thick and tough as a warship's anchor cable, which held the spines of the millstone-sized vertebrae together. With a horrid rending noise — similar, but magnified a thousand times, to the noise made by a dog tearing and crunching a bone — the ligament was ripped free from the spine. Then a wire rope from a winch beside Hamish's bone-saw was passed round a bollard and attached by a heavy double iron hook to the 'tail' of the vertebral column. Hamish gave the quick toss of the head which I was coming to recognize as the signal to heave away, and the winchman brought the great mass of bone and tendon whizzing across the deck to come to rest under Hamish's saw. The saw, a heavy steam-driven fifteen-foot blade rattling back and forth, began to descend in response to Hamish's finger-tip control before the vertebrae were even under it, and, as the backbone slid into place, the blade ripped accurately into the very place where Hamish wanted it, to cut off a chunk just big enough to go down the four-foot hole to the 'cookers.' In a few seconds the blade had hacked through the bone; then it stopped just before it cut into the deck. Hamish touched a lever, and the blade rose up vertical again. He wagged his beard once again, and each of the ten men spread around knew exactly what to do. Four leaped in with whale hooks, seized the severed piece, and hauled it off to the cooker a split second before the fifth, the winchman, opened his throttle and pulled the backbone another two feet along the deck; the sixth pulled out the double hook and thrust it deep into the next vertebra as soon as the winch stopped; the seventh and eighth, two little gnome-like lemmers, dashed out of the steam and made some intricate scurrying cuts at the backbone with their curved knives to enable it to bend round under the saw; the ninth, Hamish himself, brought his immense saw blade slamming down again into the next cut; and the tenth, the doctor, cowered a bit closer against the bulwarks behind the saw to avoid the flying machinery.

It took about twenty cuts and three minutes of time to reduce the huge pyramid of dead matter to sizable lumps which could be stowed down into the cookers, and then Hamish had a few minutes in which to light his pipe and give the ignorant doctor some instruction in practical whaling. Although we had started badly when first we met, Hamish and I were now fast friends, and, like most of the other whalemen, he was always ready to go to endless trouble to explain his job and yarn about whaling.

'As yon fellow Melville pointed out' (Hamish, like nearly every other modern whaleman, had read the whaling classics) 'we're nae mair than butchers on a gran' scale. The butcher selects his beast for size and kills it with a humane killer; then he tak's the carcass, skins it, splits it, quarters it, an' then cuts it into convenient pieces for cooking. And that's exactly what we're doing on this deck here. D'ye know the Norwegian name for a factory ship, doctor? They call it a *Flotten Kokerie*, and, though it's kinda unromantic an' no' a very glamorous name, it describes the whaling business better nor the sentimental writers about whaling do. If I were writing a book about whaling, doctor, like some of us suspects you're goin' to do, I'd start off with a description of the butcher's shop in Peterhead, and tak' some coloured pictures o' Andy MacTavish, oor village butcher, killin' and sawin' up a cattle beast; then I'd show by further photographs and illustration that there's nae mair to whalin' than there is tae Andy's job — except the beasts are bigger an' the slaughterhouse is in a kinda inconvenient place down here in the ice.'

'And the dangers and excitement of this job are rather more than in Andy's job,' I suggested.

'No more — just bigger an' more spectacular, like the beasts we're butcherin' compared wi' Andy's beasts. It's all a matter o' proportion. Andy's just as likely tae have an accident wi' his bone-saw as I am wi' mine: but, when he does, he'll lose a finger or two, whilst, if I make a mistake, as like as not I'll nick the head off that little lemmer there.'

As he spoke, the backbone of the next whale had come sliding across the deck, and his fifteen-foot blade was already descending to meet it. He went on with his work, and from my point of vantage and comparative safety I observed the other operations going on in the gigantic butchery.

The liver of the whale had been removed and hauled (it weighed nearly a ton, and needed a powerful winch to haul it) to a corner of the deck, where a man was engaged in chopping it up into small chunks and popping it into a special hole leading to the 'liver plant' below. The stomach and intestines had been similarly hauled aside, not to a hole leading below, but to a break in the bulwarks through which they were to be cast into the sea, the only bit of the whale other than the flukes and the baleen to be rejected. But, before they were heaved overboard, Davison, the bosun, arrived on the scene, armed with a flensing-knife, and he slit the enormous stomach open and spilled its contents on the deck. Then he drew a grubby notebook from his trousers pocket and wrote something down with a stub of pencil. I braved two twisting ropes and ten tons of wildly swinging flesh and bone to get over beside him to investigate this mysterious going-on.

'The law and Commander Gyle, the whaling inspector, insist that we do this,' he explained as we stood looking down at the hundredweight or so of little red shrimps spilled out on the deck. 'I'm writing down the contents of the stomach, which we've got to do for every whale we take. The point is that the biologist boys still believe — though any old whaleman will tell them they're wrong — that the whales come down to the Antarctic following their grub, and they reckon, if they can track down the krill which the whales eat, they can work out the migrations of the whales. So I write down in my book: "Stomach contents: Krill," and the biologists say: "Aha! That whale had a full belly of shrimps when he was killed in latitude sixty-eight south; therefore he went there to have a good meal" — which, if I remember my schooling, is what they call a *non sequitur*. The commander agrees with me, but he still makes me do it.'

Having got the information I wanted, I dodged back into my nook behind the saw and resumed my conversation with Hamish, but in a few minutes Davison came along with more curiosities to show me. Our whale was a female, so he brought over the ovaries, each one the size of a soccer ball: he brought the pituitary gland, as big as my fist, though in the human it is the size of a pea; the pancreas, a yard and a half of healthy sweetbread weighing about six pounds, compared with our miserable little two ounces of insulin-loaded tissue; and, the thing I had asked him to get, a blue whale's eye, with all the muscles attached, for the research man in Oxford. This got us talking about research and the routine scientific investigations made on the whales that are taken, for, though others gave the orders, Davison was in charge of the practical side of all such work.

The date, time, and position of every whale taken had to be recorded. The length of every whale was accurately measured. The sex was noted, and, in the case of females, whether pregnant, and, if so, the size and sex of the foetus and whether the cow whale was producing milk. The point of all this I could understand, and also why in these days of expensive hormones the biochemists should be interested in the collection of internally secreting glands of great size, such as the whale's pancreas and pituitaries.

'But *why*, in the name of God,' I asked Davison, 'do you make a collection of ovaries? I've noticed that you have hundreds of them all neatly pickled and stowed in barrels up forrard there.'

He chuckled. 'There's a man you haven't met yet,' he told me, 'but he'll be waiting for the ship when we get into Liverpool. He comes south with us every few years, and he's a damned nuisance, holding up production to make his researches when we have him aboard. We call him Ovary Joe, and we all get along well with him, though as a matter of fact he's a very distinguished London biologist. But he's got a bee in his bonnet that you can tell the age of a female whale by examining the number of ruptured follicles in the ovaries. Well, Joe gives me threepence for every pair of ovaries I bring back to him the years he's not with us, so I collect and pickle them from every whale — perhaps mainly because a few thousand threepences is quite a lot of money, but also because Joe is a good chap, though his ideas are maybe cuckoo.'

I found, during our discussion, that Davison — the practical though intelligent whaleman — adopted a tolerant but mildly contemptuous attitude toward all whaling research; but on one aspect of it he became scathing and even profane — the researches carried out by the Royal Research Ship *Discovery II*, the vessel of the Royal Oceanographic Society, which is permanently engaged in investigations in sub-Antarctic waters.

'She spends all her time wandering round the edge of the pack ice,' he averred, 'shooting little silver harpoons about six inches long into all the whales she sights. The harpoons are marked with the date and place the whale was sighted, and the idea is that we recover them and send them back to London, so that they can work out how far and in which direction the whale has travelled between meeting *Discovery II* and being killed by us. A very fine theory, and there's a reward for sending in the silver markers, although I've never collected it yet. But, if you go down aft there and listen to the blubber-slicing machine, which is exactly the same as a kitchen meat-chopper, you'll hear it humming along, then suddenly snarl and come to a full stop with a broken blade, and we know when that happens it's another of those bluidy *Discovery* harpoons. And when the repairers have worked for two or three hours extricating it from the blades and getting the machine working again, the marker will be a twisted lump of metal, and the date and place engraved on it couldn't be read by a hieroglyphic expert.'

'Are ye finished with these guts yet, bosun?' an irritated voice interrupted us from out of the steam, closing our scientific discussion, which had been verging on that major crime aboard a whaleship — 'holding up production.'

'Aye!' replied the imperturbable Davison, and a winch clanked in the distance; a rope tautened, and a mountain of smelly whale's innards slid toward the ship's side and dropped into the sea far below with a slobbery plonk.

I leaned overside to see the fate of this part of the whale for which man could find (as yet) no use. It was not long a-coming. What seemed like — and maybe was — a million black-and-white Cape pigeons descended on and gathered around the filthy mess, and in a few moments each one had ripped off his small piece and was swimming around for a hundred yards or more, tearing at his dinner. An occasional albatross glided down into the mêlée, chased off some of the shrilly complaining pigeons, and made a silent and dignified meal before making his long runway on the water to rise and glide off again. And all the while a cloud of Wilson's petrels, the 'land birds condemned to a life at sea,' were fluttering in the air over the guts, darting down occasionally to take a tiny beakful of the rich fodder and rising into the air again to digest it. But the birds did not get the entire feast by any means. For the most voracious thing in the Southern Ocean appeared to get his share, and a large share it was.

Five killer whales, each twenty to thirty feet long, with huge black fins rising rhythmically from the water as they swam toward the ship and evil black-and-white snouts broken by malignant fang-filled cavities rising occasionally above the water, advanced upon the meal. Only hyenas on land and vultures in the air can convey the same sense of remorseless ill-will against all creation that killer whales convey as they slowly approach their loathsome victuals. This pack was about five hundred yards out when I saw them first. They rose to blow, scarcely rippling the water as they did so, puffed each one once, then slid below the surface again, their horrible sickle-shaped fins following them like a hunchback's hump. About ten seconds later the performance was repeated — ugly snout — jet-black fin — puff — and glide beneath the water again, but a hundred yards nearer the ship. Again: snout — fin — puff — and disappearance, a hundred yards closer still, but not a ripple to show for it. Then the last appearance, fifty yards off their food, and by now I could see their cold, black little eyes. They disappeared, but suddenly all the birds gathered around the whale offal rose squawking into the air. There was a great swirling of water beneath the filthy mass, an occasional black fin showed for a moment or two, and chunks of the mess, a ton or so at a time, began to vanish beneath the water.

One killer, made more confident by the ease with which he

was obtaining his dinner, pushed his snout above the water and grabbed a hundred-pound titbit of coiled intestine floating high on the sea. He never drew his meal below the surface. From the wing of the bridge overhead there was the sharp crack of a rifle. The killer, drilled neatly behind the eye by a heavy ·303 bullet, leaped half out of the water in his death spasm, then sank in a whirl of spray and blood.

'There's Mark at his favourite sport again!' Davison remarked at my shoulder. 'He hates killer whales with a loathing quite out of proportion to the damage they do to him and his bonus, though they do tear out the tongues and the best part of the oil from half the whales we catch. He'll be happy all night, now that he's killed that one. If you want to get along with Mark, doctor, borrow a rifle from the bridge and take up the sport of killer-hunting.'

I stayed with Davison and Hamish Gordon for the rest of that day and all through the night as the fourteen whales were 'dealt with.' As Davison had promised, we were all clear by morning. In something less than an hour after the last whale had been hauled up the skidway, not a vestige of it remained above board except the slippery blood lying in clots about the deck and — since the last whale was nearing the thirty-three-hour limit when it was hauled up — the smell.

Just as the early Antarctic dawn was breaking, the little gnomes hauled the iron covers over the holes leading down to the cookers, and clamped them securely down. The steam straight away cleared. The winchmen heaved in their loose ropes and shut off their winches. A gang of Shelties appeared and hosed down the decks with high-pressure hoses to clear the blood and filth. A young cadet went up to the platform on the starboard side and checked over the stores, spare harpoons, and ropes laid out for the next catcher or corvette that might appear with whales. A little mess-boy swayed across the deck with a drink and some supper for the mate and the whaling inspector, who were in the office down aft arguing about the size and timing of the whales that had been brought in. Hamish Gordon was greas-

Men who go a-whaling

With the huge mass of material required for the whale hunt cluttering her decks and seven hundred whalemen idling below, the factory ship steams southward through the tropics

Leith Harbour, South Georgia
known to whalemen as the 'slum of the Southern Ocean'

Under critical scrutiny from the factory ship, a catcher brings in the results of a day's shooting

Sighting along his harpoon gun, this gunner looks what he is—a remorseless hunter in the world's biggest game hunt

ing his immense saw and tuning it up for the next day's work. And the hundred-odd men who had been on the deck a few minutes before, working like slaves, were slipping off to their cabins or mess-rooms, tired, silent for the most part, and but slightly richer than they had been twelve hours before.

The butcher's shop was closed for the night.

I, too, was tired, though I had done nothing but stand around watching one of the modern world's mightiest labours, and I was not sorry to go bedward. But, before I left the deck, I heard yet another burst of rifle fire from the bridge overhead, and I knew that one other person was still wide awake on the now apparently lifeless ship. Mark, whiling the time away as he conned our huge ship through the freezing dawn, was indulging his semi-reasonable hatred against the killer whales.

VII

BARRELS! BARRELS! BARRELS!

All parts of whales delivered to the ship by the ships attached thereto, shall be processed by boiling or otherwise, except the internal organs, whalebone and flippers of all whales, the meat of sperm whales and of parts of whales intended for human food and for feeding animals.
—*The Whaling Industry (Ship) Regulations 1951*

THE whaling industry seems remote from politics, and it would appear unlikely that the decisions of ambitious little men in the chancelleries of Europe could have their effect on that 'most perilous mode of hardy industry' away in the Antarctic seas. And yet it has happened often that political changes in the north have altered the lives and prospects of the whalemen in the far south, and occasionally in queer, indirect ways the political whims of men who would not be given employment even as Whaler Group VIII's on the whaleships have changed the whole industry.

In 1888 Wilhelm II became Kaiser of Germany. In 1890 he got rid of Bismarck, and it became apparent to one and all that Germany was going to need a large supply of explosives for many years to come. A large supply of explosives meant a constant flow of glycerine, and the only source of glycerine in those days was dead animal matter, which had to be boiled. So in 1893 a man named Hartmann sat down and designed a pressure boiler that could extract enough glycerine from dead horses to enable Kaiser Wilhelm to embark on his schemes of world conquest by high explosive.

But a more peaceful character, a Finnish engineer named Nils Kvaerner, who happened to be living in Oslo and listening to all the talk about the revival of the whaling industry through the medium of the harpoon gun, visualized another harmless and remunerative use for Herr Hartmann's boiler. By making slight alterations, he adapted the Hartmann Boiler to become the Kvaerner Cooker, the first pressure cooker for the production of whale oil. Straight away the old copper boilers or try-works, which all whaleships had been using for centuries to extract the oil from blubber, joined the hand harpoon, the outboard flensing-platform, and the back-breaking 'heave-pawl' in the whaling museums of Mystic and Dundee. The new Kvaerner Cooker, along with the Sven Foyn gun, the Andersen *hval kla*, and the Sörlle skidway, became established as an essential tool of the modern pelagic whaling industry. So Kaiser Wilhelm, like many other types whom the whalemen despise, made, unknown to himself, his contribution to the industry.

One cannot sit for five minutes in the top saloon of a whale factory ship — or in the lower saloon or on the mess-decks, for that matter — without hearing the two words *barrels* and *Kvaerner* at least a dozen times. In the top saloon of our ship this 'talking shop' began as soon as Old Burnett, the chief engineer, entered for a meal and took his place on the right of the manager.

'How many barrels yesterday, Mansell?' he would always shout across the table as soon as he sat down. Mansell would reply acidly that our score the day before had been only a thousand or so, but might have been double if Burnett's department would supply some decent water and a proper head of steam now and again and if the idle and ignorant engineers would do something about Number Two Starboard Kvaerner, which had been on the bum since we took the first whale. MacDonald, the junior chief engineer, would then rise to his chief's defence and remark that it was difficult to keep machinery working when a half-witted mate allowed his flensers to put anything from wire ropes to unexploded grenades into the Kvaerners along with the blubber. Young Evans, the chemist, would take Mansell's part and swear that there was more rust and lubricating-oil than whale oil in the samples he had tested that morning. Andra, the mate, would sway back and forward in his seat, humming an old English lullaby and occasionally informing all and sundry that they were talking 'a lot of crap.' The table in a moment or two would be surrounded by ten red-faced angry men shouting at one another about barrels and Kvaerners, and the efforts of the manager, the whaling inspector, and myself to divert the conversation into less explosive channels, such as the weather or the execrable quality of the food, would not avail to halt the flow of invective. However, half-way through the meal, when it began to look as though Mansell and the chemist were about to heave their plates full of whale steak at the engineers and the deck officers, Tom Archibald usually saved the situation by coming in from his radio room, late as always, and announcing that the Chinese had invaded Korea, or England had defeated Scotland in the rugger match, or some equally devastating piece of news that, for the moment, would make barrels and Kvaerners seem relatively unimportant. But soon somebody would again mention *barrels*, and off would go the interminable technical argument on the production of whale oil.

One day I decided that, if I was to take any part in saloon chatter during the season, I had better have a look through the factory and examine these mysterious barrels and Kvaerners and things which gave rise to such endless heated arguments among my shipmates. So I arranged for Mansell and MacDonald to spend an afternoon in the intricate maze below decks and explain to me something of the process of production of whale oil and by-products. It was a matter of tact to ask them both, for, if I had asked only one to show me the works, the other would never have forgiven me for getting an interloper to conduct a tour of what each regarded as 'his' factory. Gyle, the whaling inspector, decided to come along, too, partly because it was his duty to go below decks occasionally to ensure that the International Whaling Laws were being complied with in the depths of the factory ship as well as on deck and on the high seas, and partly because he anticipated the fun of seeing Mansell and Mac-Donald together on the actual battlefield.

So, in the way that dates are always arranged among whalemen, the four of us met in my cabin after lunch and discussed a bottle of my whisky prior to going on our tour. Mansell had brought along a fistful of papers (he is one of those people who always carry a dossier to back up their words), and, referring frequently to his 'black and white,' as he called it, he gave us a brief lecture on the production of whale oil, and some very interesting information on the 'quota system' and how this affects the reimbursement of the whalemen.

The whale quota for the Southern Ocean season, decided upon by the nations in convention at Sandefiord, was '16,000 blue whale units.' The 'blue whale unit' meant one blue whale (the largest species) or what was deemed the equivalent number of the smaller baleen whales, the finback and the sei, which would equal one blue whale. Humpbacks — the nice friendly little whales, which have not yet recovered from the holocaust to which the whaling barks early in the century subjected them — were restricted to only one thousand to be taken by all expeditions in the south. Sperm, we could take as many as we could get, provided we did not hunt them for longer than six months.

That was the quota for all expeditions, but we had a quota of our own, measured in oil, on which depended the pay of all our men. This quota was the average production of oil and by-products made by our expedition in the previous three years. At least half the earnings of all members of our crews, except the medical and scientific staffs, was dependent on this figure. If we reached or exceeded the quota, all hands would be well paid. If we did not come near it, the whaling trip would be a dead loss to most, for the bonus would be small and would not bring the wages paid by the company to anything approaching a sufficient recompense for eight months' incessant slavery away from civilization. But (here was the bait!) if the quota was exceeded, the bonus automatically increased by 50 per cent, and the whalemen would return home with thick wads of folding-money in their pockets.

But what the poor dolts couldn't see, Mansell told us, banging my table and nearly upsetting the whisky, was that the whole system was a hoax! If they worked hard and did very well one year, they'd be well paid; but their hard work would raise the quota for the next year, so they'd have to work twice as hard to make the same money! *And,* since there is the general limit of sixteen thousand blue-whale units for the southern fisheries, if one whaleman did well in some part of the Antarctic, another one — maybe his cousin — would suffer by his success in another expedition. A whaleman spending, say, twenty years in the industry would come out in the end exactly as though he had been paid a minimal salary; and, though he'd have had his excitements of good and bad years and striving to reach his quota, he was not the person who in the end would come out financially better off as a result of the 'quota' and 'bonus' system.

But, whoever was going to win or lose over it, the quota for our expedition for this season was 131,000 barrels of oil and 3,200 tons of by-products (mainly meat and bone-meal). Other small items counted toward the quota. For example, one pound of ambergris, if we were lucky enough to kill any sperm whales with bad guts, would count the same as a ton of meat-meal toward the quota; but, since ambergris, the fine ounce, was worth at the time a little more than the fine ounce of gold, it was not a bad exchange, from the owners' point of view, for a ton of manure. Similarly, a hundredweight of liver oil, each gram of which contained enough Vitamins A and D to keep a child free of rickets for a month, was reckoned as worth one ton of meat-meal — to the whalemen who extracted it down there in the ice, that is; though what the comparative value is when it is made up into capsules and sold to the vitamin-deficient children of Europe, only a businessman would know.

The season was more than half-way through, and we were nowhere near half our quota when I went on my conducted tour of the factory. Everybody below decks, Mansell told us, was on his toes striving to catch up with and exceed the production of oil over the past three years.

'What's a barrel?' I asked him when we had finished the whisky in my cabin and were climbing down the slippery ladder leading from the flensing-deck to the after end of the factory. The rungs of the ladder were wrapped in tow for the benefit of blood-stained sea-booted denizens of the upper deck like ourselves who might occasionally want to desecrate the clean, oily world of machinery below, and Mansell stopped half-way down the ladder, with his sea-boots a few inches from my nose, and answered my question — in accurate detail, as was his custom whenever any query concerning whaling was put to him.

The British barrel, he told me, was 170 kilograms, and there are 5·97 British barrels to the long ton. The American barrel, on the other hand, was slightly less, containing only 31·5 gallons. And different from both was the barrel of fuel oil, of which there were 6·5 to the ton. No whale oil was actually put into barrels today — it was kept in tanks — but the barrel measure was still used in computing the oil. The price of whale oil today was £100 per ton, and over the past ten years had varied from £60 to £110; and dried meat-meal fetched £45 per ton . . .

'Are we spending the day on this ruddy ladder?' inquired Gyle, whose feet I could see on the rung above Mansell's wagging head; and the lecture on the economics of whaling was postponed while we slid down onto the factory deck.

Now, a tour of a factory of any kind can be, and usually is, a most boring experience, and a description of such a tour is more boring still, so I will not attempt to explain in detail the technical and industrial processes carried out below decks in a whale factory ship. But, briefly, the factory consists of a section for boiling, or 'trying out,' oil from the blubber (the best obtained from the whale); another section for boiling oil of lesser quality from the bones; a third for extracting oil from the meat; then a fourth for extracting the last vestiges of oil from the 'glue water' and *grax* remaining when the first three operations have been performed; also machinery for drying, pulverizing, and bagging the 'meal' remaining when all oil has been extracted from meat and bone, and some smaller plants for special processes, such as the extraction of the vitamin-loaded liver oil. The principles underlying all the processes are simple, and consist in: (1) cooking the bits of dead whale in Kvaerner- or Hartmann-type boilers (which are identical with the pressure cookers every housewife uses to-day except that they are about ten feet by twenty and develop a pressure of six hundred pounds of steam, which would blow the housewife's cooker and her kitchen into Kingdom Come); (2) centrifuging the liquid produced by the boilers, to separate oil from glue water and *grax*; (3) centrifuging everything again, lest a pint of oil be lost; (4) drawing off the now dry meal and putting it in bags to be sold to the farmers at more than £30 a ton; (5) throwing away nothing if there remains a pennyworth of oil to be squeezed from it, and reluctantly, at the end of the process, pumping overboard the few gallons of evil-smelling water and the few handfuls of useless *grax*, which is all that remains of the mighty whale.

'That's enough about the industrial side!' the inspector and the doctor now announced to the engineer and the production officer. 'Now tell us what all these men are doing hanging about down here. None of them seem to me to be "on tiptoe"!' Gyle added sarcastically.

The factory was on 'full cook' — working all-out, that is — during our visit. There were eight whales in the cookers, and another four on the deck above in process of coming down through the manholes. That meant there were some eighty men working on the shift in the factory. The shift was long — twelve hours, with occasional brief breaks for meals — but, as Gyle implied, we saw no evidence of back-breaking labour such as the flensers and lemmers were performing up top-side in their effort to reach the quota. In fact, most of the men in the factory seemed to have jobs that consisted in sitting on a stool reading a book and, every five minutes or so, glancing at a dial, whereupon they lazily got up, turned a knob or two, glanced at the dial again, then returned to the stool and the book. I taxed MacDonald about their apparent idleness, and remarked that the whalemen in the factory seemed to earn as easy a living as any workmen I had seen.

MacDonald got indignant. 'D'ye realize that each of these

men is looking after thousands of pounds' worth of material passing through his machine every hour?' he expostulated. 'In the past twenty-four hours we've prepared and stowed fifty thousand pounds' worth of oil and by-products, and every twenty days on full cook we put a million pounds sterling in the holds! And, if one of these fellows muffs his job, it will cost the company something fantastic and will probably lose us most of our bonus earnings. So don't disparage my fellows working down here because they're not running around all the time. Their job's not just brute force and bloody murder like the work of the mate's men up on deck.'

I still saw no evidence of great intellectual activity or laborious exertion on the part of the factory workers spread out in that dim conglomeration of machinery; in fact, I watched about ten of them for several minutes, and not one even looked up from his book. But, when I knew more of the job below decks, I allowed that the factory men earned their pay, if not as hardly as the catchermen and the deck gang, at least more strenuously than any worker in any factory ashore. For the day of this conducted tour was still and no sea was running — a rare state of affairs in the Southern Ocean. And even in the usual Antarctic swell the men would not be able to sit on their stools, far less read books, but would be dashing around amid scalding steam and crashing machinery in an endless struggle to keep their gear working and the flow of oil running smoothly. And, in anything approaching a gale, keeping the factory working was, as one of the workmen put it to me: 'like trying to operate the San Francisco power station at the height of the earthquake!'

The trade names of the men in the factory were more mundane, but just as interesting as those on deck. The kings of the underworld — equivalent to the bosun, the plan foreman, the head flenser, the chief lemmer, and other aristocrats of the upper regions — were the leading cooker, the first separator, the meat-meal foreman, and — away down in dark depths which I had not yet visited — the head pumpman and the tank bosun. Most of them were friends of mine, for I had met them as they nursed their wounds or sucked thermometers in the sick bay, but now, on their jobs, their appearance was very different from that of the patients I knew. They got up from their books and greeted us as we passed through, and at the request of MacDonald, who was still anxious to persuade us that he did not command a gang of loafers, they explained their jobs to us.

The leading cooker was a small, alert Norwegian of Jewish background. He showed me what a Kvaerner was and demonstrated its mechanism. He tried to explain to me what his men read from their dials, and pointed out, amid much talk of 'colour indices' and 'cam-shafts' and 'temperature-pressure coefficients,' that the job was more complicated than appeared to the observer — and, in fact, was so complicated that I could not master it in twenty seasons with my unmechanical brain. But this pleasant little chap also had an unmechanical interest in life which far transcended his zeal for whale oil and Kvaerners. This was trade-unionism.

He was the accredited representative of the Norwegian Seamen's Union with our expedition, and this was his religion. Every conversation one had with him, whether it began with a discussion of his asthmatic symptoms in the sick bay or with the ideal gearing ratio for the revolving pressure boilers, would finish in a debate on labour-management relationships. I had met this obsession frequently before, but almost invariably among Reds, so during our conversation on this occasion, after he had shown off his machinery and inveigled us into talking about the relative compensation of the man producing whale oil in the Antarctic and the man selling it in the north, I asked him outright in front of my three companions whether he was a Communist. His reply was interesting.

'I'm a Socialist, doctor,' he told me, 'the same as the majority of the men in the factory and the men on deck, too, British or Norwegian. I'm not a Communist, and I can tell you this: there's not a single Communist in the whaling industry on this expedition nor the rest of the expeditions, other than that crowd of Russian poachers who have come down here this year. There's enough wrong with the way some whale owners treat their men to make the whalemen seem fertile territory for Communist propaganda and intrigue, but there's not a Bolshie amongst us. Why? First, because the average Bolshie is such a poor human specimen he couldn't stand one season in the south, and, second, because the boys know they'll eventually get a straight deal through ordinary industrial bargaining once the folk up north know that a whaling industry exists and the value of it; and, if the lads found a Bolshie amongst them, they'd heave him over the side with the rest of the *grax* — because, frankly, whalemen and Bolshies may both be rebels, but they're rebels of a different type, rebelling against completely different things, in a different way.'

On first hearing, I took our little Norwegian workers' representative with the grain of salt I reserve for politicians of all shades, for I have often heard a man disparage his party — especially the Red one — when it suited his purposes; but later in the voyage I came to realize that this man's industrial and social religion was indeed something very different from Communism. In fact, when differences arose between the medical department and the workers on the ship, I came to call not on the captain as arbiter of the dispute, but on this sensible little trade-union man, who, if a reasonable case were presented to him, would back management against labour as vehemently as, in theory, he backed the workers. And the Whaler Group VIII's were more afraid of him than they were of the captain, for, not only was he trade-union leader, but he was a Whaler Group III, nearly at the top of the whaling hierarchy, which ranges from Whaler Group XIII, the newly joined mess-boys — the dregs of the whaling society — to Whaler Group I — the bosuns, chief flensers, and other aristocracy of the whaling world. 'Anyway,' said MacDonald as we left the leading cooker, 'whatever his politics may be, he's the best damn cooker that ever sailed on a whaleship, and, if all trade-union blokes work as well as he does, I'd like to man the factory with worker politicians!'

The first separator, the man in charge of all the intricate centrifuging machinery, was a very different type. He was a tall, dark, bespectacled Scotsman. The kind who doesn't turn round until you clear your throat and nudge him, and then turns very slowly. He looked at Mansell and MacDonald, his two superior officers, as though he had never seen them before, then turned back to his machinery. Myself and Gyle he ignored completely. But Gyle had known him for many seasons, and had discovered his weak spot. This was his hobby, which, in the usual incongruous whaleman's way, was taxidermy, or 'burrd stuffin',' as he called it. So Gyle mentioned something about a penguin skin he was drying out, and an entirely different first separator turned round, genially this time. Leaving the two of them to discuss some technical point of avian necrophily, the other three of us wandered off unmolested around the separating-plant.

The other separators were a cordial, cheery bunch when the 'king penguin,' as they called their boss, was out of the way, and they started to prove to me — as every whaleman tries to do when demonstrating his job — that they were the key men of the whaling industry. I was soon, as usual, lost in a morass of technical jargon, but I was intrigued by the names they gave their machines as they patted and fondled them. The principal one seemed to be a high-speed centrifuge that went under the name of the 'G.V.K.' But no one could say what these ominous-sounding initials stood for, and the separators admitted that, though they had worked the machines for years and used the initials a hundred times a day, it had never occurred to them to find out what they meant. Mansell, of course, solved the mystery. It seems he had installed the machines years before, after a long argument with the owners about the relative merits of two types of centrifuge. This model had the catalogue number gvk — no more than a filing symbol. But Mansell had spent months extolling the virtues of the gvk model against an ogu or some such equally forbidding symbol, and the name was taken up by others until, when the machines Mansell wanted were eventually installed, the name became general throughout the whaling industry.

'Accurate information, as usual,' muttered MacDonald behind me. 'Story of Mansell's being the leading participator in the biggest advance in whaling engineering of the decade — complete boloney, as usual!'

To try to describe a whale factory ship without frequently digressing to report the pungent smells that pervade it would be like describing a painting without mention of colour. On deck the olfactory situation varied from hour to hour, depending upon the age and condition of the whales being dissected and the direction of the wind, but down here on the factory deck the odours were fixed and constant, each section of the processing-plant having its characteristic smell.

I discovered that the two worst-smelling parts of the factory had the freshest and sweetest names. There was the 'Butterworth,' which had a most yummy sound but, on inspection, turned out to be a great, ugly hunk of machinery dripping fetid whale oil from every pore and discharging clots of dirty grey sick-making *grax* from a vent in its vitals. And there was the 'Rosedown Plant,' which sounded as though it came straight out of an English spring but was in fact a quaking mass of netting onto which dropped mashed overdone whale meat and foul-smelling gravy, and which spattered slobs of the horrid mess on all who came near, as it vibrated rhythmically under the control of a greasy attendant whose job it was to separate the meat from the gravy. This man was called 'Rosedown' by his companions, and the name fitted him as ill as it fitted his machine.

But alas for the romance of modern whaling! These two delightfully named bits of machinery, and likewise the men who operated them, were named, not to bring fragrance into the rancid atmosphere of the whale factory, but after the engineers who had built them. However, to this day I cannot solve the psychological puzzle of how two men named Butterworth and Rosedown could spend their lives designing and producing reeky whale-oil machinery.

Nevertheless, there were small touches of romance even amid the separating-machinery and the grimy men who worked it. Some of their books showed flashes of it. Mostly they were reading what Gyle called 'whodunits' and 'duzzie-shaggers,' the two classes of literature which made up the bulk of our ship's library, but occasionally in a corner of the machinery we would come across a man on a stool reading Shakespeare, or studying palaeontology, or learning an obscure foreign language. And I knew at least one whose reading was confined to the Greek classics, and another for whom even ten seasons in the bowels of a factory ship had not destroyed the romance of medieval poetry. He was immersed in *Beowulf* on this occasion when we found him, but cheerfully left that hero a while to talk to us of whale oil. It was he who initiated me into a whaling secret and showed me another of those strange little anachronisms that permeate the modern industry.

Every now and again he would get up from his stool and his book and go over to a spigot on the side of his separating-machine, from which he would half fill a cigarette tin with whale oil. Then he would solemnly spit into the tin and gaze at his spittle descending through the oil for about half a minute. He would then heave the tinful of oil into the scuppers and, taking a sterile boiled glass flask from a shelf, he would fill it from the same spigot, mark and seal it, and send it up to the ship's laboratory to be analysed by young Evans and his assistants. But he was not going to trust the exact mathematical scrutiny young Evans would make of his sample. First, with the aid of his cigarette tin, he was going to make his oil pass the spittle test, used by British whalemen for centuries before the first chemist went afloat to assess the grade of their oil. And I understand that the separators' spittle test was seldom wrong in diagnosing exactly the standard of oil the machinery was producing. 'In fact,' young Evans confessed to me at the end of the voyage, 'it was a good check on my results, and the spittle men often queried my findings and put me straight when I'd made a bloomer in the lab.'

What is the test? Well, it must be a cylindrical tin, two inches by two and a half; you fill it just over half-full of oil, then you spit into it. And what happens then and how you judge the grade of oil from what you see in the next thirty seconds is a secret that

American whalemen have tried to extract from their British colleagues for many decades. The secret of the test seems to lie in the time it takes for the spittle to break the surface tension of the oil — and that is all I can say, for, not being a separator, I know no more about this mysterious trade secret.

The extracting- and separating-machinery did not by any means constitute the whole of the factory, for below us were still two decks filled with drying-, processing-, and sorting-machinery for the various by-products of the whale, and below that again were the tanks and holds where our loot was stored.

'I wanna see a *barrel* !' I kept saying petulantly to Mansell and MacDonald as we wandered around, so eventually they took me away into the depths of the ship to examine Number Two Starboard Wing Tank, a modern equivalent of the old whale-oil barrel. It was an iron pit about the size and shape, it seemed to me, of a large grain elevator. Its capacity was, according to MacDonald, 'only about five thousand tons — around thirty thousand barrels, that is.' But at the time I saw it it was nearly empty, which meant there were a mere thousand barrels or so (a good cargo for a New Bedford bark at the end of a four-year voyage!) swilling about at the bottom.

Our tour of the factory finished in one of the meat-meal holds, where thousands of sacks of dried dead whale were stacked silently, ton upon ton, from deck to deckhead. There was a queer spooky atmosphere in this mausoleum of whales' ashes. Absolute silence, though ten thousand tons of machinery were banging away within a few hundred feet all round us, except for the swishing of the Antarctic sea against the steel plates on which we stood fifty feet below its surface. And this immense stack of dumb matter that, some of it a month ago, some of it a few hours ago, had been sporting, feeding, and loving in that sea. Dumb? Those bags shouted at us, in that dim cavern, the question: 'What's it all about?'

VIII

THE PSYCHOPATHS

> If a man does not keep pace with his companions, perhaps it is because
> he hears a different drummer. Let him step to the music which he hears,
> however measured or far away.
>
> —THOREAU

SOMEBODY — I cannot find out who — expressed Mr. Thoreau's thought even more neatly in the couplet:

> There are some who hear a different drummer,
> And who march a different pace.

This couplet I kept framed above my desk in my comfortable cabin on the whaling ship.

I kept it there, not to apply to myself or to justify my flight from regular practice to the strangest medical job in the world (although I must confess that even to me the faint tattoo of the different drummer was more audible in the far Antarctic than in any place I have been), but to remind myself that my whalemen patients were to a man marching a pace very different from that set by the orthodox drummer of the northern hemisphere.

Old Burnett, during one of his gay, sociable phases, admonished me on this subject, and, though I believed I had gained sufficient insight into the whalemen's character to make his warning unnecessary, it is worth repeating to any of those who march in step and have never heard the other drum.

'You won't get to know us, doctor, in the short time you'll be with us,' he cautioned me, 'and, when you come to write about us, it will be very easy to make us out to be a mob of half-crazy malcontents whose only aim in life is to see the bottom of every whisky bottle. But try to give a fair report on us, even when you come to tell about the way the whalemen drink. After all, though the kirk and the owners and the folk at home say we drink too much, we bring the whales back to them.'

I have labelled the whalemen psychopaths, but by that I mean nothing derogatory. I do not mean that they were mentally unbalanced or sick, nor do I mean that they suffered from any defect or neurosis or psychological inferiority. Often laymen who do not understand the term, and even psychiatrists who do not understand the type, use the word *psychopath* to mean these things. But I use it rather as a term of superiority. The psychopath — the 'man with the suffering mind,' to analyse the word etymologically — is a type I have spent my life studying, and my conclusion long ago was that his mind is healthy — too healthy to be acceptable to, or to accept, the civilization into which he was born, and therefore doomed to alienate itself from that civilization in some way. Some such minds, like those of Dostoevsky, Kafka, and Thoreau, have found their escape through letters; others, many thousands of them, have escaped through art, and even some, like Galileo, Newton, Darwin, and Freud, through science; and many, like Socrates, have got out of the human jail by philosophy's door. But the great majority of such incompatibles can find no talent or technique which gives them a spiritual avenue of escape from civilized humanity while they remain physically in its midst, and this huge army of unskilled psychopaths is forced to make an actual material getaway to some of the few remaining parts of the world where they will not encounter, and so will not clash with, their orthodox, average, and usually intolerant fellow humans. Some of these displaced persons from civilization, like Ernest Shackleton, Robert Peary, Marco Polo, Columbus, and others of the great explorers, have left their fellow men to follow a dream; others, like the Pilgrims, or the Latter-day Saints, have set out to found new communities where, with others like themselves, they hope at last to be compatible; but a vastly greater number have left civilization in covered wagons, on sledges, and — most of all — in the fo'c'sles of ships, and especially whaling ships, to seek in the lonely places of the earth that thing they could not find, or were not permitted to find, in the crowded places.

It was thus as refugees from civilization that I diagnosed most of my whaling shipmates, and, though their response to the rhythm of the faraway drummer was ruder, coarser, and often less intelligent than the echo made by the great men I have mentioned, I believe they heard his tapping as distinctly and as insistently.

Mansell, of course, was the most obvious psychopath of the lot, as any psychiatrist who got to know this lovable old whaleman would agree, and as he admitted himself when I had explained the term to him. A glance at his background and history — and one never got more than a glance — was all that was needed to prove it.

This we, his friends, knew about him, and I think no man knows more: he could speak English, but was obviously not English- or American-born. The Norwegians told us he spoke good Norwegian, but they could not make out what his accent was. He could chat with Chippy and Thor, the only Swedes aboard, in fluent Swedish — Chippy said with a German accent, but Thor thought it was Russian. He had once been a consul in New Orleans, we all knew, but no one knew what flag had flown over his consulate. I learned some more personal details during intermissions in the long course of instruction on whaling lore he gave during our long voyage. I knew about, or at least had been given fleeting insight into, a tragic romance dating back to his days in New Orleans; I had heard a passing admission from him that his dominating ambition since his school-days had been to master some one subject, totally and alone among men, and that whaling was the only one he had succeeded in finding for which he felt mentally equipped. I deduced from his statements and reactions to his shipmates that he held an ineradicable belief that all men were honest and nobly motivated, and that, if Mansell was bluffed or hurt, it must in some way be Mansell's fault. And I knew from his behaviour to man and beast that he had a fear, amounting to horror, of physically or mentally hurting anybody or anything himself.

All these things that I knew about him gave hints of why he and civilization had found themselves mutually incompatible, but no one of them gave the explanation of why he had spent the greater part of his life on the fringe of the Polar ice — the only place on earth, according to the great Darwin himself, where all competition between the living things of nature ceases. I could with ease give a wordy, plausible, but essentially meaningless analytic explanation of Mansell and his strange way of life, but the whaling season was not far advanced before I realized that none of the Viennese psychological hypotheses hold any validity south of the fiftieth parallel. And, anyway, the analytic schools have never given an accurate description, never mind explanation, of the type I call psychopath, which I encountered in pure culture, with Mansell as the characteristic organism, when I went among the whalemen.

Their psychopathic traits showed up to greatest advantage, not when they were hunting or dismembering the whale — for then they were merciless automatons — but during their few periods of relaxation in the Polar wastes. For occasional official holidays are celebrated by these men during their seasonal grind to bring the maximum amount of food possible out of the Antarctic to the citizens in the north, and on the rare occasions when they lay off whaling to relax, I think the citizens they feed would wish no part of them, and would be horrified by their manner of relaxing.

Early in the season the Norwegians held one or two 'Prayer Days,' when they insisted that all work should come to a stop for a few hours. The first time this happened, I thought it would mean we would stop for prayer; but I saw no evidence of religious activity during the break, and the conviviality attending the celebration of the Fire of Copenhagen (I could never understand why the Norwegians considered this an occasion for prayer anyway) was at least as exuberant as that shown by the Scots on their 'holy days.' But at Christmas our psychopathic ship had its real blow-out.

All hands downed tools, and for twenty-four hours there was pandemonium on the Polar Sea. The catchers came in on Christmas Eve, not to bring whales, but to collect as much loot as they could persuade an unsympathetic chief steward to part with, and as much liquid cheer as they could scrounge from their friends with hidden supplies of whisky or private stills aboard the factory ship. Then a convenient gale sprang up, which made all whaling impossible for a day or two, even had there been anyone fit to do it, and the whole fleet, including the factory, hove to in the lee of an iceberg as big as Malta. And here the fun began

Christmas celebrations opened very stiffly and formally on the factory, and this, according to the whaling inspector, was a sign most ominous, pointing to the way the day would end. At 11 A.M. all the top saloon officers assembled at the manager's behest in the smoke-room, wearing collars and ties for the first time since leaving Tönsberg. Seated or standing uncomfortably around, we drank two vapid 'company cocktails' supplied by the chief steward, and cautiously broached a bottle or two from the manager's private stock. Our conversation was subdued and elegant, and an observer might have thought we were the elders of a Presbyterian kirk in session, instead of a bunch of tough whaling characters about to begin their annual binge in the ice. Once Old Burnett mentioned the word *barrels*, but the disapproving tut-tuts from the decorous gentlemen around him had more effect in shutting him up quickly than the blasphemous rejoinders his fellow whalemen normally made to his endless talk of oil.

About noon Mansell brought the manager's cocktail party to an abrupt end by announcing in the usual Mansell bellow: 'Now we all go and have a drink!' and in his cabin and a dozen lesser meeting-places throughout the ship the real celebration of Christ's birthday began. Callers began to arrive from the lower deck. It was a privilege of the bosun, the second bosun, the plan foreman, and one or two more of the leading personalities of the deck and the factory to call on every officer and wish him a Merry Christmas, and it was an ungenerous (and unwise!)

officer who sent them away without the customary tot. Led by Davison, that pillar of sobriety on normal occasions, the little cortège had reached my cabin before breakfast, and now by noon they had worked their way right through the after-quarters of the ship, had negotiated the long, pitching deck with a most unseamanlike gait, and were making their calls on the officers in the forward 'apartment house.' They arrived in Mansell's room just as he opened his first bottle, and in a few minutes all hands were at ease and comfortably disposed around the cabin, and, the occasion being what it was, officers and petty officers began to open out and reveal themselves more than was their wont at other times.

The motion of the ship in the gale was violent and was felt especially in Mansell's high-placed cabin, where furniture, ornaments, and frequently an unsteady seaman were being pitched about. Nobody seemed to notice it, and never a hand was stretched out to save Mansell's glasses and pictures, or even his guests, from smashing into the bulkhead. But I noticed one curious reflex action among the old seamen — each time the ship pitched extra violently, a dozen hands reached out to prevent the bottle being tilted off the table. The table itself might glide away altogether, but the bottle would be safe in the middle of the chaos, held upright by many large but instantaneously reacting hands.

The conversation was revealing. Whaling, though it was the obsessive interest and interminable subject of discussion among these men, seemed that day to be a forbidden topic. They talked of the late war — a theme practically never brought out on other occasions, though nearly every man on the expedition had been in it up to his neck for six years. Victor, the deck storeman, former bridge-player of international repute, now psychopath who had found peace on a whaleship's lower deck, sat with Gyle, discussing cricket. MacDonald and the chief electrician argued the merits of Rudyard Kipling as a poet; and the second radio-operator hauled a copy of the *Golden Treasury* out of his pocket to help them decide on the points at issue. The manager, bored with his own diminishing party, joined us shortly and was soon in a discussion with the bosun on rug-making, a form of amusement which occupied them both in their rare leisure time. I ensconced myself in a comparatively safe corner of the cabin and entered into a conversation with our toughest gunner, who revealed to me — daring me under penalty of sudden death to quote him — that his ambition was to make enough money to buy a small sheep farm in New Zealand and settle down.

Mansell, our host, was entering into several conversations at once, trying hard to make some intelligent comment on a subject unconnected with whaling, and at the same time trying to dissuade Old Burnett from giving a sermon on the evils of drink, which was his custom when the whisky got into his Calvinistic soul and warned him that he might be tempted to join those around who were enjoying themselves. But Mansell's ignorance of theology and ethics was as profound as his ignorance of every subject outside whaling, and his conversational sallies this Christmas Day were not erudite, though nearly always they were funny.

At three o'clock, by which time nearly everybody on the ship had visited its unofficial social centre — Mansell's cabin — we broke up the party and went up again to the saloon to eat Christmas dinner. The ship had been decorated in the traditional way with all the tinsel and tape and greenery that could be found, the tables were covered with the usual cotton snow, crackers, silver bells, and angels, and we sat down beneath two huge flags, British and Norwegian, with an imitation Christmas tree between them.

'What a lot of damned rot!' commented Old Burnett, as people began to adjust foolish paper hats and the usual sounds of gaiety arose from the tables. 'It's plain ridiculous to interrupt the work of the ship to pretend we're enjoying ourselves amongst all these damfool decorations!' But I knew that the best of the decorations, bunches of daffodils and green fern, the only real flowers anywhere within a thousand miles of that patch of desolate ocean, had been supplied by Old Burnett himself; and I knew the care and trouble he had expended in growing them, and the acute anxiety he had suffered during the past few days lest they should not be in full bloom in time for the Christmas dinner-table.

The dinner was a success, chiefly because most who could had contributed a bottle or two, and also because Mansell kept one table roaring with laughter as he bellowed out libellous and shockingly detailed stories of the love life of the whaling gunners, with illustrations drawn from the amorous histories of the three gunners who were present as guests, for Mansell's knowledge of whalemen was as widespread and exact as his knowledge of whaling. The other table was similarly amused by Tom Archibald, the radioman, who was a humorist of equal skill but of finer and more deadly technique, and was making an attack on the British Navy against which Commander Gyle was making a scintillating but ribald defence.

There was something lacking, however, and, gay though it was, our Christmas feast away down there in the lee of that iceberg was rather pathetic. The food was good — cauliflower soup with seaweed in it and *löbskaus*; turkey for those who could not face that Norwegian culinary horror consisting of salt fish soaked for days in caustic soda; and plum duff saturated in the company's brandy for all. But silences fell now and again when we looked around at one another and saw only a gang of tough men, flushed with whisky, wearing absurd hats and making artificial fun. We were glad we had Mansell and Tom, who, as born humorists often are, were extra-sensitive to changes of atmosphere or strain in the audience, and reserved their best cracks and stories to alleviate the tension. I saw very clearly during that Christmas dinner that Mansell had been dead right in his diagnosis of the main difficulty and cause of depression of the whalemen in the south: 'U-u-u-rgh! No women!' One girl at that party — anything of the opposite sex, even one fat and fiftyish old squaw — would have made it a festive triumph, but in her absence it was impossible to remove the slightly hollow note from the gaiety.

At the end of dinner the manager rose and gave the toast:

'Gentlemen! The King!' We all rose and drank the toast. We sat. The manager rose again and gave the toast: 'Gentlemen! The King!' Again we all solemnly arose and drank. The manager had tactfully not specified whether he was giving us George of Britain or Haakon of Norway first, and each of us could toast the monarchs in the order of our individual preference.

When we sat down and all instinctively glanced at the pictures of the two kings that hung one at either end of the saloon, I had a thought — one of those thoughts which, backed by considerable research that will never be made, would provide the basis for a psychohistorical thesis that will never be written. It was this: the greatest days of England's voyagers, explorers, and adventurous men who went to the most distant inaccessible places of the earth for years of voluntary exile were not the days of her kings, but of her queens. Might this be explained by the fact that in the days of the queens there was among them the presence of a woman, in spirit and usually in picture, dominating every gathering of officers in isolated, out-of-the-way places and standing proxy for her missing sisters at celebrations such as our sterile, rather pathetic Christmas party? Perhaps, by some psychological quirk, Drake, Raleigh, Hawkins, Livingstone, Weddell, Franklin, and the many others who toasted Elizabeth or Victoria at the end of their far-off Christmas dinners did not rise feeling so empty and foolish as we did with George and Haakon, our benign but most unfeminine symbols, looking down upon us. Maybe Columbus would not have sailed so far and dared so much for Ferdinand as he did for Isabella.

'Hum — but what about Cap'n Cook and Ernest Shackleton and all the others who carried the Geordies' flags round these parts?' asked Gyle when I submitted my hypothesis to him — thereby destroying it at birth. 'You'll have to wait until the U.S.A. has a female president's picture over the Christmas dinner-table on an interplanetary rocket. Then you can test your idea.'

'Or perhaps,' I thought, 'if I again attend or get Gyle's reports on the annual celebrations on British whaleships in the

Antarctic for the next few years, I may find fresh evidence to strengthen my idea.'

I have stressed the brief (and most unusual) display of Nordic and Britannic patriotic emotion on our ship that Christmas because of the repercussions — incomprehensible to those who do not know the psychopath — that followed later in the day. After lunch I went aft to my comfortable and isolated cabin, opened a special bottle of my own, and drank a toast to the woman whose picture hung over my desk above my couplet, then got into my bunk to compose a reply to the radiogram I had received from her that morning. After that perhaps I would write a letter or read a book. I got the first done, then awakened about two hours later. The weather had subsided, but the ship was still hove to in the shelter of the iceberg. I got up, and, going into the sick bay to see what was doing, I found Sigrid sewing up a scalp and applying compresses to a broken nose, the first Scottish and the second Norwegian.

'Is there a war going on?' I asked.

'It was declared about an hour ago,' Sigrid informed me with a grin. 'I think Norway is winning! And, if you're going forrard, doctor, I advise you to go through the factory — not across the deck.'

I wanted more information before viewing the conflict, so I rang up Gyle on the ship's phone. Battle had been joined, he told me, in the alleyways of the forward apartment house at about two bells. The combat did not seem to be strictly international; in fact, the *casus belli* was reckoned by the neutral faction to have been a remark by a Norwegian flenser to a Norwegian gunner that he shot nothing but short whales. On that, an Ulsterman foresaw trouble, so he hit the nearest Scots Presbyterian, then leaped upon an English steward. 'And now,' Gyle said, 'there's a bit of blood swilling in the scuppers, but they haven't got out the flensing-knives yet.'

Thus briefed, I went forward to take a look, and arrived just at the climax. The combatants, about thirty in number, had fought their way out onto the main deck and were filling the entrance to Hell's Gates with bloodthirsty cries and the sound of blows. There were some cries savouring of nationalism, such as 'You bloody Scots! You no good!' and 'Let the Norski square-heads have it, boys!' But in some instances Norwegian was locked in battle with Norwegian, or Scot with Scot, while many of the Shelties stood neutral and the presence of the Ulsterman and the English steward complicated the racial issue further.

Then Davison arrived, and he didn't wait to call for order or read the Merchant Shipping Act, but treated the neutral observers to a sight that I for one had always wanted to see — a bosun dealing with an unruly crew in the old-fashioned bosun's way.

We neutral spectators and Davison decided upon a drink when the battlefield was cleared, and so, of course, we went up to Mansell's cabin, there to end this Christmas Day. Gyle was with Mansell.

'Well, Davy, did you win again this year?' asked the inspector.

'I dinna ken what will happen on this ship the year I lose!' grunted Davison. 'But, anyway, gentlemen, it's been a good Christmas — quieter than most years, though.'

'And how,' asked Gyle, turning to me, 'does our learned psychiatrist account for this invariable outburst of frenzy that takes place on every whaling ship of every nation every year to celebrate the birthday of the Prince of Peace?'

'Because none of you know what peace is, and none of you ever will!' was the reply I made at the time, and I think my re-mark may have been overheard — and understood — by little Dornoch, the second steward, who was coming in and out of the cabin with glasses for our drinks.

IX

THE OUTSIDE OBSERVER

The use of the sea and air is common to all; neither can a title to the ocean belong to any people or private persons, forasmuch as neither nature nor public use and custom permit any possession thereof.
—ELIZABETH I OF ENGLAND

COMMANDER P. A. GYLE, Royal Navy (Ret.), was born in Boston, Mass., fifty-odd years ago. His ancestry was somewhat Churchillian. His father was a British naval officer of the old blood-and-thunder, 'God bless the Queen, and the Navy's not what it was since they gave up flogging' school, sprung from a line of naval officers going back to the galleons. His mother was a mild-mannered American lady, or rather, a Bostonian. Gyle himself was a midshipman at the Battle of Jutland, and fired his first shot in anger before his sixteenth birthday.

Between the two wars he served in the small ships of the Navy, wherever there was a job to be done and the prospect of some trouble, instead of serving in big ships where peacetime naval life consisted of ceremonial cruises and cocktail parties. He was with the Yangtze gunboats a while, then with the fishery-protection cruisers. He spent a year or two on the sloops up the Persian Gulf chasing pearl-poachers. He went anywhere, in fact, where he could have command of a small ship far removed from the ballyhoo of the dignified flag-showing Navy his father loved so well, and preferably to a place where his guns would be loaded with live ammunition rather than blank. During World War II he got mixed up in more trouble in and around the Mediterranean than the average fighting-sailor finds during his whole career, but at the end of the war, when the Navy was again looking for officers who could conduct themselves properly at cocktail parties rather than under shell-fire, he found himself out on the street, with a wife and growing family beside him and a pension of £450 a year to support them.

He had no marketable ability or knowledge other than a huge experience of the sea and of the ways of seamen. He did not even try to earn a living ashore, for he knew that he was totally incompatible with the creatures who compete on that element. But fortunately he heard of a job afloat, and a job connected with small ships similar to those that had been his passion in life. He went to interview an elderly gentleman in Whitehall, who, as Gyle told me himself, 'thought that whales were fish, but had around his office the finest photographs of icebergs I have ever seen.' This old gentleman liked the look of Gyle, and liked his record, so sent him off for a year to study the ways of the whale and idiosyncrasies of the whaleman — the only type of seaman he had not yet encountered. He passed with ease all tests of seamanship and personal probity required by the Whaling Inspectorate, mastered the theory of modern whaling and its legalities in the time allotted, then sailed south as a junior inspector to learn the job on the spot. Soon his worth was recognized even by Whitehall, and he has sailed to the Antarctic for seven months every year since as senior inspector.

The job is a most unusual and little-known one.

Gyle and his few fellow inspectors are employed under the International Whaling Convention. 'There shall be maintained on each ship engaged in treating whales at least two inspectors of whaling for the purposes of maintaining continuous inspection while the ship is so engaged,' says the law, and as with most international laws, there is much more implied than written in that sentence. The whaling inspectors, like many officials of international organizations today, have a double loyalty: first, to the government that employs and pays them; but, second, and no less demanding, to the international convention under which they work. Their job is mainly to curb the over-exuberant whalemen in order that the various species of whale may be preserved and, despite the slaughter, allowed to breed and increase. 'We're gamekeepers' was the way Gyle explained it, 'keeping an eye on the world's biggest and most important game reserve.'

Inspectors have a hundred or more regulations and restrictions to enforce. For example, they must ensure that no whale shorter than the length internationally agreed on for each species is taken; they must preserve the rarer species, such as the right whale and the California grey whale, inviolate; they must limit whaling to the times and seas laid down by Sandefiord, and ensure that the expeditions they accompany never trespass on the world's great whale sanctuaries. They must be seamen, zoologists, mathematicians, men of absolute integrity who can refuse bribes presented daily in sundry attractive forms. They must be detectives with the observation and acumen of Holmes; they must be lawyers, arbitrators, and often judges; and — by God! — they must be psychologists in order to impose the international law and prevent the 'title to the ocean belonging to any people or private persons,' while at the same time they remain on terms of good-will with mercenary whale owners and with hundreds of whalemen, every one of whom is trying to hoodwink them.

For doing this job and being all these things, the British government, in 1951, paid its senior inspectors £50 and junior inspectors £40 a month, and yet succeeded in finding outstanding men to undertake the work.

I say that the inspector's job is to enforce the law of his nation and the law of the International Board, but he is given no power to do so. He cannot *order* the manager, or the gunners, or any man on the expedition. He can only 'advise' them, and report any delinquencies of which he has absolute proof long afterwards when he returns home. Most breaches of the whaling laws carry, for the owners, for the master of the ship, and for the gunner or whichever individual commits the offence, a penalty of three months' imprisonment. But I have heard of no case (nor had Gyle), in my own or any other country, of a man doing time for a whaling offence. Maybe some prison warden somewhere can let me know if, among the murderers and thugs under his care, there is one man tramping round a prison yard anywhere in the world to atone for the offence of 'shooting a short whale.'

However, though Gyle had no big stick with which to enforce the law he represented, and though every one of the whalemen knew this, it was a rare one among them who did not accept and at least try to comply with his 'advice.' Most of our crews had served in or under the Navy, either British or Norwegian, and those who had knew Gyle for what he was as soon as they saw him. He was the only man I ever heard addressed as 'sir' on a whaling ship, where manager, captain, gunners, chief engineers, doctors, and the like are usually addressed by all and sundry by their first names, or, if one is popular, by a nickname. He was the only man who could commit the mortal sin of 'holding up production' on deck or factory without giving offence — and not because he was the inspector, but because he was Commander Gyle, a man who liked and understood seamen, as seamen liked and understood him.

I got to know him early in the trip. We got together mainly, I think, because we were the only two on the expedition whose future was not tied up with the whaling company, and who could take an objective view of the psychopathic whalemen among whom we, admitted psychopaths ourselves, had to live a while.

Most evenings I spent sharing a bottle with him in his cabin, or he in mine, and quickly we discovered common interests. An inquisitiveness about everything connected with whaling and whalemen was one of these, and, if we were talking whaling, we passed the code word over the ship's 'party line' telephone to Mansell, who came to share our bottle and monopolize the conversation. But whaling was but one of our interests, so, if we felt like getting away from the Southern Ocean a while, we excluded even that friendly character, and instead asked Victor, or Tom Archibald, or Sigrid, or any of many men aboard who could — their repressions, if any, removed by a couple of slugs — talk on any subject in the universe which might come up. Then we would see our senior inspector at his best.

Most of his life not spent on the bridge of a fighting-ship had been passed by Gyle with a book in his hand, and his knowledge was as wide as his intelligence was high. The whalemen, though the great majority of them were intelligent well above the average and many were knowledgeable in fields far removed from their work and way of life, did not stand a chance against a brain like this — and they knew it. Although he could give a two-hour discourse on the recession of the nebulae and showed a thorough understanding of the politics of Bolivia, he was also (next to Mansell and Micky, the plumber) the worst — or, should I say, the most pertinacious and best-informed? — gossip on the ship. And the ability to gossip humorously and good-naturedly about the men who make up one's little world afloat is one of the most valuable traits a man can take with him on an eight-month whaling voyage.

When I arrived in his cabin of an evening, or he arrived in mine, he would first extract from me a report on all the day's doings, important and trivial, from the after end of the ship where I lived — the progress of the injured men in the sick bay; what the scientists were working on and talking about in the lab.; who was sober, and who was not, among the engineers; how many killer whales had been shot at the foot of the skidway; and a hundred other matters that become important news items after months at sea. In return he would then give me the gossip of his territory, the forward end of the ship. He would report the day's incidents and talk on the bridge, the course, whaling plans, and weather prospects. He would give an account of the behaviour of the psychopaths who lived with him in the forward apartment house — of the bridge officers, the office staff, the cooks, stewards, and radiomen, and a tolerant and invariably humorous repetition of the talk in the lower saloon and the men's mess-decks, which always reached his ears in some mysterious way, even down to the latest rumours circulating among the mess-boys.

The only thing he never gossiped about, unless forced by question and answer, was his own job. No doubt this was an ingrained service habit, but I found it frustrating because, following my policy of trying to get data on each whaling job from the man who did the job, I wanted to get an inspector to talk about inspecting. Nevertheless, by doing a sort of Dr. Watson to his Sherlock Holmes day after day for months, I think I found out most of what there is to know about his odd profession.

It is not entirely confined to measuring and inspecting whales, giving advice to the manager, remonstrating with the gunners, striving to preserve the whale species, and being a symbol of the only moral force operating in the Antarctic. I watched Gyle performing strange jobs that seemed unconnected with the work of game warden and detective. In the early mornings he or his junior inspector could be seen up on the wing of the bridge, whirling a strange gadget attached to a piece of string round and round his head. When I sought information about this peculiar form of Spartan exercise, the most I got was that 'some fella in London wants a few meteorological data on this bit of sea.'

At another period of the voyage Gyle developed a sudden and intense interest in nylon rope, its capabilities and defects, and — perhaps by coincidence — his assistant developed a similar interest that lasted just as long and was equally intense. On other occasions they became absorbed in strange occupations that seemed to bear no relationship to the whale, or sought from the whalemen peculiar information that could not have been of any value in conserving the whale species, and spent hours at night entering it all in notebooks and diaries.

Micky, the plumber, reckoned he had the explanation of these strange goings-on, which the whole ship could not help observing. 'It's obvious they're still in the English Navy — both of them!' was Mickey's conclusion. 'This whaling inspectorate's just a blind, and it gives the English government a fine excuse for sending trained men down to the Southern Ocean each year to see what's going on.'

When, during one of our sessions in his cabin, I told Gyle Micky's hypothesis, and advanced certain theories of my own to account for the extra-curricular activities of him and the junior inspector, he looked at me with exactly the expression Holmes

A blue whale foetus is often post-humously delivered on the deck of a factory ship. The whalemen are superstitious about this, and the foetus is invariably thrown back into the sea instead of into the cooker to make oil

'D'ye want a side o' bacon to tak' home, Doc?', the bone-saw man calls to the photographer

The catcher fleet waits in an inhospitable bay in South Georgia for the opening of the whaling season

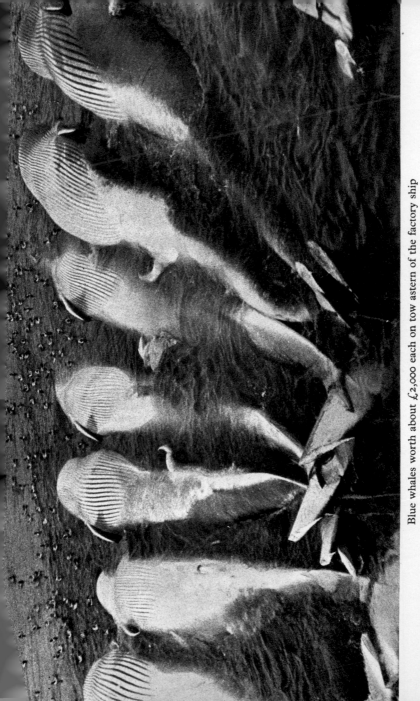

Blue whales worth about £2,000 each on tow astern of the factory ship

Huge steam-press boilers have replaced the copper kettles used by the old-time whalers to extract the oil from the blubber. The score marked on the side of the boiler is the number of barrels of oil extracted so far during the season

Laboratory work on board a whaleship is a fascinating occupation, but by no means an easy one during the Southern Ocean gales. Here, a whaleman by profession, but a keen young chemist too, checks on some oil samples from the day's catch

must have used to Watson when the latter attempted to make deductions. But his reply was, if more terse, certainly in language Holmes never used. 'Balls!' he said.

Gyle was as interested in the lives and manners of the whale-men with whom we lived as I was myself, and often he was the keener observer and better commentator on their personalities. He agreed that the generic term *psychopath* fitted our shipmates well, and that they were a distinct species within that genus. He made comparisons between the whalemen and the other pro-fessions manned almost exclusively by psychopaths, in which professions he included fighter pilots, submariners, lumberjacks, coal-miners, and even press reporters. 'All the jobs, in fact, which John Citizen insists shall be done but is not prepared to do him-self are manned by psychopaths, and each job breeds its own peculiar species of psychopath.'

'Whaling inspectors?' I ventured to ask.

'Yes — and stray psychiatrists we find wandering about the Antarctic Ocean! I'll recognize even that species of psychopath if ever I encounter it again. But it's my belief' (this was one of Gyle's favourite themes and he warmed up to it) 'that, before you understand the psychopaths who carry out — and carry out magnificently — the dangerous, unusual, and ill-rewarded work in out-of-the-way places of the world to maintain John Citizen in comfort in his armchair at home, it's first necessary to take an objective view of that specimen, and a very different one from that he takes himself. He likes to tell us this is the age of the common man. He believes it himself, and certainly he's coming out of it rather better than the uncommon men who have the misfortune to live in his age. Imagine him sitting reading his paper at his fireside in London or Edinburgh or Chicago right now. . . . The man who hewed the coal to put on his fire and keep him warm was no common man. The fellow who felled the tree in the Canadian forests which made the chair John Citizen sits on was a hard-drinking psychopath whom John wouldn't allow into his sitting-room, but without him there would be no chair. John reads his newspaper and protests that the news is dull, with no heed to the difficulty and often danger a thousand psychopaths have undergone to bring him that dull news. Reporters, viewed from his armchair, are unreliable fellows, prone to exaggeration, who sit around hotel bars and drink too much. And so he is prone to criticize the men — uncommon and psychopathic, all of them — who go out into the world to do things and find things which will interest him in his dull life in his armchair, just as he criticizes the men who wrest direct from nature the raw materials that make his comfortable life possible.

'Take the whalemen's contributions alone — does John ever look around his house and count the necessities of life brought to him by the eccentric types who prefer going to the Southern Ocean every year rather than join him in the armchair opposite? Never to my knowledge! He doesn't know or even bother to find out that his soap, his margarine, the cattlecake that fed the beef he had for supper, the fertilizer that grew the wheat for his bread, the feed he gives his chickens, the vitamin pills he gives his kids, the glaze on his photographs, the oil in his watch, the tan on his leather belt, not to mention over seventy different pharmaceutical preparations that appear in his bathroom medicine chest regularly, have all been found for him down here in the Southern Ocean by the lads whom we know and like, but whom he would regard as half-crazy drunks unfit to associate with him in the north.

'And he *really believes* that men take up jobs like lumberjacking, mining, or whaling because they are inferior beings incapable of doing his superior civilized work in office or factory or shop and have been forced by circumstances into their *outré* occupations. He seldom stops to think that somebody must have killed and brought home the sperm whale that provided the oil for his wife's lipstick or that there must be some thousand whalemen finding for him a hundred necessities and a thousand trivialities that he finds in every shop. But if he ever thinks of such men, *he's sorry for them* — because, in his view, they haven't succeeded in being like his superior self, and have failed in his endless struggle to find a well-paid cushy job. God help him . . .

But it's time I went on watch. Come on down on the plan, and I'll show you what a really uninteresting and routine job that of a whaling inspector is.'

We went down on deck, and Gyle disappeared into the little cubby-hole opening off the flensing-deck aft, known as the 'mate's office,' to take over from the other inspector, get an account of all the whales that had been brought aboard in the past twelve hours, and settle himself in for another twelve-hour battle to uphold the law.

A whale was being brought aboard — a female fin whale that looked rather small and needed no straining of the whale-winches to bring it up the skidway. As it lay on the deck and the flensers were attacking it, the second bosun emerged from the mate's office bearing a notebook, two spikes, and a measuring-tape of the kind used by surveyors. He went to the tail of the whale, counted the notches in the stumps of the flukes, noted the number down in his book, hauled out an old hunter watch from his greasy breeches, noted the time, inevitably glancing skyward and then round the horizon in the way of seamen as he did so, though no information from there was required. He then stuck one of his spikes into the deck, more or less in line with the tail of the whale, tied his measuring-tape to it, then walked forward, letting out the tape, to affix the other end to his second spike, stuck ostensibly opposite the snout of the whale. He made more notes.

Then Gyle emerged from the mate's office, also with note-book in hand. I should point out that the flensing process was by this time in full swing, and the Gaunt Stranger and his minions were heaving blocks and tackles and wire ropes and tons of blubber in all directions with complete disregard for the safety of the bosun or the law; but the second bosun and Gyle were well accustomed to moving about in this inferno, which I have tried elsewhere to describe, and even I could move about in by now with moderate security.

Gyle also examined the notches in the flukes, noted the time, and, being a seaman also, glanced automatically around at the weather and the state of the ship as he did so. Then he picked up the after spike and — without any comment from him or from the second bosun, who watched him — moved it two feet along to bring it really in line with the whale's snozzle in a just and legal position opposite the point of the lower jaw. Then, going forward, he moved the other spike eighteen inches to bring it alongside the notch in the flukes — not the end, but the point decided upon for measurement by the nations assembled in solemn convention at Sandefiord. Walking aft again and reaching up over his head to the port-side mammary gland of the dead cow whale, he gave a squeeze. A jet of milk, enough to fill a gasoline can, shot out from the huge udder as he did so: and when this happened, he looked for the first time a bit disconcerted, even angry.

We went into the mates' office, where one of the mates sat 'with the aquavit running out of his ears,' as Gyle put it.

'Who's the gunner of Number Three catcher?' Gyle asked him in the abrupt, attention-compelling tone used by naval officers when they are angry.

'Wha' ya say, 'spector?' the mate fumbled, realizing vaguely that something was wrong. 'Ogi Jansen's gunner Number Three — good gunner, Ogi——'

'He may be a good gunner, but he's also a first-class scab. And I'm gunning for him now. That bastard's taken me in too often,' said the angry inspector. 'Five short whales this season; two mysteriously broken whale lines, which were cut as cleanly as ever I've seen ropes cut; and now a lactating fin whale!'

The anger concerning the lactating whale was because it must have been accompanied by a calf, which, as we were speaking, must have been swimming in loneliness, searching for its mother and starving to death.

'But the really interesting thing, Robertson,' the inspector said when he had calmed down somewhat and Mr. Ogi Jansen had been duly logged, 'is the biological rather than the legal point. Come and look at this whale again.'

That it was under sixty feet was indisputable; it was nearer fifty. And that it was lactating was also incontrovertible. Gyle got a cup and squeezed another mighty gush of milk from one of the two udders. He invited me to taste it. I confess that, quite irrationally, I could not stomach it, and the very idea of drinking dead whale's milk nearly made me vomit. Gyle, however, had a stronger stomach, and he quaffed the cupful with apparent relish (as do many of the whalemen, who drink it whenever the illegal killing of a lactating whale gives them the opportunity). He then explained the biological point to me. Apparently all the books and authorities say that there never was a finback whale that became pregnant under sixty feet in length. Yet here lay one before us, fifty feet and already a mother. For that was milk, if ever we had seen, smelled, and tasted the stuff, as Gyle said.

We re-examined this unfortunate, diminutive mother again and thoroughly, but could find no abnormality other than her size.

'I wonder what rotten old bull took advantage of this poor little thing's innocence,' remarked Gyle, and he seemed really sorry for the small whale. 'If Ogi Jansen could swim, it's him I would blame! It's the sort of foul trick he would play!'

On another occasion, instead of the inspector demonstrating to me the anomalies of the whale and the misdemeanours of the whalemen, I brought both to his notice — but too late. One day I was going forrard for my lunch. Since there was but one whale (a large blue) on the deck, I ventured the length of the ship top-side to go to my meal, instead of going through the factory deck to avoid the ropes and knives. The mate and inspector had also gone to lunch, leaving the deck in charge of a gangling and not-very-bright Shetly of middle age who spent most of his time gazing over the ship's side, whistling eternally. On this occasion, however, he seemed to be studying the whale with great interest, so, when the flensers had stripped the blubber, I joined him to find the cause of his unusual industry. He asked me if I had ever seen anything like it, and waved a hand at the huge mass of flesh lying before him.

I had seen something very like it. The flesh and blubber and organs and even the bones of the whale were studded every inch or two with cysts about an inch in diameter, filled, as we found when we cut some open, with yellowish, cheesy, amorphous material. I had seen exactly the same thing in autopsies of children who had died of advanced miliary tuberculosis — that form of the disease which gets totally out of hand, breaks down all resistance, and attacks every part of the body, forming small, cheesy cysts in the few days before it kills.

I was extremely interested, so, forgetting my lunch a while, I dashed back to the sick bay, got a couple of microscope slides, and took scrapings from the cysts in the foul and leprous flesh. When I had done so and had deposited the slides in the dispensary, I went off to lunch, without its occurring to me to ask the gangling Shelty what he proposed to do with the whale.

I sat next to Gyle at the table, but I had delicacy enough not to describe my experience until he had finished his lunch. Half an hour later, when I did so, he, too, was very interested, for neither his books nor his experience had taught him anything of tuberculous or similarly diseased whales.

The first question that the inspector part of him wanted answered was what they were doing with the whale. He hurriedly wiped his mouth and left the saloon table, telling a steward to get hold of the chief chemist and the biologist and send them after us.

When we got down on deck, there was not a vestige of whale anywhere, and the decks were clean, well hosed, and free of blood and oil.

'What have you done with that diseased whale?' Gyle demanded of the Shelty.

'What diseased whale?' asked the Shelty in a mystified tone, looking at me as though seeking some clue as to what the inspector was talking about. He then went back to the ship's side and resumed his whistling. But the cookers in the factory below us were churning away.

I took Gyle up to the dispensary to show him the slides of thick pus I had taken from the whale's flesh. He told me on our way there that I should stain and preserve them very carefully, for very little was known of the pathology of whales, and disease of whales seemed to be so rare he was quite sure that his friend MacBlank (he named Britain's greatest cetologist) would be very keen to have them. When we reached the dispensary, the slides had vanished.

It would be absurd to suggest that the coincidence of the failure to report to the inspector a strange disease in a whale being flensed, and the disappearance of the unique slides from my dispensary, constituted a conspiracy on the part of any of the whalemen. For, after all, why should they conspire? The law demands that 'All parts of whales delivered . . . shall be processed by boiling or otherwise, except . . .'; and the exceptions allowed by law do not include diseased whales; so if the whalemen did not put this whale into the cookers, they were probably breaking the law, and the inspector would have been bound to reprove them.

But I have no doubt, had they asked Gyle's permission to put this particularly nauseating carcass over the side before (as I hope!) they did so, I am quite sure the official eye would have been opaque to the technical breach of the law. And if the slides had not disappeared from my dispensary, I would willingly have submitted them as medical evidence to support a change in the law to force it to recognize diseased whales amongst the exceptions which need not be processed.

But the exception is the test; and although reports made by a veterinary surgeon who accompanied a whaling expedition since the war indicate that a cystic disease of whales such as I saw is by no means rare, neither the International Whaling Board nor the Ministry of Agriculture and Fisheries has yet, so far as I know, taken any precautions to prevent diseased whales from being processed and added to the numerous whale products used and eaten by the British public today, and no whaling inspector has yet been instructed to turn the blind eye should a whaling company ignore the law and throw a diseased carcass overboard.

But that is the whaling inspector's job — trying to make

people comply with the law, and lacking all power to enforce the law; and often enough being placed in the position of having to agree with those who break the law that the breach makes much more sense than the compliance.

But, if they are all like Gyle, their main job of protecting the whale species, and also 'the title of the ocean,' is one they do well, despite the strange things that sometimes happen on whale-ships.

X

BLOOD AND ICE

When ye were sleeping on your pillows,
Dreamed ye aught of our poor fellows,
Darkling as they faced the billows,
A' to fill the woven willows?

—Scottish Song

Lest it be thought that I was no more than a passenger on the whaleship, let me tell something of my own job and of the difficulties a doctor encounters when trying to conduct a fairly heavy industrial practice several thousand miles and several months removed from any hospital or specialist assistance. A whaling practice is undoubtedly the most isolated medical job in the modern world. It is also unquestionably the practice where the doctor is likely to be faced with the strangest accidents and medical emergencies, and under the most unusual conditions.

Take a typical case — admittedly the worst and most dramatic I had to handle, but the sort of thing that is commonplace in the whaling industry, and of which we might have had a dozen similar instances, had our expedition not been an exceptionally lucky one.

One afternoon Gyle and I sat gossiping in his cabin. A sudden gale had got up, a fierce sou'westerly wind straight off the ice, with low clouds scudding no higher than the masthead. It had not blown long enough to raise a sea of any consequence as yet, but the elements were beginning to growl and snarl all round us in a way that made obvious even to my un-nautical instincts that we were in for a damned bad night. Gyle, I remember, was telling me that even after thirty-five years at sea he hated high winds without the accompanying high seas, and that the sound of wind in the rigging still gave him the chills and the grues when he heard it.

In came our very correct and proper little cadet whom Gyle had named 'The Admiral.' This laddie spent a good deal of his time searching the ship for the doctor when something had gone wrong, and his smart sailor-like rat-tat on the door usually signified trouble.

'Pardon the interruption, Commander Gyle, sir! May I speak to the doctor? . . . Sorry to trouble you, doctor, but manager's compliments, and would you speak to the gunner of Number Six catcher on the blower? Understand there's been a bad accident, and it's rather urgent.' And, with a click of his heels to Gyle, he withdrew.

'I tell you, winds of gale force getting up when the sea is still always mean disaster for somebody. I probably won't see you for two or three days,' was Gyle's cheerful valediction; and he was right.

The report from Number Six catcher was vividly descriptive but not very illuminating surgically. It was that 'the mate had got tangled up in the whale line, which had a large fin whale on the end of it, and the lower half of him looked as though he'd been through the blubber-chopper.'

The gunner was a chum of mine, and a good fellow, I knew. His ship was racing full-speed for the factory as we spoke, and we were lumbering toward him with all of our twelve knots, but it would take him several hours to get in, and he admitted frankly that neither he nor anybody else on the catcher had any clues about what to do with the smashed-up mate or with all the funny little gadgets in the ship's first-aid chest. In fact, their treatment so far had been to carry the mate below, heave him into his bunk, and place by his side all the rum and other strong drink they could find aboard.

I tried, as best I could, to give over the blower an elementary lecture on first aid, and some detailed instructions on stopping haemorrhage, splinting, giving morphine, and treating shock, but I stressed that the most important thing was to get him to the factory as rapidly as possible. The gunner assured me he would do this, though the weather was worsening rapidly and there would be a sea 'like bloody hell' running when he got in; but he promised — and, as it was Gunner Oen talking, I knew he meant it — that he would come alongside or 'sink his ruddy ship trying to do so.'

It was dark when he got alongside, and one of the worst nights the Southern Ocean had yet treated us to. I was waiting on the harpoon platform, a wooden structure built out over our starboard side, from which the small craft were loaded and unloaded as they came alongside. This platform was the domain of The Admiral, and he had everything organized in the way that only an efficient seventeen-year-old can organize things. He had — with the aid of all the Shelty seamen, who had turned out unasked — rigged a coffin-shaped box, padded all round to break any jolts. This was slung to the derrick that normally hauled the 'basket' up and down, and fixed by an ingenious system of ropes, which would keep it vertical no matter what happened. He proposed to drop this contraption on the deck of the wildly tossing catcher when opportunity presented, to be loaded with the injured man and slung back aboard the factory. An additional derrick had been rigged, carrying the basket, which stood on the platform out of the way. The Admiral explained to me exactly how he proposed to ship the wounded mate, and said that he had talked to Gunner Oen and it was all arranged. But in the middle of his explanation old Davison climbed up onto the platform and took me aside.

'I wouldn't try to bring a stretcher case aboard tonight, doctor, if I were you,' he said in his quiet, hesitant way. 'With the sea that's running now and this gale, we'd most likely kill him before we could heave him clear of the catcher deck.'

'What d'you recommend then, Davy?' I asked, knowing from experience that this old man's advice was the best I could listen to.

'Get the manager to turn the catcher round, and steam down into the ice, both of us. It's only about a hundred miles away, and the sea will be manageable down there. . . . And, if you would want to be going with the catcher yourself, doctor,' he added more hesitantly still, 'it'll only take us two minutes to un-rig the cadet's stretcher sling and put the basket back on the derrick.'

I would most definitely *not* want to be going on the catcher in weather such as would deter any gunner but Thor or Oen from coming alongside, never mind attempting a transhipment, but I saw the sense of the old man's advice, and it was the only thing that could be done. So I told him to go ahead and rig the basket, which he proceeded to do, explaining in his kindly way to the disappointed Admiral that his complicated stretcher sling would be just the very thing needed to bring the injured mate aboard when we got down to the ice. I dashed up to see the manager.

'I was hoping you'd suggest that, doc,' the manager said when I put forward Davison's ideas. And he gave the necessary orders over the phone to bridge and engine room. When I returned to the harpoon platform, the catcher was alongside and had just managed to get a rope aboard. A large, tough sperm whale lay between the two ships, the great and the little, but, even so, they were grinding and smashing at each other like two canoes be-fouled in a mighty rapid. Everything on the platform had been rearranged, and old Davy had persuaded The Admiral that it had been that little cadet's own idea to change the plans, so things were going smoothly — if that term may be used for happenings on an insecure platform, tilting and swaying like a roller coaster, with a tiny ship alongside, sometimes far below the platform, and sometimes rising, on a huge sea, level with or even above it.

Sigrid was there with my gear. He had packed the basket with everything that could possibly be needed — the emergency sur-gical box, additional morphine, splints, my catcher clothing, enough cigarettes for a month, and even the book that he knew I was reading at the time. I got into the basket on top of all this gear, more scared than I had been since the Salerno landing, and commended myself to whatever gods may be. But by now Mark had come down from the bridge to supervise things himself. The Admiral handed over his command, and, with Mark choosing the moment and old Davy himself taking the winch, I was swung out on the derrick and somehow deposited on the deck of the crazily pitching little catcher with a bump no greater than a well-oiled elevator would have made. A pair of heavy, expensive fur gloves landed beside me as I crawled out of the basket. The little Admiral had noticed at the last moment that Sigrid had forgotten to equip me with gloves, and had pulled off and heaved down his own.

Although it was freezing hard and the gale tearing off the ice was bitterly cold, Gunner Oen was pouring sweat down his bearded face when I climbed up onto his little bridge beside him. His seamen were already letting go the two wire ropes that held us straining to the factory, and his intention was to sheer off as quickly as possible while the miracle of preserving his tiny ship as it banged against the plates of the factory continued.

But the manager's voice, bellowing above the gale through the loud-hailer on the bridge far overhead, ordered: 'Don't cast off yet, Oen! Basket's coming down again.'

Oen howled with fury, telling the manager he was a crazy bastard and would kill us all with the delay; but a moment later he was grinning. The basket swung out from the factory again and, under the co-operative control of the two finest seamen on the expedition, landed gently, though God knows how, on the gyrating deck of the catcher. A seaman dashed through the heavy seas that were breaking over the deck of the little ship and grabbed the contents out of the basket. It was two large flagons of Navy rum. Even the Intolerable Ho, our unpopular chief steward, had come out trumps in this emergency, and this unprecedented showing of humanity on his part made Oen grin and admit the dangerous minute's delay had been worth while.

Immediately the two straining ropes were slackened and cast off; the telegraphs of both ships clanged; propellers thrashed; and the little ship sheered away from the greater like a mouse scuttering from under the feet of an enraged elephant. As soon as we were clear, and headed southward at full speed and to hell with the weather, Oen took me below to the unfortunate mate. As we went below, I saw how crazy it would have been to attempt to tranship the injured man that night. He had been placed in his own cabin, a tiny cubby-hole tucked away below the water-line at the after end of the ship, at the foot of two vertical ladders. It was quite an adventure for us two fit, active men to cross the coping of the engine room, hanging onto the wire lifelines, for the seas were breaking even over there, the highest part of the little ship, and everything below that was most of the time submerged completely; then to swing down one ladder, which twisted and jerked in every direction, threatening to throw us off into the racing engines adjacent to the ladder; then round two sharp corners, stooping as we did so to pass through a breast-high doorway; down another vertical ladder and round another bend into the mate's cubby-hole. I saw that it was going to be an extraordinarily tricky job to extricate a badly hurt man from that iron rabbit-trap even in a flat calm, and, as Davy had warned, to start moving him that night would have been to sign his death warrant.

I did not know Helgen, the hurt mate, but Oen had told me as we struggled down the ladders that he was a tough egg and would take a lot of killing. And he was! He lay on the settee of his tiny cabin, roughly bandaged from the thighs downward, his badly splinted lower legs flopping about with every motion of the wildly pitching ship. An empty rum bottle and a tin of cigarettes — all his kindly but unimaginative shipmates could think of in the way of medical comforts — were in the rack beside him, and he gave me a cheerful, half-drunk greeting as I went in.

My civilized colleagues in orthodox surgical practice would have been horrified at the rum being allowed in a case of severe trauma with shock and haemorrhage, but I had no qualms about it; for I believe that the denial of alcohol to the grossly wounded is one of those medical rules of thumb based on slender theory and a modicum of prejudice without any scientific investigation to back it, and I believe that the relaxation of anxiety a few hearty slugs can give a gravely injured man far from hospital more than counterbalances any slight physiological ill-effect. Anyway, I always gave plenty of alcohol to the wounded in war before I started hauling them about, and I believe they were the better for it. So, acting on my own experience rather than the rule of thumb, when Helgen asked for another shot, I gave it to him. But this time it was mixed in a pint of hot tea which the catcher steward miraculously brought across the deck and down the two ladders, and it was accompanied by a double dose of morphine.

As we were waiting for this to take effect, Oen told me the story of the accident. The weather had still been fair when they shot the large fin whale. When the harpoon struck, the whale neither dived nor ran, as ten thousand whales would do, but did the ten-thousand-and-first thing. It took out a short line — about fifty feet of the unbelievably strong and elastic nylon fore-runner — then swam below the ship and came up immediately astern. Seeing what was happening, Oen rang for full astern, and the ship moved quickly backward to clear the whale. But it was too late. The rapidly turning screw fouled the nylon rope, and in a moment everything was a tangle beneath the counter of the ship, with the whale still tugging and straining with the force of a railway engine at the end of the bar-tight rope.

Immediately Oen saw the situation, he ordered the line cut. This is a dangerous job at any time with elastic nylon rope, which lashes back at the man cutting it with the force of a thousand stock-whips, so Helgen, the mate, went aft to do it himself. But just as he was about to cut in a safe place, the propeller of the ship cut the rope for him. In a second there was a chaos of twisted iron, wood, and blood, and the moaning Helgen lay on the deck with the remnant of a now harmless-looking silky rope wrapped like a python round his smashed legs.

By the time Oen had told me what had happened, the rum and morphine were taking effect on Helgen, and he was lying back on the settee telling us over and over again that he had promised to take his wife some nylon stockings from Aruba on the way home, but he wasn't 'goin' to support that —— —— industry any more!' I gave him another shot of morphine and some scopolamine, and in a minute or so he was pretty well stunned, so the gunner and I started hauling him about. We had to unscrew the cabin table and jam it against the other wall of the tiny cabin to brace ourselves against it and maintain some balance in the heaving little box. Then we cut away the crude bandages and what was left of the mate's trousers.

The mess of torn flesh and splintered bone underneath was such as I had not seen since the war. But now I had no well-organized line of evacuation and expert surgical aid awaiting my patient as I had then. Only a kindly but ham-handed Norwegian gunner in an ill-lighted gyrating closet racing through a gale down to the Antarctic ice.

However, Oen soon got the hang of the job. Once he understood that he could do no damage and cause no pain by pulling hard on the legs as I wanted him to do, but only by bending them, he applied and sustained with his tough Norski muscles a traction on both legs such as normally takes two nurses on each leg to produce in the operating-theatre. As he did this, he shot out a foot now and again to save me from crashing against the opposite wall as the catcher nearly turned upside down, and he also kept track of scissors, forceps, sulphonamide powder, and all the rest of my tools and equipment, which were sliding from end to end of the cabin floor and sometimes leaping a foot or two into the air when the ship lurched. At times, with an extra sudden and heavy roll, I would go over backward, despite Oen's steadying foot, and our patient would start sliding off the settee, which had tilted to sixty degrees. But when I picked myself up and came back, Oen, both the mate's ankles now grasped in one huge viking hand, would still be maintaining the traction on the legs and, with his other hand, had caught the patient by his belt in mid-air and thrust him back onto the settee. Other assistance we could not use, because there was no room for a third to work in the tiny room, but at one point we called in one of the several men outside the door and got him to edge in between us and lash Helgen down to the bunk. This made our operation easier thereafter, but even then, under these appalling conditions, it took us about three hours to clamp a few spouting arteries, roughly cleanse and bandage the wounds, and splint the legs — an operation that would have taken perhaps twenty minutes under normal conditions. And it is, I think, a tribute to our crude, extemporized surgery, as well as to the anaesthetic properties of a mixture of morphine and ship's rum, that Helgen was fast asleep when we finished and remembers nothing about the bloody horror of being fixed up in that little box-sized cabin behaving like a barrel going over Niagara Falls — as it had every right to do, for it was ten feet below the surface of the Southern Ocean in one of its foulest and craziest moods.

Well, the end of this apparently melodramatic story is that Helgen survived. He survived not only the rough surgery to which we subjected him but a post-operative day, when he should have been lying on a hospital bed in dead silence with continuous blood transfusions but instead lay on that same settee with another bottle of rum while the catcher crashed about in the continuing gale, searching for a bay in the ice where he could be transferred to the factory. He survived his journey up the ladders to the deck of the catcher in the special type of stretcher designed during the war for extricating badly wounded men from tanks. He had a comfortable transhipment to the factory, thanks to The Admiral's ingenious sling, when the two ships were at last well inside the pack ice, where the force of the gale could not greatly affect the sea, and where we saw old Davison's advice to be so consistently right. ('Aye!' said Davy when I later thanked him. 'It's a good whaleman's rule, which you can apply to life as well as whaling: If things gang agley, don't hurry north to the crowded places seeking help; get down into the ice, where at least it's peaceful!')

Helgen's troubles were by no means over when we got him aboard the factory. He still had to survive a more complicated operation — this time with proper anaesthesia, however — and then he lay in plaster in my sick bay for some weeks until we could send him to South Georgia after another mid-ocean transhipment. On South Georgia he lay rotting in his original plasters while company officials in the far north found excuses to avoid taking him through an open sea to Montevideo and flying him home to a hospital in the U.K. or Norway, as I advised by radio. They eventually hit upon the incredibly absurd excuse that they could not detach a small ship from the lucrative whaling for a few days to take the man smashed up in their service home as I suggested, 'because the difficulties of transhipment at Montevideo would be too great.'

When I read their radiogram, I thought of the little Admiral and his Shelty seamen on that harpoon platform; of Davison and Mark performing a transhipment such as no one from Montevideo has ever seen; of kindly ham-handed Oen doing the job of surgeon's assistant in that wildly lurching little box below the Antarctic more gently than an operating-nurse ever did it. And I damned the comfortable men in the north, who know so little of the 'tough eggs — hard to kill' in the south.

I do not want to give the impression that medical practice in the Southern Ocean consisted entirely, or even largely, of such dramatic incidents. The bulk of it was no more interesting or exciting than that of an isolated country doctor, who has to do his own surgery, treat accidents, and make all his own diagnoses and trust his own judgment with only an archaic selection of apparatus and an X-ray machine fit to be a museum piece to help him; and no consultants. The country doctor must be able to pull teeth, cook and prepare special diets, go to the blacksmith's shop and supervise the hammering out of any special splints he needs, and do a thousand other things for which no medical school or university ever prepared him. So, also, the whaling doctor must know, or quickly learn, to deal with any peculiar thing connected or unconnected with medicine which comes along, and deal with it alone, except for a devoted but not properly qualified Norwegian assistant.

The 'sick' of the factory ship assembled twice a day, at 8 A.M. and 6 P.M., in the sick bay away down at the after end of the ship. Sigrid would marshal the twenty-odd men who would appear; sort them out; sew up the minor wounds; take the bits of grit out of the eyes, unless they were metallic splinters or embedded in the cornea; hand out aspirin and Epsom salts to those whose heads or bowels demanded them; throw an obvious malingerer or two down the alleyway; then come into my adjacent cabin and ask me to see the hard core, usually about half a dozen, with whom he thought I should deal.

The half-dozen might be a group like this: a Whaler Group VIII with syphilis, which he had been concealing and trying to treat himself since he left the arms of his last dusky woman in Aruba; a flenser who had scratched his hand on a wire rope and neglected to have it dressed straight away, with the inevitable result that the wound, contaminated by bits of long-dead whale sticking to the wire, was soon a burning sepsis; the liver-chopper, asking for a recommendation to the mate to have his job changed, on the grounds that he had done nothing but chop liver for twelve hours a day for four months and was going nuts; a Norwegian laddie with a cough from smoking too much, but terrified, like all his countrymen, that he was dying of tuberculosis; and — inevitably — a surly and insular Glasgow engineer who wasn't going to tell any bloody Norwegian such as Sigrid what was wrong with him, but insisted on seeing me, and was going to write to his union about it if denied the privilege.

The 'sick parade' attended to, I would go into the tiny 'hospital' — a room the size of an average hospital bedroom, with six built-in cots around the walls and fittings for two more in the centre of the room for emergencies. Here the more seriously ill or injured were stowed, and, on an average, we would have four occupants. Three of these would be quite serious cases, but the fourth was a perfectly healthy little mess-boy who appeared daily on the ship's medical return as suffering from some new and terrifying Latin disease that required a further week or two under treatment in hospital. The point of this, of course, was that the company made no allowance in the ship's complement for anybody as unproductive of whale oil as a hospital steward, and the Intolerable Ho would never lend us steward assistance when we wanted it. So — as inevitably happens to those who are foolish enough to cross a doctor — he lost his best and brightest mess-boy for the duration of the voyage as soon as that co-operative little character crossed the door of the hospital and agreed, in return for an easy job and hospital food, to suffer from 'Balaenoptera Musculus' or some such hideous disease for the next few months.

So far I have accounted for only about two hours of my working day, and often enough this would be the sum total of my labours; but it was not always so. Accidents happened — much more rarely than I had expected when I first saw the type of work the men were doing and the apparently total disregard of all Board of Trade and Factory Act safety regulations as soon as a visit from an inspector became impossible for six months or so. But happen they did, at all hours of day or night, and frequently in the most bizarre ways. A young Norwegian lad, who converted me to the modern hypotheses of accident-proneness more firmly than all my reading had done, fell into a cooker, with tons of blubber on top of him, four times. The first three times he was hauled out by his mates unscathed, but the fourth time he was scathed badly enough to become a permanent resident of the ship's hospital, and remain there, wrapped up in plaster, until we were able to put him in hospital in Norway several months later.

Another young Scots boy, a Whaler Group VIII who worked in the factory, saw no reason why he should walk the length of the factory deck on the firm's business when he could ride on the travelling belt that conveyed the bags of meat-meal from one end of the ship to the other. He successfully made the journey about twenty times a day for many months, but one day he pushed his foot between the belt and the rollers. Of course, in typical whalemen's way, nobody knew how to stop the belt, and MacDonald, who had started it and presumably knew how to stop it, might be anywhere on the huge ship. So they stood around for a few minutes, discussing this predicament while the belt sawed remorselessly through the lad's ankle, and then decided to send for the doctor and, of course, for old Davison, who was sent for whenever any predicament arose anywhere on the ship.

The boy became another permanent resident in the sick bay, not so much because of the semi-severance of his foot, but because the putrid remains of many a long-dead whale, teeming with bugs that laugh at penicillin and all the -mycins, were deeply embedded in his ankle joint. I hope his wound is healed up now. It was not when I bade him farewell months later and sent him away from the unbelievable sepsis of the whaleship at last.

And then, of course, Helgen, the mate of the catcher, became our third seriously injured permanent boarder in the sick bay.

They were a cheerful threesome for the first few weeks, but gradually the boredom and strain of lying painfully and uncomfortably around that viewless and cheerless little room, with no prospect of release from it for months to come, began to tell on them, and we had three very surly and crotchety patients to deal with. Their shipmates did their best for them. Every book or magazine on the ship eventually found its way into the sick bay, and I became quite accustomed to highly embarrassed old salts coming up to me on the deck, twisting their caps and thrusting an old pack of cards or a grubby year-old copy of the *Reader's Digest* upon me with the comment that 'maybe the sick lads could find some use for this.' We had on board a cinema apparatus and five films, which were shown over and over again to the crew in their mess-rooms and to the officers in the saloon; but for every show given to the general public there would be two shows given to my 'incurables' in the hospital. Nearly every night when I went in, I would find a Norwegian lad (named Yogi because he had let his hair and beard grow untouched for eighteen months) setting up the complicated apparatus and screen and preparing to give a two-hour performance to my patients — all this immediately after he had come off a back-breaking twelve-hour shift on the flensing-deck. In a similar rough, comradely spirit, any man who had managed to scrounge more than his entitled whack of rum out of the Intolerable Ho, or who had succeeded in manufacturing a specially good bottle of plonk, would smuggle half of it — unknown to Sigrid and myself, he thought

— into the sick bay, and my three patients would have a royal and usually extremely beneficial party.

Before I went a-whaling I had met and talked to but one former whaling doctor, a rather stuffy and humourless character who (heaven help his unimaginative self!) had been utterly bored when he was down south and thought modern whaling and whalemen a most unromantic and uninteresting proposition. This fellow gave me lots of advice, some of it good, but when I find myself in the same position, giving advice to any doctor who is joining the whalers, the advice I shall give will be very different.

I shall advise the 'experienced physician, over the age of thirty,' whom the whaling companies require, to learn to pull teeth and acquire a fair knowledge of dentistry before he sails. He need not learn to do fillings or any complicated conservation work, but he should take the electric drill and all the complicated dental apparatus with which the company will clutter up the sick bay. He will find it useful if he adopts the whaleman's hobby of carving sperm-whale teeth, and it will be in great demand by all hands for their scrimshaw work. He will have to learn to take and develop his own X-ray pictures. He would be wise to learn enough Norwegian and enough Lowland Scots to discourage the whalemen from blatantly discussing in his presence the best and easiest ways of taking him in. He should learn a little plumbing, a good deal of carpentry, and some metal work. He should — absurd though it seems, as he is going to the South Polar regions — brush up his tropical medicine, especially on malaria and the tropical forms of venereal and skin diseases, for, after the ship visits the oiling ports on the way south, these will form a large part of his non-surgical practice. Likewise, he should read up on heat-stroke as well as frostbite, for his ship, built for the ice, must pass twice through the tropics, and many of his patients will work for weeks in temperatures such as the sun never made.

His friends on board should be the bosun, the junior assistant secretary, the second electrician, and the deck storeman. To make friends with the heads of those departments will be impossible, as it will be with the chief engineer and the chief steward, yet there are many things he will need to make his life and work comfortable, and there are no department stores in the Southern Ocean.

I would advise him to take his own library. He will find many books worth reading in the ship's small library at his first visit, but he will never see them again, except in quaint and unexpected places, for he must realize that there are many intelligent and educated men even among the Whaler Group VIII's. (I have seen, for example, the ship's only copy of Ibsen's plays lying for weeks, and well read, beside the bed of a fireman/greaser when I visited him to treat his burns.)

Coming back to his work, he should not be impressed by the vast quantity of medical equipment and stores the company will put aboard before he sails, but should insist on having more of every commodity — in some cases twice as much, and in some cases ten times. He will need it all and more before he returns to medical civilization in eight months, and, anyway, it only costs the company a penny per man per day to equip its ship's hospital, and all drugs, dressings, and medical attention given to any Norwegian whaleman are paid for by the Norwegian government, while any medical expenditure on British seamen is subject to rebate on the Income Tax. So our new whaling doctor should not be hoodwinked by the company's apparent generosity in the matter of equipment. He will find it is the bare minimum — and not even that, unless he belly-aches a good deal before he sails.

The last and perhaps most important advice I should give the 'new boy' is that, unless, like all the other professional men and craftsmen who accompany a large modern whaling expedition, he is prepared to subordinate his professional instincts and prejudices and be a whaleman first and a doctor a long way afterward, he should not go a-whaling.

Whatever his professional leaning or specialty, there is much to interest and often fascinate the whaling doctor. If he inclines to

183

surgery, he will see accidents and injuries such as no other surgeon has ever seen. If he be a bacteriologist, he will encounter germs and pathogenic agents — brought aboard by, and breeding in, the dead whales — which have never been investigated or cultured in any laboratory. If he is an allergist, he will see allergic reactions to whales and whale products which surely no man has yet studied, and he will find old Moby Dick, the ancient sperm whale of the Antarctic, responsible for most of them — which will give him to think, if he is a doctor who can still think. If physical medicine is his bent, he can absorb himself in a study of man against a hostile environment such as he will find nowhere in the orthodox professional world. And if, as in my own case, mental medicine is his main interest, he will find himself incarcerated with several hundred psychopaths for months on end, and with an opportunity of studying the most bizarre and unassimilable human types in an environment and on a job where they are of incalculable value to John Citizen, and where John Citizen, his average predictable respectable self, could not last a month.

My psychiatric sessions on the whaleship occurred seldom, and my official psychiatric cases were few (many fewer than they would be in a similar group of six hundred and fifty in a shoreside industrial practice). But some of the lads did come along with complaints and disabilities that were obviously psychological, and occasionally I would pick from among my patients one who seemed even more ill-reconciled to the modern world than his unusual shipmates, and would put him on my equivalent of 'the couch.'

There was, for instance, a young Norwegian mess-boy who was incurably and miserably seasick in fair weather as well as foul from the day we left Tönsberg until we were well out in the Southern Ocean two months later. I knew of no physical remedy for seasickness (and, as none of the old whalemen knew one either, I will stake my life none has yet been discovered!), but this lad was becoming seriously ill as a result of his constant vomiting, so something had to be done. Some simple psychotherapy was tried. His trouble was easily elicited, even through an interpreter. Incredible though it seems in a Norwegian, a large part of that trouble was that he had never seen the sea until he stepped aboard our whaleship for an eight-month voyage. He had been born, and had lived all his fifteen years, on a farm near the Swedish frontier, as far from the sea as it is possible to get in Norway. Now he found himself in a very inferior position among the dozen or two hardened mariners in the mess-boys' dormitory — lads who had spent their lives beside the sea, and who had been brought up among ships and small boats. As soon as I suggested to him several lines of conversation, and got him to inquire of his little shipmates how many of them could ride a horse or drive a car or ski down a real mountain or do any of the things that had made up his life until he was introduced into this strange element, the sea, his seasickness cleared up. He became one of the best and spunkiest lads we had aboard, the hero of the kids' mess-room, and, before the end of the trip, he was pleading to go on the catchers because life aboard the factory was too steady and dull.

Then there was the stoker who had worried himself into a jittery state of illness. He and several others were working several weeks on a complicated job on the evaporators above the main boilers, in a belated attempt to produce some decent water on the ship, and he thought his mates were beginning to look at him and say that he 'couldn't take it.' I went below to the stokehold to find out exactly what it was he and his jeering mates had to 'take.' Had I not taken my own thermometer and found to my medical amazement that they were on that job working twelve hours a day and continuing to survive in a temperature of 140 degrees Fahrenheit, I would not have believed it physiologically or psychologically possible. An interview with the manager, and a direct order to the Intolerable Ho to give the stokers almost unlimited rum to mix with their regulation lime juice while the job lasted, cured my patient straight away. And, if I understand properly the vascular action of alcohol and its psychological effect on stokers, it prevented further breakdowns among the men working in that tiny inferno.

One of my favourite patients was the man who boasted (perhaps rightly, though old Julius, the catcher engineer, disputes this) that he was the oldest man in the Southern Ocean whale fisheries. This was old Alec MacDougall, the boilermaker. Gyle once asked Alec, a quiet, courteous old Scots Highlander, if he had ever made a boiler, and Alec admitted that he never had and wouldn't know how to start. But all large ships carry such a tradesman, and his principal job seems to consist in grinding hot metals in various parts of the ship. Alec came along to me every day or two with a metallic splinter — invariably of brass or some metal that the magnet would not extract — deeply implanted in his left eye.

'Alec,' I told him one day, 'if you come along with another splinter in your eye through not wearing your goggles, I'm not going to put you on the table and take it out; I'm going to put you on the couch with half a gram of pentothal inside you and talk it out — and find out why you keep trying to destroy your sight.'

Alec grinned and agreed, and, sure enough, back he came in about a week with another splinter in his much-scarred eye. I did not put him on the couch, except figuratively, nor did I give him pentothal; but I did learn much of Alec MacDougall and why he seemed insistent on blinding himself.

Then there was Dornoch. I knew him well by the time he came to consult me, and we had spent many hours discussing photography and birds and, occasionally, abstract subjects. I liked him, and I think he liked me, but, when he came along late one night, long after the routine sick had departed, to complain vaguely about his ear — which was not paining him, nor deaf, nor giving any trouble that he could adequately describe or I by examination could detect — I got slightly exasperated with him and packed him off to come back next morning. But next morning — to the disgrace of one who should have had the psychiatric insight to know that with a quiet, shy character like Dornoch there was something much deeper he wanted to talk about than the triviality of his ear when, all out of character, he troubled a doctor late at night — Dornoch was not there. He had taken himself and whatever overwhelming problem he had wanted to discuss overboard and into the ice for ever.

Why he did so I shall never know. It had been a sad but not a gloomy night, and we went to bed in peace and in security as sound as the Southern Ocean can ever offer. Five hundred tired and healthy whalemen slept solidly, and I, their doctor, had no worries to break my sleep.

At 4 A.M. we were awakened. The brassy, peremptory shout of the ship's siren sounded even more than usually urgent and frightening, in contrast to the quiet dawn ending the uneventful night. Eight short blasts — pause — eight more short blasts!

I was awake and beginning to realize that eight blasts meant 'boat stations' — a piece of nonsense which we practised on Monday afternoons at three o'clock when there was nothing really important to do, but quite out of place at eight bells in the middle watch, when all but those essential to the running of the ship were sleeping.

Eight blasts again! And this time the metallic stutter of the engine-room telegraph breaking in between the blasts! Something strange was going on up on deck, and I, in my bunk below, began to be a bit frightened. I fortified myself by the thought that some five hundred other men would be lying in their bunks awake and as frightened as I was, but still not frightened enough to overcome the fear of appearing foolish if we should leap for our life-jackets and dash to our boat stations, as Board of Trade regulations demanded we should do. After all, I thought — as no doubt did my shipmates — this was a whaling ship, and nobody on whaling ships pays any attention to the Board of Trade, so we lay a while in our bunks and considered what might be happening.

My first hypothesis was that one of the mates was drunk again and had got near the siren cord when nobody was looking. This was not impossible, as he had once summoned us to boat stations when the ship was securely tied up in Leith Harbour and the whole crew was ashore hunting for penguins' eggs. . . . But the ship was heeling over and changing course to starboard at top speed — a highly dangerous procedure in an overladen factory ship. No bridge officer would risk it except in case of grave emergency. So that hypothesis was abandoned, and the second more frightening one took its place: the radar had let us down, the look-out had fallen asleep, and a huge iceberg had appeared out of the dawn ahead, too close to avoid, and the watch-keeper on the bridge was rousing us up before the crash.

I reached for my cigarettes — my usual escape mechanism in emergencies — though I badly wanted to reach for my life-jacket. Five hundred other men like myself, awake in their bunks, waited. The crash didn't come. But now the ship, as I saw by the wash through my porthole, was turned right around, steaming full-speed back along the course she had been on a minute before; and something stranger happened — eight short blasts on the siren *again*! Obviously the bridge was badly alarmed about something! Then the telephone beside my bunk buzzed urgently.

It was Gyle, the whaling inspector, who wanted to know what the hell was going on — though how he expected me to know in my cabin right down aft when he slept under the chartroom about ten feet from the bridge was somewhat mystifying. But I was relieved to find that he, the most experienced sailor on the ship, was as scared as I was. We were discussing various possibilities, and had just agreed that undoubtedly somebody was drunk somewhere, when the bridge cut in on the phone. It was Mark's voice, and that meant it was something serious, and no drunken prank: 'Doctor and Commander Gyle — will you both come up to the bridge, please, straight away? Better bring some warm clothes.'

Gyle got there in about ten seconds. It took me nearly two minutes to make my way the whole length of the ship, and, as I ran forrard, an occasional tousled and half-ashamed head stuck out of a cabin door to ask: 'Is there anything wrong, doctor?'

Mark, with the Norwegian manager and the whaling inspector beside him, was searching the sea through binoculars when I

188

reached the bridge. He spoke to me without taking his eyes from the glasses.

'Man overboard,' he explained briefly. 'Silly bastard jumped for it just after I came on watch. Saw him go. Wanted a boat's crew in a hurry, so I called all hands to boat stations. Water temperature's only a degree above freezing, so he doesn't stand a chance — but we've got to go through all the drill. . . . Should be just about here he went in.' He banged the telegraph to full astern, then stop, and the massive ship came to. 'Would like you to go away with the commander's boat, doctor, if we see anything.' 'Who was it?' was my only question. Mark grunted the man's name, and I felt slightly sick when I heard it. The man whose heart was making its last few feeble pulsations somewhere in that icy water while the tense group on the bridge of the whaleship did all that was possible to find and save him was a friend — a whaleman whom I had thought I knew and understood. He had been my patient, and had in fact consulted me the night before; perhaps he had tried to tell me of his trouble, which — though doubtless in greater degree — was that trouble which affects all whalemen who choose the world's most desolate sea as their retreat. And now, having failed to tell me or failed to make me understand, rather than try again to rehabilitate himself within the human race, he had chosen to remain in the sterile Antarctic silence for ever.

Long after hope was gone Mark lowered his glasses. 'Not a ruddy chance! He's a gone gosling!' He turned to the second officer, who had joined us. 'Take over, Mr. Jensen. Turn to starboard. Ring for full ahead and resume your course. You can dismiss your boat's crew, commander. Sorry I had to trouble you, doctor. Come an' give me an entry in the log in the morning. Good night!'

XI

WHALE IN A TEST TUBE

Science carries us into zones of speculation where there is no habitable city for the mind of man.

—Robert Louis Stevenson

'THE trouble with the whaling industry today,' grumbled Old Burnett, 'is that there are too many damned intellectuals mixed up in it!'

His definition of the term *intellectual* was wide. It included the scientists aboard — two chemists and a biologist; it included Mansell, in his capacity as statistician: all whaling inspectors, and anyone whom Burnett ever saw 'fiddling with damn silly toys and gadgets' not directly concerned with the production of whale oil. It included the radar expert and another young university man who sailed with us to try out a new type of gyrocompass on the catchers and fit them at sea. In fact, it included every man with the expedition who was not directly engaged in killing or cutting up whales, or cooking them into oil to increase Old Burnett's bonus.

I was considered to be on the fringe of the despised intelligentsia, but I never qualified as a full intellectual — principally, I think, because, when I treated the old man for his various aches and coughs, I gave him all the mustard plasters and black draughts and rubbing-lotions and other museum pieces I could find in the ship's medical stores, and was never tactless enough to prescribe any treatment less than a hundred years old. If I had, he would most certainly not have taken it, but would just have damned me as 'another of those modern intellectual doctors who don't know any real physick!'

The battle between conservative or traditional whaling, with Old Burnett in the van of those forces, and modern scientific whaling, with the chief chemist leading the intellectuals, went on throughout the voyage. The chief chemist was a worthy opponent to the old man and his followers — the 'entrenched forces of reaction,' as the politicians would call them. He never got angry, as the entrenched forces often did, but — sitting in argument at the saloon table, with Mansell, the senior but most progressive whaleman of the lot, at one elbow to help with statistical and historical information, and with young Evans, the youngest but scientifically best educated whaleman, at the other — the chief chemist would quietly tie Old Burnett and Andra, the mate, and anyone else who backed tradition against research, into a tangle of unanswerable logic from which their only method of escape was an angry outburst and a damning of all intellectuals.

The chief chemist often, in his remorseless way, succeeded in infuriating even his fellow intellectuals and those who would in general back him against the reactionaries. 'God spare me from a man who's *always* right!' was Gyle's outburst one day when the whole saloon, even Mansell and Evans, had called the chemist to question over some point not even remotely connected with chemistry and the chemist had shown that he knew more about it than any of the rest of us. Similarly, he would challenge me on some medical matter, and quickly I learned to go and consult my books before giving him a reply. Invariably, to my chagrin, I found that the book showed him to be correct. He was like that horrid little boy who sits in the front row of every class and corrects the schoolmaster — to the delight of the class, but to the fury and despair of the master. Gyle applied to him Plutarch's description of Caesar's barber: 'A busy listening fellow!' and this perhaps described him best. He looked like a barber, too.

But, though he knew the jobs of all of us better than we knew them ourselves, we had to admit that he knew his own and knew it better, possibly, than any scientist afloat. So we were all secretly rather proud of him — even, I suspect, Old Burnett. It was only necessary to visit him in his laboratory high up on the poop of the ship to see his worth. There he dwelt in a new world of progress and ideas and speculations connected with the whale and whaling products — the obvious master of a new science.

'What are you doing, chemist?' I inquired one day when I went up to the laboratory to pass an idle half-hour and found him and the Norwegian biologist in the middle of a forest of flasks and test tubes.

'I've just asked this dumb Scowegian a simple question which he can't answer,' he replied, nodding towards the grinning Oslo University man. 'I asked him what whales drink, and how, and he says the question never occurred to him before. So I'm trying to find out for myself.'

All the body fluids of the whale — blood, lymph, oil, milk, and the rest — are no more saline than the same fluids of a mammal living on land, he explained. They have a salinity much lower than sea water, and much lower than the semi-permeable membrane of his intestinal wall between sea and body fluids would warrant.

'Now, a large blue whale,' he continued, 'doesn't sweat out salt the way every land mammal does, and his urine's no more saline than yours is; and, unless he licks the ruddy icebergs, he's got no supply of fresh water to keep down his salinity. So somewhere in his body he must have an evaporator as big and efficient as the evaporators that produce fresh water on the catchers. But where it is, and how it works, this pseudo-scientist over here and his colleagues never seem to have inquired. Same with the seals and the penguins and all the other warm-blooded animals that live in the sea. How and when do they drink, or how otherwise do they keep a negative salt balance in their body fluids compared with the environment in which they live? Maybe I'll tell you in a month or two.'

He did not tell me, and I am not well enough up in the biology of the cetaceans to know whether anyone can answer the question, but I could see that it was a fascinating academic problem.

At other times when I visited the laboratory the problems of the day would be different:

Why has no female sperm whale ever been sighted or killed in the Southern Ocean, though many thousands of old males are killed there every year? Is it blighted romance or plain greed that divides the sperm-whale sexes? Perhaps, our chemist thought, a hormonal assessment of the old Antarctic bulls' testes would give the answer. It did not — and nobody knows the answer today.

At what rate would whale tendon from the flukes be absorbed by the human body if it were put on the market in huge quantities of twenty-foot strands to replace the rare and expensive kangaroo tendon presently used as surgical sutures to repair hernias? Our chemist wanted to try it out on my patients, but I dissuaded him.

What is the nutritive value of a properly cooked fin-whale steak compared with the best cut from the ox? Much higher, the chemist reported after a few days' work.

How could one make the whale — as it should be — the world's main supply of the immensely valuable new pituitary and adrenal hormones? I believe our chemist contributed work to this end which may soon have big results and may make the whaling industry even more valuable to the modern world.

All these and a hundred other queries occupied our chief scientist and leading intellectual when he abandoned his routine oil-grading and vitamin-assessments and plankton- and krill-examinations and began 'wasting the firm's time,' as Old Burnett put it.

But one special and particular academic problem occupied him throughout the voyage. It was Gyle who posed it.

'Chemist,' he said in exasperation one day when the busy fellow had been more than usually right, 'tell me why Moby's blow-hole is invariably on the port side, and I'll accept all your peculiar scientific hypotheses on any subject hereafter!'

By 'Moby's blow-hole on the port side' Gyle meant, of course, that, while the nostril or blow-hole of every other type of whale is plumb in the middle of the 'forehead,' that of the sperm whale is invariably off-centre and invariably to the left. Other asymmetries occur in the whale family. The finback whale has baleen pure white on one side of its mouth, midnight black on the other, which nobody has yet explained; and even less have they explained why on the inside of its immense mouth the colours are reversed, or why, to reach the verge of crazy incomprehensibility, the fin's smaller cousin, the sei whale, prefers to be black only a quarter of the way down one of his gums before it changes to vivid white.

Gyle and I had discussed this phenomenon of the asymmetry of the species of whale at great length. I was no zoologist and he described himself as, at best, a 'practical' cetologist, but the two of us had searched our scientific knowledge for months, seeking some other example of a regularly asymmetrical animal. Other than left- and right-handed man, we decided, after searching all the books available, that there is no mammal except the whale and a one-horned type of reindeer now extinct — and there are very few animals of non-mammalian orders — which is not exactly the same on the left side as on the right. (I had to wait until I came to America and met a more acute observer than myself to be reminded that, when the tailor measures a customer for trousers, he asks: 'Which side do you dress, sir?') And there was no explanation we could find in the books of the asymmetry of the three species of whale. So, epitomizing the greatest mystery of the whaling world since the species decided to leave the land and return to the sea, Gyle challenged the all-knowing scientist with his question: 'Why is Moby's blow-hole invariably on the port side?'

'Is it?' was the first reaction of the scientific mind. 'Can you show me evidence that no sperm with a blow-hole to starboard has ever been taken?'

'Yes!' interjected Mansell, who was also, after several months, a bit fed up with our saloon-table know-all. He promised to answer the inspector's question himself if the scientist found no explanation within a week.

As is usual whenever an argument or a challenge arises on a whaleship, bets were passed, Science standing to gain a bottle of Scotch if he produced the answer in a week, and Production and the Inspectorate a bottle of best Laboratory-Made Plonk apiece in case of failure, provided they themselves could put forward an acceptable hypothesis.

For the next few days the chief chemist was seen sneaking into the little ship's library to withdraw nearly every whaling book it contained and pore over them with young Evans to help him. He was also seen in long conversations with Davison and some of the other old whalemen whenever there was a sperm whale on the deck, and strange anatomical diagrams were found lying about after such conversations. But at the end of the week, when zero hour for the settlement of the bet came round, he had for once to confess that he was beaten and could not explain the asymmetry of the whale — 'nor can anyone else,' he added to justify his unwonted ignorance.

Mansell, however, rose to the occasion and gave an ingenious if probably quite unscientific explanation, which I shall not attempt to reproduce in his characteristic speech. 'The Antarctic Current flows from west to east, doesn't it?' he shouted, waving his arm counter-clockwise round the water jug to emphasize his point, and the chemist assented. 'And there are more large bull sperm found at the edge of the Antarctic ice than anywhere in the world, yes? And every one of them has a white, phosphorescent jowl of a very peculiar shape, with teeth only on the lower jaw. Just about as ill-adapted for underwater feeding as it could be, is it not, although all the authorities say the sperm dives deeply and feeds on the sea bottom — this on the evidence of one which was once brought up from five hundred fathoms under the Atlantic, tangled in a cable. And the sperm whale has a large blunt head filled with spermaceti; and that spermaceti floats in oil taken from down aft of the beast — try that in your laboratory if you don't believe me — and that means its head is much lighter than its tail, which would make diving damned difficult. The sperm feeds entirely on squid, which come to the surface at night and are adapted for swimming into the current to get their food. And maybe you won't find this in your books, chemist, but I know it from my records: sperm are fatter and have more oil in them just after the full moon than at any other time of the month. So it's obvious now, isn't it?' Mansell paused and sat back in his chair, as though his point were made and his case closed.

'Whatever is supposed to be obvious, isn't!' the chemist grumbled, and at this stage the rest of the listening 'intellectuals' agreed.

'Well, it's obvious to me,' Mansell leaned forward and continued, 'that the sperm is a surface and not a depth feeder. Is he going to be such a damned fool as to dive down to the sea bottom — where he must be uncomfortable, to say the least of it — for his lunch, when the squid are going to come up immediately after dark and hand him as much supper as he can eat on the surface? His principal feeding ground is the Southern Ocean, and it seems obvious to me that he hangs vertically in the water, kept in that position by his light head. He does this at the edge of a piece of ice — usually the pack, but often a berg or even a floe — with his flat snout just awash, and waits for the squid at night, especially on moonlight nights, to swim up-current toward his phosphorescent jaws, which, under those circumstances, would be admirably adapted for lapping them up. *Now* is it obvious?'

'A tenable hypothesis so far,' the chemist agreed, 'but what's that got to do with his blow-hole being well forward on the port side?'

'It would have to be well forward, wouldn't it,' Mansell exploded, 'if he floated vertically in the water with only his snout awash?'

'But *why* on the port side?' insisted the implacable scientist.

'Because' — Mansell played his trump card, but it was only a deuce — 'if he lies at the edge of the ice for a few million years with his jaws pointing east all the time to catch the squid swimming against the clockwise Antarctic Current, and with a mass of ice just above his right ear, he's going to learn to puff out sideways and to the left, isn't he?'

'Hum — I'll only give you half a bottle of plonk for that idea, and not the best plonk either,' the chemist conceded.

'Mansell, you're full o' crap!' was Andra's opinion of this involved and (I thought) most ingenious hypothesis, and Old Burnett made a noise of disgust as only one with a strong Scottish accent can make such a noise. But all the 'intellectuals,' in argument afterwards, were agreed that Mansell's explanation of the sperm whale's weird anatomy and feeding habits was at least as feasible and well founded as the usually advanced one that it dives many hundreds of fathoms to do battle with giant octopuses on the sea floor, ill-adapted as it is to do so.

Young Evans asked what about all the wicked scars and slashes that every male sperm has on his flat nozzle, which are supposed to be given him by the beaks of the squid in his dim submarine battles.

Mansell, as usual, was not beaten for an answer: 'You try floating vertically in an Antarctic swell with tons of ice crashing about, and you'd soon have a good many scars on your noggin! And you'd be glad to have a ten-foot-thick pad of spermaceti between the banging ice floes and the part of your head where you get the headaches!'

Gyle summed up this discussion. Maybe, he allowed, Mansell had been talking a lot of nonsense, but the real point at issue was the almost unique mammalian asymmetry found in certain species of whale. It had been known since the days of Benjamin Franklin that whales were peculiarly interested in ocean currents, and were found in greatest profusion at the edge of currents or at the edge of ice fields, and this asymmetrical environment of current and ice, comparable to nothing we shore-side mammals ever encounter, probably in some way determined or accounted for the weird lopsidedness of certain whale species. The 'intellectuals' unanimously agreed, and the chemist went off and produced three bottles of best Laboratory Plonk, which Andra and Old Burnett assisted in consuming.

Mansell's theories of the whale, unorthodox and far-fetched though many of them were, usually had some scientific basis. Those of some of the other whalemen often enough had not. The part of the whale's life history that intrigued them most (and the aspect of whale life of which least was known by either scientists or whalemen) was, of course, its sex activities. 'How in the name of God do they do it?' was a very frequent starting-place of argument and speculation when two whalemen were discussing the whale.

Theories varied. Nobody had ever actually seen it, but everybody knew somebody who knew a man who had. Some said that the bull whale swam on the surface while the cow dived and floated toward him upside down from below. 'Ridiculous!' said the opponents of this theory. 'Woman and the bee are the only female animals known to take the initiative in this matter. And, anyway, if the time taken over the job is proportional to the size and unwieldiness of the apparatus, Madame Whale would have to come up and blow now and again, and this would be impossible in position one.'

The next school of thought upheld the theory that the bull whale swam up by the cow whale, tipped her half-way over with his flipper, and then rolled half over himself and, as the seamen put it, 'made fast alongside.' Mark was the principal antagonist of this theory. 'Maybe that's so with the sperm, where the female's half the size of the male,' he conceded, 'and maybe the sperm has his blow-hole on the port bow so he can pant a bit in that position; but with blues and fins, where the female's much bigger than the male, I can't visualize it. It would be just like a tanker coming up alongside the factory ship — and you've all seen how much full ahead and full astern and turn to port or starboard I have to do before I can make fast to a tanker. It would take the whales at least half an hour before they could get a line aboard from one to t'other — and no female of any species is going to wait that long!'

Mark headed another school of thought — the 'pessimistic' school, as Gyle termed them. They believed that there was no 'laying aboard' at all, but that Monsieur and Madame Whale merely swam in the same patch of ocean, the one impregnating the water, the other being impregnated by it, and neither getting any more fun out of it than do the salmon. 'In fact,' said Mark in support of his hypothesis, 'the day in his mighty growth when the force of gravity overtook and nullified his desire was the day the whale reluctantly left the land and returned to the water.'

Mark had given much thought to the breeding habits of the whale. In fact, he had worked out to the last detail a project that was going to save the whaling industry against all its competitors and preserve it for another century at least. It was this:

He proposed to capture alive two blue-whale calves, one male and one female, and transport them home in a specially designed tank ship. Then ('It wouldn't take a quarter of the capital needed to finance a single whaling expedition!' he averred) he was going to start the first whale farm, and the obvious locale for it, he thought, was Loch Ness in Scotland. He had an answer to every objection.

How would he capture the whale calves uninjured? 'With a blunt-headed harpoon, of course, which would deliver a non-lethal jolt of only about a thousand volts. This would put the calves into an electric convulsion that would render them unconscious long enough to be made fast and hauled aboard into the special tank; and, incidentally, would improve their mental condition and make them more amenable to domestication.'

How would he prevent their running amuck and smashing the special tank and the ship on the way home? 'Two hundred gallons of morphine and hyoscine solution — the same stuff the doc pushes into the gunners when they run amuck — pumped aboard them each day through the compressed-air machine would keep them somnolent until they reached Loch Ness.'

But Loch Ness was fresh water, was it not? 'And so what? Whales are not fish, and they could live as easily — maybe more easily — in fresh water as in salt; and, anyway, most of us have seen the Loch Ness monster, which is only some kind of whale of the smaller species and has lived there happily since the first American tourist fell for the story.'

What about feeding the whales on the Loch Ness whale farm? 'Easy! There's a variety of fresh-water shrimp almost identical with the krill eaten by the blue whale, and in one year you could have the loch well stocked with whale grub.'

But what about breeding, asked the 'intellectuals' and others who criticized the scheme, thinking mainly of the in-breeding from one pair of whales and the degeneration of the stock that would result. 'At the worst,' Mark riposted, 'you'd have to send a ship down to the Southern Ocean every few years to capture another calf and bring in fresh blood — but even that won't be necessary when we start artificial insemination!'

I will leave to the imagination the details of the artificial insemination of the whales, which Mark had worked out with the co-operation of the British Navy, represented by Gyle. It involved the use of a destroyer, with high-speed torpedoes loaded in the warhead with special capsules instead of high explosive. Mark was to load the warheads with a pedigree strain supplied and guaranteed by the not yet existent Department of Cetogenics of Edinburgh University, and Gyle undertook to register on or in the target area with at least one salvo in three. And thus new and bigger and better varieties of whale would be bred in domesticity than ever were hunted in the broad liberty of the ocean.

'You fellows talk more damned nonsense than anybody I ever listened to!' remarked Old Burnett, who eavesdropped upon, but seldom joined in, the discussion of such projects. 'But, if you're going to start breeding whales in test tubes, you'd better get a Clydebank engineer to design an' build the first test tube for you. And, if you want a milking-machine to take two hundred gallon off each o' your cow whales twice a day an' keep the whole of Scotland in milk — you just let me know!'

Not all the ideas of Mark and the 'intellectuals' were as crazy and fantastic (or should one perhaps say far-sighted?) as the Loch Ness whale-farm project. Certainly Gyle's idea of training a pack of killer whales to hunt down the blues and the fins, with the corvettes acting as whips and the catchers following with a 'View Halloo!' was away beyond the crazy side of fantasy. But another of Mark's schemes, though he produced it amid laughter, had just enough credibility to make it worthy of consideration outside the madhouse or a whaleship saloon. It was to collect certain sex secretions from female whales taken during the period of oestrus. Bucketfuls of this (to bull whales) delightfully attractive substance would be dumped into the sea at selected points of the Southern Ocean. The catchers would wait around the area, and in a very short time all the excess male whales from hundreds of miles around, whose demise would not affect the future of the whale race one-tenth as much as the destruction of a single potentially prolific female whale, would gather in the trap. As Mark pointed out when he advanced this not ill-considered scheme, the salmon-poachers of Scotland have recently learned a very similar dodge and are taking ten times as many fish out of the lochs since they began scattering salmon spawn in selected bits of water out of sight of the police.

There was a common feeling among both scientists and whalemen that, though whaling was great fun and certainly the most dramatic way of tapping the vast food reserves of the ocean, it was really a wasteful and unnecessarily laborious way of doing so. The principal exponent of this idea was the young Norwegian biologist, who was specially interested in plankton. This vast reserve of minute plant and animal material fills all the oceans of the world, and the biologist lad maintained that, properly utilized, it could solve for centuries to come the ever-increasing problem of human nutrition. His father and grandfather had been whalemen, and — perhaps because of this — his ambition in life was to put all whale owners and whalemen out of business for ever by finding an economical means of dredging, and a palatable way of using, this plankton. As he put it to me when discussing the matter: 'It's a case of "*Warum einfach wenn es kann so schön kompliziert sein* — why simple when it can be so beautifully complicated?" Why put a bucket over the sea wall of New Bedford or Dundee or Tönsberg and draw all the protein and oils and vitamins you need to feed your cattle and poultry and make your margarine, when you can organize expeditions to go twelve thousand miles away with beautifully complicated apparatus to hunt whales — whales that have fed on krill which in its turn fed on plankton almost identical with that we find around our coasts — and, after a long industrial process, break the whales down again into end products that contain less protein, oil, and vitamins than my plankton?'

I do not know how this lad is getting on, and I am of two minds whether to wish him luck in his researches. The whaling company, at the behest of some Norwegian research foundation and not realizing that it might be nursing the seeds of its own destruction, gave him passage with us and left him at the end of the season in South Georgia, where he was to remain for eighteen months. I think, on the whole, that I hope his researches on that island have failed, for the world today is humdrum enough already, without his dull coastal fishermen with their plankton nets displacing the last twelve thousand peaceful adventurers remaining in our midst.

Also on our ship — but sent by a commercial, not a scientific, concern — was a Norwegian fisherman who had never before left Norway and had never seen a whale, but who also had designs on the whaling industry, to destroy or replace it. His intention was to investigate the possibilities of the Antarctic fisheries —a hitherto unexplored commercial and nutritional project. The Southern Ocean teems with fish. It is only necessary to bait a cod hook with the smell of bacon and throw it overside anywhere in the inlets, or over the banks surrounding South Georgia or the other southern islands, to haul up a large and most repulsive (but, when properly cooked, tender and delicious) meal for six men. There is only the one species of edible fish (called the 'toskin' by the whalemen), but it abounds over vast stretches of ocean as the cod used to do over the limited area of the Grand Banks. It is eaten extensively in South Georgia and on all the whaleships in the south, but is unknown in northern markets, where potentially it could displace the cod, and it is sufficiently abundant, if taken and processed as the whales are today, to produce much more protein and animal oils than does the whaling industry. A Norwegian company, wise enough to trust a simple fisherman's intuition and his catch over a season rather than the reports of the 'intellectuals,' sent this old chap south with us. He was going to Husvik Harbour, South Georgia, where he was to be given a fishing-boat identical with the vessel he had used for many years at home. On his report and the results of a summer's fishing, it was to be decided whether it was commercially feasible to start tapping the Antarctic fisheries and transporting the harvest so many thousand miles through the tropics to the hungry modern world.

The whaling companies are most peculiar in this matter of competition. Since they have a monopoly of transport to the Southern Ocean, they are often asked to convey potential competitors such as our young plankton expert and the Husvik fisherman to the south, and at this stage they are singularly obtuse and willingly give them passage. But, as soon as they realize that the purpose of the visits to the Antarctic (which they consider their private property) is commercial, they turn and often enough abandon their one-time protégé quicker than Mr. Arbuthnot drops his hot bricks.

There was the tale of a young Frenchman who was transported by a whaling company to South Georgia to study penguins. He was treated with the greatest consideration and courtesy by his whaling hosts before and on arrival on the island. But, when it was disclosed that his researches into the multitudinous penguin species consisted in boiling the birds down and comparing the oil he obtained from them with the oil obtained by greater labour from the whale, he was straight away given the cold shoulder — and South Georgia is not a place where one would choose to be given the cold shoulder by the whaling companies. It was related to me — with more than the usual allowance being made for the whaleman's incorrigible habit of improving on a good story — that this unfortunate character wandered round the island for two years from whaling station to whaling station, living off the whalemen. They gave him their charity at the risk of incurring the displeasure of their employers, while he sought in vain for a passage back to the mainland in any whale-company-owned ship. Ultimately, I am told, an Argentinian company reluctantly gave him passage to Buenos Aires, from which time nothing has been heard of him. Whether it is true that, before leaving the island, he was made to sign a document forswearing any interest in penguins for the rest of his life, I cannot say. Anyway, I gather that the French penguin-oil project — potentially as great an industry as modern whaling — was stillborn.

I hope that, when the slow-thinking whale owners realize what they are up to, the young biologist and the stolid old Norski fisherman are not treated to the same fate as the Frenchman. None the less, on this occasion I am on the side of the whale owners, and wish no luck to any project that is going to mean the end of whaling.

Perhaps my 'intellectuals' do not sound a very laudable bunch of scientific brains, and they may appear to deserve much of the contempt Old Burnett continually poured on them, but that is because I have not touched sufficiently upon the importance and seriousness of their day-to-day routine work in their crazily pitching little laboratories away down in the ice. Testing and grading oil under difficulties that would appal a shore-side scientific worker, they daily and hourly ensure that nothing of poor quality goes into the British diet. They assess the vitamin content of the whale products, thereby keeping up the nutritional standards of much of the cattle and poultry of the U.K.; and they do not hesitate to expose any attempt to tamper with the whale products, or any illegal contamination or pollution of them that is brought to their attention which might have detrimental effects upon the health or nourishment of any human or animal. Apart from some serious gaps in the law, which under certain circumstances permits stinking, rotten whales to be added to the cargo, and apart also from the occasional hoodwinkery of the whalemen, which often deceives the scientists as it does the inspectors, the cargo brought home at the end of the season is pure and of good quality, and it is the floating scientists who must be given the credit for this.

Before leaving whaling science, I must report the major scientific discovery *I* made in the south, which was in the science of nutrition. It is that whale meat not only is edible, but, properly cooked, is delicious and infinitely preferable to the meat of the ox. Properly cooked, I say! And, as it is now appearing in New York restaurants, where it is variously described by the customers as tasting like cod-liver oil and long-dead hippopotamus, I will end my chapter on science in the south by reporting in detail the manner of cooking it.

Take a ten-pound cut from the rump of a finback whale, just aft of the dorsal fin. (It must be a fin whale or, if you can find one, a humpback. If any New York waiter offers you blue whale, take it in preference to beef, but complain about the absence of fin from the menu; and, if any man tells you he has eaten sperm whale, or that any stomach could tolerate what even the Cape pigeons and the killer whales spurn, give him the lie, even though his name be Melville.) Hang your cut of fin rump steak up on a hook, preferably in a fairly warm spot exposed to the sun. Leave it there for three days. The horrid black mess you will see when you return at the end of that period may put you off whale meat for the rest of your days, but do not be deceived or discouraged. Hold your nose, cut away all the black crust and bury it deeply far away from your house. In the centre of the cut you will find about two pounds of fresh, juicy, oil-free, fatless steak. Put this under a scorching broiler and char it quickly on both sides. Then put it on the table and cut from it the finest pound of medium-rare steak you ever ate in your life. Bury it under a mountain of fried onions, and eat it with roast potatoes.

And I maintain that you will then agree that it was worth while travelling forty-seven thousand miles on a whaleship and passing six months out of sight of land, even though I brought back nothing but that valuable scientific discovery. Even Old Burnett agrees with this, though neither of us expects the whale companies to give us a percentage on the increased sales of whale meat which should result from our propaganda.

XII

THE MEN BELOW

To the ignorant the great results alone are admirable; to the knowing,
rather the infinite device and sleight of hand that made them possible.
—ROBERT LOUIS STEVENSON

GUNNER LARSEN and Gunner Olsen saw the whale at the same
moment. Their catchers were steaming on a parallel course
only a few hundred feet apart on a clear, cold, grey Antarctic day
in perfect whaling weather. The whale, a large blue, rose between them. Larsen turned sharply to port, and Olsen turned the
same degree to starboard. Both saw nothing but the whale and
perhaps another seven and a half pounds sterling waving airily
above it. When Larsen reached the spot, the whale wasn't
there; but Olsen was. And Olsen, instead of finding a fat blue
whale and a nice addition to his bonus, found himself looking
along the sights at Larsen, who was also well armed and angry.

Fortunately the shock when the bows of the two little ships
met at twenty-eight knots put both guns out of action, otherwise
a long overdue civil war between the Olsens and the Larsens
would have opened with an artillery duel at point-blank range
in the Scotia Sea. As it was, the battle was verbal, conducted first
for a few minutes across five yards of ocean from one smashed
and twisted fo'c'sle head to another, and continued for half an
hour or more after the two severely damaged little ships had
drawn apart, across the radio telephone.

Those on the bridge of the factory ship a hundred miles away
who understood Norwegian listened at first with delight, but
soon with alarm, when Larsen, in between his vituperation
against Olsen, announced that his ship was already two feet
down by the head and only his forrard collision bulkhead was
keeping him afloat. Olsen replied that it would serve Larsen

bloody well right to sink with all hands, but he would stick around until the factory came up.

The factory was already turning in the direction of the position where the furious gunners thought they were, but it would take her eight hours to get to them. So, when Larsen announced that his ship, too, was taking water, Mark did that thing which a bridge officer does, or dares to do, but once or twice in his career: sent his compliments to the chief engineer and told him to come up on the bridge immediately.

Old Burnett, give him his due, was there almost before Mark had laid down the telephone, for he knew the summons portended some extraordinary emergency. In ten seconds he had grasped the serious situation of the damaged catchers. 'Pit those two hysterical gunners off the blower, an' let me talk to the engineers!' he told Mark. 'An' we'll maybe get some sense from them!' he added in the inevitable Burnett mutter.

When the two catcher engineers came on to the radio-phone, he got from them an exact picture of the extent of the damage by means of half a dozen terse technical questions. Then he gave his instructions:

'Now, you will both do this: You will empty your forrard fuel tanks — pump the oil into the sea, an' to hell with it — and that'll trim you by the stern enough to raise your cracked plates sufficiently out o' the water to enable you to put those twelve bags o' cement ye didn't want to load but I insisted ye should carry in your stores, down in the fo'c'sle where you're takin' water. Give it half an hour to set, then tell the gunner he can make three knots — no more than that, mind! That'll bring ye alongside us an hour earlier than if ye stay where ye are. If you're there when we reach you, I'll know ye're fair-to-middlin' engineers. If ye're not, I'll know ye've learnt nothing I ever tried to teach you, and ye deserve to drown!'

The two catchers were still there, but limping badly, when we reached them. But the Southern Ocean, with its invariable bad taste and malicious humour, had decided to produce a mighty swell from some far-distant gale, and, as always seemed the case when emergency arose on the small ships, it required prodigies of seamanship to bring them alongside and make them fast.

On this occasion, by a miracle, nobody had been hurt. This was a case of injured ships, and I was able to stand back and watch, with interest and a good deal of sympathy, while others coped with the damage.

Old Burnett, as required by honour and tradition, went over in the basket first, aboard the most seriously damaged catcher, and 'examined the patient.' His was the decision whether the injured ship should be withdrawn from the expedition and sent back five hundred miles to the repair shops at South Georgia, accompanied by another healthy ship, at enormous loss to the company and the whalemen, or whether repairs could be carried out down there in the ice. He had not appeared to do a hand's turn of work in the previous two months, but, being able to empathize with him, I knew that, in the half-hour from the time he entered that crazy little basket until he came up again with his decision, he was going to earn at least two months' pay.

'We'll do it here!' he said to the expectant knot of engineers and idlers who waited for him on the harpoon platform when the basket was slung aboard again. 'MacDonald! You'll hand the factory over to Gunn there, an' you'll repair the two catchers well enough to finish the season safely.' And with that the old man seemed to lose all interest in the emergency and went off to his Bible and his whisky bottle in his cabin down aft — as fine an example as I have seen of a chief who believed in the absolute delegation of responsibility once the decision on policy had been made by himself, provided — as in this case — he had trained his lieutenant himself.

We all now watched MacDonald. He also went down in the basket, inspected the damage, and came back as confident as his chief. 'Michelsen! We'll need two new plates. I've chalked the ones that are beyond repair. And here's four places that need welding — get Gavin to do that and give him three men to help him. Leave the cement where it is, but put in another eight bags

208

when you've finished the job. Micky, you've got two days' work by-passing all the pipes forrard of that bulkhead. Jack, lend me a couple of electricians to rewire the gunner's telegraph, which is good and buggered. Alec, dismount that harpoon gun and give him a new one. There's not much wrong with the old one, but, if we don't replace it, Olsen will blame us for every whale he misses for the rest of the season. Gunn, come up to my room in an hour and I'll hand the factory over to you — this job's going to take three days. Doc, have you got a slug in your cabin? Because I need one badly.'

For three days in a heaving swell the engineers worked on those damaged catchers, carrying out a job that even I in my ignorance could see would be tricky enough in a dry-dock at a home port and, when undertaken at the edge of the Southern Ocean ice pack, verged on the crazy or the miraculous. Michelsen and Gavin were the heroes of the job. The former was a crafty little Norwegian mechanic who did no work whatever unless he was plied with drink, but who more than justified his pay and bonus during his weeks of idleness by his ingenuity and skill when something went wrong and he was bribed by six large shots of rum to put it right. Gavin was a large, quiet, awkward Scot — the kind who would work patiently over his lathe for several hours shaping the screw of a tiny bolt to make it fit perfectly in its socket, and who would not even swear if the ham-handed repairer's mate dropped the bolt into the sea before it reached its socket, but would quietly return to his lathe and make another one.

These two and their small group of helpers worked day and night hanging over the bows of the catchers, soaking wet most of the time, and later, when a hard freeze-up came, sheathed in solid ice along with their tools and the steel plates on which they worked. MacDonald went over in the basket every hour or so to see how the work was going, never interfering, never giving his advice unless the artificers asked for it, but giving silent encouragement.

Once in the middle of the night I went over with him, for

209

Michelsen and Gavin were both chums of mine and I had heard that it was one of the sights of the whaling industry to see them working together. It was! I wished as I watched them that we had an artist on board who could paint the weird scene of these two ice-clad figures working silently together by the hideous violet light of their electric welder. It was a subject worthy of a great brush or a lens more nimble than mine, even had it been staged in a Glasgow shipyard; on the tiny heaving fo'c'sle-head of a three-hundred-ton ship a thousand miles from the nearest repair shops and as near the South Pole as a man had ever used an electric welder before, the scene seemed to my unartistic eye to have some strange significance worthy of perpetual record. I think the men on the job vaguely felt this themselves. They could, had they wished, have demanded their trade-union rights, stopped work every few hours to eat, and insisted on being relieved after a twelve-hour shift, but they would have been outraged had MacDonald or anybody else suggested it. Michelsen and Gavin had been commissioned to perform a work of craftsmanship — which, according to one reputable if old-fashioned definition, is synonymous with a work of art — and, believing, probably rightly, that they were the only two artists in the world capable of the task under the set conditions, they would have deeply resented the suggestion that any others could take over for them.

They worked silently, for they had no word of common tongue and could communicate only in the international sign-language of mechanics; but they were as efficient and methodical as though they were working in a well-heated machine shop at home. And, if Gavin put out a hand, Michelsen knew just what tool he needed; or, if Michelsen gave a Scandinavian grunt, Gavin knew, either by telepathy or by the instinct of men who work with inanimate metals and materials, that the bolt was too tight or maybe — though the grunt seemed exactly the same to me — too loose.

At the end of nearly three days Michelsen and Gavin got up off their little stools, took off their welding-goggles, gave the beautifully finished new bows of the second catcher a kick, in the way engineers always do when they are satisfied with a job, wiped their frozen hands on a sweat-rag, and nodded grinningly to each other. The large audience up on the harpoon platform, including MacDonald, most of the other engineers who were off watch, and an idle doctor, knew that the job was finished and the whaling could now proceed with our full complement of catchers.

MacDonald sent up word to the saloon, where the wordy battle between Olsen and Larsen was still continuing after three days, that the little ships were ready to sail, and the two gunners descended and went aboard their catchers. Neither spoke a word of thanks. They glanced at the completed work, omitting even to ask who had done it, though Olsen found some criticism for an ingenious piece of outboard patchwork on the grounds that it might in some remote eventuality interfere with his shooting, then went up to their bridges and prepared to cast off. But, before they could do so, Old Burnett appeared on the scene with the surly remark: '*I'll* pass the ships before they sail!'

His way of 'passing the ships' was to go aboard each catcher in turn, give the gunner a blistering in front of Michelsen and Gavin, pointing out that it was only good engineering that compensated for poor seamanship and made modern whaling possible, and then invite the engineers of the catchers to come up to his cabin and share a bottle with MacDonald and Michelsen and Gavin and everybody else who had been concerned with the near-disaster except the gunners. The gunners fumed and cursed inaudibly, but made no protest at the delay, for even their dim intellects could grasp that the modern whaling industry is at base controlled, not by the reckless fishermen, but by steam and electricity and the slide-rule, and by the men who understand these things.

I do not agree entirely with Old Burnett, who maintained that all romance had gone from modern whaling and that it was no longer a job demanding fine seamanship and an adventurous spirit, but was merely a large and complicated problem of engineering. Nevertheless, though I know less about engineering than I know about the Trobriand Islanders, even I could see that our engineers were performing work which I would have deemed impossible had I not seen them at it, and I could see that the industry was dependent upon their skill and ingenuity at every turn. And, though their work does not appeal to the imagination as does that of the dashing gunners, they knew themselves that it was more difficult, required more grit and guts, and was, for those who could see, much more romantic.

Tales of the miracles wrought by whaling engineers in the Antarctic are as manifold and — when the conditions under which they work are realized — as exciting as any tales of the whale-hunt. For example: to replace the screw of a steamship is a big, complicated job requiring under ordinary circumstances a well-equipped dry-dock, cranes, a casting-foundry, and the like. But it has been done by whaling engineers down in the Antarctic pack ice, the forward compartment of the ship being flooded until the stern was lifted right out of the water until it was level with the engineers, who fitted the new propeller, working from a large ice floe. Repairing leaks, or almost rebuilding engines, or improvising spare parts weighing tons out of crude materials, are routine jobs for the whaling engineer. On one occasion some years ago, which the engineers still talk about over their drinks, a factory ship struck a large iceberg head-on at full speed and within a few minutes was flooded to her watertight doors and sinking rapidly. But no *Titanic* disaster resulted. The engineers had anticipated this very contingency; by sundry ingenious devices they kept the ship afloat and built a new bow on her out of solid concrete. Not only was she not lost, but she finished the season and (maybe the story here has the whaleman's usual addition) far exceeded her quota of whales taken and processed.

Even the day-by-day running of the machinery and plant of a modern whaling expedition is, to the layman, an awe-inspiring work. To take only one small aspect of it: the expedition requires some two thousand tons of clean fresh water every *day* during the season, and every drop of this must be evaporated from sea water. The supply of water was a constant source of anxiety to our engineers. More and better water was the constant demand of everybody — from the factory engineer, who wanted as much piped into his factory daily as would supply an average small town, to the doctor, who wanted merely to keep himself and his patients clean and develop his films. As the season advanced and the demands on the evaporating-machinery became heavier, water rapidly became a commodity second only to alcohol in value.

Fortunately I quickly discovered the procedure for getting my whack of the valuable commodity, and a little extra. It was useless to talk to the stony-hearted engineer who had charge of the evaporating-plant. 'I only distil the damn stuff,' he would say, 'and my evaporators have been working to capacity since the day we sailed, so don't blame me if you're short. And, if your water is coming out of the taps as black as coffee and full of *grax*, again don't blame me, because anyone who could distil dirty water would be a bloody genius!' It was Gyle who gave me the tip when I asked him why he always had clean, plentiful bath water in the inspector's quarters while the doctor and the ship's hospital bathed and operated and dispensed the medicines and played at photography with only a thin trickle of mud for hydration. Gyle advised me to discuss the matter with Micky, the plumber — over a bottle. This I did, and the next day Micky carried out some 'repairs' in the pipes between the hospital and the alleyway. When he had finished, a gush of clear, healthy water came out of all my taps; and I was sympathetic but mystified when I heard the engineers, including the fellow who 'only distilled the damn stuff,' complaining bitterly to one another because all the taps up and down their alleyway and in their baths had shrunk to a slimy ooze. For the remainder of this voyage, though it involved occasional alcoholic consultations with Micky, I got my fair share of the precious daily tonnage of water.

But I have no wish to jest about the astonishing job done by the whaling engineers — though that is their own custom. I would rather recount some of their other feats, which amaze the uninstructed but are considered by the engineers themselves to be dull, routine jobs. They keep the main engines of the seventeen ships of the expedition running for — in the case of the factory ship — forty-seven thousand miles from the time of leaving the last repair shop until return to the home port, with never a half-minute's delay on account of engine failure or breakdown. And it is not straight chug-chug along, with a 'Stand By' signal precursing changes in speed, as in the case of ordinary merchant vessels, but 'Slow,' 'Half Ahead,' 'Stop,' 'Full Astern,' 'Full Ahead,' all day and every day, and every now and again the signal known only to marine engineers in naval ships in action and whaling ships in the ice: 'Full Astern, for Christ sake!' which has its own special ring on the engine-room telegraph, a ring that the officers on the bridges of fighting-ships and whalers, and their engineers below, know very well. And forty-seven thousand miles under this constant strain on the men concerned meant an even greater strain on the machinery, for — as our junior chief engineer told me after bringing his slide-rule out of his pistol pocket and making some rapid calculations — it involved some fifteen million revolutions of the ship's twin screws, and never once did the screws fail to turn in the direction and at the speed demanded by the officer on the bridge.

Other 'routine' jobs of the engineers were equally dumbfounding to the uninitiated. Our chief electrician, with the help of his three assistants, maintained in perfect order a mileage of wire which would have stretched many times round the earth, and treated as easily understood toys a bewilderment of electrical apparatus ranging from Asdic depth-sounding gear and a weird monstrosity called the Tchernikov Electrical Log, to my X-ray apparatus, which no doctor, despite his allegedly higher education and supposedly superior I.Q., has ever succeeded in understanding yet.

It was also a source of wonderment to me how the whaling engineers managed to maintain not only the main engines of our seventeen ships, but also an equal number of steering-engines, some sixty-eight steam or electric winches and donkey engines

214

(the sudden failure of any one of which might have cost men their lives), and the other ten thousand gadgets that make modern whaling possible on its huge scale.

I once expressed my astonishment about the wonders of whaling engineering to MacDonald. 'Doc,' he said, 'when you were a wee laddie, did you once get a real model steam engine as a Christmas present?' I thought back and admitted that I had. 'And could you ever make it go?' And I had to admit that I never could. 'Well,' he said, 'don't pass any opinions of engineers or engineering, for or against, until you understand and can work that model engine!'

I think he had something there regarding the engineering, but, thinking it over since, I am inclined to believe that the engineer himself is a subject I can study and discuss, even though I do not understand the workings of the simplest overhead cam-shaft (whatever that might be!) on a model steam engine. For the engineer, though he would like to think he is, is not a machine calculable upon a slide-rule, even though the inanimate things with which he works might be. I saw the most illuminating example of this aboard our ship.

Machinery does break down, even though it has the most devoted and ingenious men attending to it. On this occasion it was the main whale-winch that suddenly died. This was a mighty engine placed on a high platform amidships of the factory ship which hauled the whales out of the sea up the skidway on to the flensing-deck. It had hauled up several hundred whales without a hitch, but one day, when a big blue monster was half-way up the skidway, the winch emitted peculiar noises reminiscent to me of the expensive noises my car used to make when it was time to turn it in for a new one, and came to a jarring stop amid roars of escaping steam. It was obviously a bad breakdown, and liable to be a costly one, for all whaling must necessarily come to a full stop until this vital piece of machinery was repaired.

To the imperturbable Gavin was given the job of repairing it. Climbing up onto the high platform, he made an inspection of the wreckage while an anxious knot of engineers and mates and disappointed whalemen collected below. His inspection was brief, but his expression was gloomy when he leaned over the rail to make his report. 'Eighteen to twenty-four hours — maybe longer!' he shouted down, then set to the job.

He and his two assistants were up there continuously through the night and well into the next day, taking out huge chunks of mangled machinery and inserting spares. They were covered with oil and sweat, though the temperature stood well below freezing. A procession of apprehensive and sometimes irate whalemen, who stood to lose mightily on the bonus as a result of the hold-up, wandered across the deck below them, occasionally shouting up to ask how it was going, but not daring to go near the harassed and dead-tired mechanics up on the high platform.

Then a little mess-boy, the youngest and cheekiest on the ship, wandered down aft, bearing a sperm-whale tooth in his hand and demanding in his impudent treble: 'Where's Mr. Gavin?'

'What do you want Mr. Gavin for?' asked MacDonald, who was standing with a group of very glum engineers at the end of their alleyway.

'He promised to mount this whale's tooth in white metal for me, and he hasn't done it yet,' replied the boy.

'Well, look, sonny,' said MacDonald with a straight but twitching face, 'Mr. Gavin's up there beside the whale-winch. He's been there all night and half today sitting on a lump of frozen steel, with no sleep and nothing to eat. Why don't you go up and ask him about your whale's tooth?'

And amid the first laughter heard down aft for eighteen hours the boy went off. But, instead of going forrard to his quarters, he *did* climb up the ladder amidships, and his tiny figure was seen talking to Gavin away up beside the winch. In a minute or so he climbed down again, and MacDonald, now laughing openly, called out to him: 'What did Mr. Gavin say, son?'

'He said to leave the tooth on top of his locker in the machine shop, and he's going to fix it directly he's finished the job he's on now— and what are you all laughing at?' the lad inquired innocently.

What, indeed, were we laughing at? We should have remembered that Gavin was the most serene and patient of a group of men whose occupation, the maintenance and repair of whaling machinery under Southern Ocean conditions, demands more serenity and patience than any job I have ever encountered. Before dark that night the whale-winch was working again, hauling the hundred-ton carcasses up on to the deck regularly every half-hour with never a hitch. The money was rolling in again, the bonus was mounting, and the whalemen were all smiles; and the little mess-boy was proudly displaying his whale's tooth, now mounted in white metal on mahogany with delicate care and obvious good taste.

Marine engineers are a race apart, and the whaling engineers are the aristocracy of that race. I would that I were the 'Robbie Burns to sing the song of steam' for whom Kipling's McAndrew prayed, but I can only give a simple account of a few unusual and talented men as I saw them doing an incredibly difficult job under brutal conditions. MacDonald running a huge factory turning out millions of pounds' worth of products on three crazily swaying decks five hundred miles south of the Horn; old Julius sitting, at an age I reckoned to be eighty, in the bowels of a speedboat leaping after the whale amid the drift ice; MacTavish, the junior chief, whom I have never mentioned because he was the type of man whom nobody ever does mention, keeping the main engines of the factory ship running for forty-seven thousand miles with never a hitch, and keeping his greasers and stokers happy and laughing when they worked at a temperature of 140° in tropical waters, as also when they worked at below freezing in the Antarctic; Jack, the chief electrician, who would turn into his bunk after a fifteen-hour shift at the masthead realigning the D.F. aerial and would turn out again half an hour later with a cheerful 'O.K., doc!' when my operating-room light was giving trouble; Gavin and Michelsen taking on every day a repair job such as no engineer had ever tackled before, and doing it without complaint under conditions that no well-paid trade-union leader could survive for two minutes; and, over them all, the brooding, cantankerous figure of Old Burnett, whose best testimonial is that the whaling engineers fight in the offices at home to sail under him.

This old scoundrel I got to know slowly, and my respect for him increased with my knowledge. One day our acquaintance took a huge jump. We sat in the saloon over lunch, everybody a bit gloomy, for the whaling had not been brisk and we were far behind our quota. Old Burnett was the gloomiest of the lot, for he had been on the wagon for a fortnight and had been spending his time in his cabin alone with John Calvin instead of John Haig. But it was he who broke the gloomy silence:

'Ye know,' he said, 'I would like fine today to go to a bull-fight!'

He blinked around solemnly through his thick glasses as the laughter at this masterpiece of incongruity in the Antarctic Ocean died away, then added: 'Well, since I can't do that, mebbe I'll entertain the doctor. Doctor — ye'll be welcome in my cabin this evening!'

'For tea?' I politely inquired.

'No! For whusky!' And he got up and ambled out of the saloon.

I reported to his cabin as ordered, at what I reckoned to be 'whusky' time, and I passed there one of the most interesting evenings of my life. I got his life story — you invariably get that when you are entertained by a shipmate in his cabin at whusky time — and that alone would make a book. Born of whaling people, he had the sea in his blood, but, not having money enough to get there in the Navy or on the bridge of a merchant vessel, he had served his apprenticeship in the shipyards of Dundee, the old whaling port, at five shillings a week (one dollar in those days) and later completed his marine-engineering education in the yards of John Brown of Glasgow when the *Queen Mary* was still a dream on the drawing-boards of that famous company. And then to sea, and to sea with the whalemen (he said because the money was better and he had a lot to repay his family for his education, but I think perhaps the blood of his ancestors was as impelling a force as the pounds, shillings, and pence). World War I interrupted his career — 'it was a dull time, that; I was third on one of the banana boats running to South America, and we got torpedoed but twice' — then back to the whaling. Between the wars he made himself the master of the engineering department of the British whaling industry, but the Second World War came along — 'and that was kind of a bloody nuisance! They converted all the factory ships into tankers an' put them on the transatlantic run carrying high-octane petrol. I advised against it, for what chance does a blunt box with fifty-foot freeboard and a maximum o' eleven knots stand against a submarine? However, I sailed as chief on the first one they sent across. I mind there was a ladder to the upper deck outside my cabin door, an' I kept thinking to myself: "Burnett, it's comin' — an' when it does, if you can't find the ladder, you've had it, and, if you can, you might stand the chance of a snowflake in hell." Well, doctor, every night I switched out the light when I turned in, and made a practice dash for that ladder in the dark. An' I came so I could be on the upper deck in around five seconds. We got across with only a few scares and nothing serious, and we nearly got home again. But at the mouth of the Firth of Forth they got us. Well, I had practised my drill, and I reached the ladder two seconds after the explosion — only the ladder wasn't there. The torpedo had hit just aft of my cabin and blown my ladder to buggery along with a lot of other things. I'm not quite sure yet what happened after that, but it was then I got all those burn scars you saw when you examined me. I lost two more ships under me later in the war, but I must admit that first was the worst experience I ever had. And now, doctor, we'll have another glass of whusky, and I'll tell you something about the engineering o' the whaling industry, as it's obvious you're going to write a book about us, and, as sure as there's a living God, your chapter on the engineers will be the most cock-eyed of the lot.'

He told me much. He told me a bookful of stories of what the Scots whaling engineers had done, and the only credit he took himself was that he had 'trained all they lads.' He was the first who put to me a tolerant hypothesis concerning the owners and shareholders of the whaling companies, people whom he knew better than any of his colleagues did. 'They just don't know — they don't know the job the lads do for them,' he asserted; and I hope he was right.

As we were drinking our last whisky, his cabin telephone rang, and I had another brief glimpse of how this old Calvinistic, Kiplingesque character earned his pay.

'Aye, Mac, what the hell are ye wantin' at this time o' night? ... The steam-pipe's blown between the Coastguard an' the Rosedown, has it? Well, I thought it might do that. Put Ernie MacGowan to mend it. He did a job for me just like that around nineteen-thirty. An' look, Mac, I don't want to interfere, but maybe if you made the angle of that pipe where it goes through the deckhead a bit more obtuse it wouldn't burst again. . . . Aye! I'll be here. I'm just biddin' good night to the doctor, and then I'm turning in; but give me a call if you haven't got it fixed when the watches change, or if your pressure on the Coastguard drops below a hundred.'

I bade him good-night; and I think by the flicker in his eye he knew that I was beginning to understand that modern whaling is largely an engineering problem, and that he, sitting with his Bible and his whisky bottle, was the key man on whom the success or failure of our expedition depended.

XIII

ALL WHALING SHALL CEASE

And the Lord spake unto the fish, and it vomited out Jonah upon the dry land.

—JONAH ii. 10

THE southern hemisphere baleen whaling season was scheduled to close on April 16, but it was one morning late in March that Gyle came into the saloon waving a marconigram from Sandesfiord and announced: 'Gentlemen! With effect from midnight next Sunday, all whaling shall cease!'

The officers assembled for breakfast expressed no enthusiasm at the announcement; in fact, all hands were downcast. The early closing of the season meant that the sixteen thousand blue-whale units permitted to be taken from the Southern Ocean each year had been exceeded long before the estimated date. That signified that other expeditions had done much better than ours and had exceeded their quotas, while we were still far short of ours and had only a few days left to make it up.

'We can't do it!' said Mansell after making some Mansellian calculations on the tablecloth, and the gloom increased, for everybody knew what he meant. 'It's that damned English ship *Balaena* again!' was his guess. 'Every year she do better than anybody because she sail out of Cape Town and fish west while we puddle around Scotia Sea and South Sandwich Islands!'

Certainly, as it turned out, the *Balaena* expedition of London (as nearly every year) had beaten all other pelagic fleets and was already on her way home with her tanks and transports full to capacity. But there were other theories advanced for the sudden termination of the season. One was that the Russian expedition, which had been fishing in our vicinity all season, and with which our gunners had often nearly made war on the high seas, had been putting in false figures to Sandefiord in order to limit the whaling of other convention-observing nations while it cheerfully disregarded the terms of the convention itself. We knew from visual and photographic evidence that their catchers had started taking whales, blue whales, long before the season opened, and we saw no reason to accept their reports and returns at the end of the season, when, by claiming more than they had taken, they could end the whaling for everybody for another year. But, whatever the reason, Sandefiord declared that after seven days the whales would be reprieved until the next December and all the whalemen could go home.

And what a seven days those were! Every man made one last furious effort to achieve the quota in his own particular small niche of the expedition, each one determined that, if we failed, it would not be his fault.

The gunners scoured a vast area of ocean, killing as many whales on each of the seven days as the factory could deal with inside the legal time limit (and maybe a few more, Gyle suspected, when he saw badly 'burned' whales coming aboard; but, if the gunners did kill extra whales during those last few hectic days and stow them quietly behind icebergs until they dared to report them, the official eye was benignly opaque).

The flensers and lemmers stripped and stowed the whales as quickly as Davison could haul them aboard, and there were seldom fewer than four being worked on the deck at any time of the day or night. The men in the factory below forgot their grumbles and their 'seamen's rights' during that last week; led by the little Norwegian trade-union representative, they worked double shifts, and to hell with the overtime money and the union rules!

Whaling inspectors, mates, the chief engineer, the Intolerable Ho, and all the others who had succeeded in keeping their hands clean and their nails well polished throughout the trip, started doing work, even simple pulling and hauling, which would have been far beneath their dignity in normal times. There was no more talk of who should do which jobs, but only of how near we could get to our quota. Even the doctor at last discharged as cured the mess-boy with the strange disease who helped in the sick bay, and the medical staff (or at least the Norwegian half of it) started getting up at 6 A.M. to see the sick, lest any man who might be working be delayed from going on the morning shift.

Half-way through the week the intensive effort showed some result. To reach all our oil quota of 131,000 barrels was now hopeless but we were close to our quota of 3000 tons of meat-meal and by-products, and at midweek Mansell and Mac-Donald informed the saloon that they had passed that figure. That meant that every ton of by-products now counted as double on the bonus of all hands, so there was jubilation that night. Mansell, MacDonald and Gunn (who, during normal times when there were no damaged catchers to cope with, was the by-products engineer) were the heroes of the saloon; and on the lower deck Rosedown, Butterworth, and the meat-meal storeman were being similarly fêted. The Intolerable Ho released an unprecedented flow of rum to celebrate the occasion, and all hands relaxed from the final fury of work for an hour or two.

It was in the middle of the party, just after Old Burnett had passed his first words of praise to all and sundry by saying that we were not going to get the quota after all in oil, but there was no man on our ships who hadn't done his damnedest, 'but it was the will o' the Lord!' when Tom Archibald brought into the saloon and handed to the manager a radiogram from a business-man interested in whale oil.

'Is it urgent, Tom?' asked the manager, who was enjoying the brief party with the rest of us.

'No,' admitted Tom, 'but the lads might like to hear it if you read it aloud.'

I expected some sort of congratulatory message, but this com-munication was to express 'disappointment with our results for the season' and 'grave dissatisfaction' with certain technicalities of our conduct of the whaling and the engineering, which were presumably much better understood by the comfortable gentle-man in his office than by the men who had sweated blood over the problems all season, and a score of seasons before, on the Southern Ocean.

The radiogram, to my astonishment, did not upset my shipmates or spoil the party. I think the sender might have saved the expense of the radiogram, had he known how little effect it would have on those who knew they had done as much as men could do, and who expected no more nor less in the way of thanks. I think I was the only one in that saloon who felt any bitterness, and that was because I have never become accustomed to John Citizen's ingratitude for the things he owes to those who follow strange and hazardous occupations in far places in order that he may continue his comfortable life at home.

Mansell's statistical comment was that the balance sheet for this voyage would show a gross profit of only two and three quarter million sterling instead of three!

Then the whalemen went on to talk of things more interesting to them than a businessman's opinion. But I started to draw up another balance sheet for our expedition, one very different from that the company auditors would pass when we got home. My balance sheet, on the credit side, showed not only the huge exchange of sterling between the British housewives, the Ministry of Food, and the whaleship owners. I also had on my sheet an entry showing the thirty-thousand-odd tons of protein we had taken from the sea — enough, when it had been dealt with in various ways, to feed half a million children and keep them in vitamins, many medicines, soap, and a hundred other necessities of life until the whaling recommenced the following year and men set off again to the other end of the world to bring them more. My balance sheet mentioned also a more intangible credit — the benefit to the human race, in this age of softness, resulting from a battle successfully fought by six hundred and fifty men, not against other men, nor against any office-devised quotas, but against the worst that nature could devise in her warfare on mankind. And I took note of the still more intangible spiritual profit gained by the individual men through their comradeship and co-operation as the Southern Ocean did its worst.

On the debit side I put, first, my little friend Dornoch and his terrible, lonely, and inexplicable death in the icy sea. This was in no way the fault of the owners, but would they, I wondered, mention his loss as an item of consequence when they computed the results of the voyage? I saw a hefty viking, maimed for life, and some others badly hurt, lying in my sick bay, enduring their pain and discomfort cheerfully at first, but gradually reduced to moaning babes as the months wore on and their evacuation to comfort and proper treatment for their injuries was considered 'impracticable' by company officials who were 'thoroughly satisfied' with the medical service 'they' provided. I saw a procession of lesser injured men who had only lost a finger or two, or scarred themselves with burns, or damaged an eye, or broken the odd bone, in the struggle to reach the quota. And I saw an immense labour by hundreds of dog-weary men, going on for months without slackening for cold, or gale, or blizzard — without much financial reward, and with no reward in the way of thanks.

But when I presented to Mansell the vague outline of my balance sheet, he queried this last item. 'Sure — the owners appreciate what we do!' he maintained. At the end of twenty-five years' service each whaleman receives a letter of thanks and, of course, the alarm clock. 'That's mine on the shelf over there. It must have cost them about seventeen shillings and sixpence!'

Nevertheless, the balance sheet I made out for the whalemen, like that made out by the owners, showed a huge profit at the end of the season; and their quota, reckoned in hard labour, resistance to difficulty, cheerfulness, and capacity to endure, had been far exceeded.

Came Sunday, and we were still five thousand barrels short, but at midnight Gyle 'advised' the manager to cease all whaling. A signal immediately went out to all the catchers, instructing them to come in with any whales they might have taken before midnight, then refuel and proceed to South Georgia for refitting and laying up for the winter. By a strange coincidence, though the night was 'blacker than the heart of a whaling inspector,' as somebody put it, and the weather was fairly heavy, nearly every gunner had succeeded in killing a whale just before midnight struck; so the factory had a dozen or so whales to deal with on Monday morning.

Thor, as he had brought in the first, delivered to us the last whale of the season. Then he came aboard the factory himself, the first time in five months he had left his tiny ship, his job completed for another year. I was an interested eavesdropper when Gyle and Thor, senior inspector and leading gunner, met on the flensing-deck beside the last two whales. They had not seen each other for months, though their radio communications had been frequent and at times blasphemous.

'Well, Thor,' Gyle opened the conversation, 'it comes to around fifty-two years this season, by my reckoning!'

'Na-a-a-w, commander! Not a day over thirty-five, I promise you,' Thor protested, looking most distressed. I, the eavesdropper, who knew some things our astute inspector did not know, was inclined to think that even Gyle was making an underestimate, for the period of years they were discussing was the total prison sentence Thor had earned through the season for technical breaches of the whaling convention, at the mandatory maximum of three months for each offence — always provided the inspector was able to prove his offences and chose to report them.

'What about the sei whale that "got away" when you were fast-fish on the twenty-second of January?' Gyle asked with assumed nonchalance. 'Leading gunners don't take sei whales, do they? They consider themselves above such small game, and to bring one in might have spoiled your reputation.'

'The rope broke, commander, I swear it.' Thor looked like a novice making his first confession.

'I saw the rope,' Gyle interrupted him. 'The cleanest break I ever saw — and, if it should have been assisted by a knife, that alone would be worth five years' clink on various counts, wouldn't it? And by the way — how the hell *do* you cut a nylon fore-runner with a whale on it without killing yourself as you do so?'

'You don't use a knife, you use an axe,' Thor began to explain with enthusiasm to his fellow seaman. 'You carry the rope round a bollard, then you stand on top the bollard with your axe like this.' He leaped on an adjacent projection from the deck to demonstrate. 'But I didn't cut that sei whale adrift, inspector! You ask my boys——'

'I know if I asked them their story would be identical with yours,' Gyle remarked dryly. 'But what about these two whales you've just brought in? That fin's two feet under length, if ever there was a short whale, and that makes your fifteenth under size this season — though you've never shot a lactating whale with calf, I will admit, which is the only reason I remain friends with a hardened criminal like yourself. . . . And that other whale's not more than three hours dead, although the season finished twelve hours ago. I *thought* I heard a harpoon gun bang somewhere sou'west of us around breakfast time this morning!'

'Na-a-a-w, inspector! I got that fin about eleven o'clock last night, and the blue half an hour before that — you ask my lads!'

'You're training your lads up to be poachers just like yourself,' said Gyle. And then he was serious: 'But look, Thor! This is your last season of carrying on the way you do. Next season every offence, however trivial or unavoidable, is going in the log, and you *will* be for the high jump when we get home. You see, I want to put in a report against the outrageous way the Russians seem to be ignoring the convention, and how the hell can I do so when you leave *us* wide open to criticism the way you do? Stick by the rules a bit more next year, for Christ sake, even though some of them are ridiculous, and even though you know I can't catch you out when you break them.'

'I'll try, commander' — Thor was honestly repentant when it was put to him this way — 'but, when they're blowing all round you, it's difficult not to let fly. Look at those two bastards out to port now, inspector. If you weren't here, I'd be off to take a crack at them right now, even though some clerk in Sandefiord says I mustn't!'

He pointed to two whales spouting close to the factory and

lying carelessly awash, enjoying life, as though they also had received word — as perhaps in some mysterious way they had — that the season was over and the deadly little catchers clustered around were now harmless small vessels with unloaded and dismantled guns.

'I know how it is, Thor,' sympathized Gyle, seaman and whaleman himself. 'And, by the way, I haven't congratulated you yet on your catch this season. I'm glad you beat that ill-mannered, ignorant clod, Gunner Jansen, who's sent in three lactating females this season. . . Now let's have a look at this blue of yours; it's the last whale of the season, so I won't point out that it's a day or two older than twelve hours and certainly wasn't done in last night. Off the record — how long have you had it stowed to leeward of an iceberg?'

'Only a couple of days, inspector. I never keep them longer than that. But mine's not the last whale, remember. There's still the fender whale to come, and that's five days old if it's a minute.'

He was right. When his two whales were dealt with, and when all the catchers and small craft had refuelled and departed, there still remained the really last whale of the season — that one which had lain alongside the factory for nearly a week, acting as a buffer between large and small ships. The law stated that all whales shall be on the deck of the factory ship within thirty-three hours of their killing except 'those whales used as fenders'; for them there is no time limit within which they may be added to the edible or other oils.

At the risk of making my reader sick, I shall try to describe this whale as it went down into the cookers.

It had 'exploded' some two days before. That is to say, the accumulated gases from the decay of its intestines had burst its mighty belly wide open with a report like a cannon shot and an outrush of putrid fumes like the discharge from fifty morgues. The blubber, last thing to decay, was in fairly good shape, but I saw one flenser — a hardened man of many years' experience — go quietly to the rail and vomit overside when he stripped off the first piece of blubber and encountered the stinking mass beneath.

The flesh was grey, semi-liquefied, and fell in slobbers on the deck as the blubber was removed; but it was being put down the cookers, into the oil, while inspectors, chemists, and a disgusted doctor stood helplessly by, frustrated by an absurd quibble in an otherwise sensible and beneficial international law.

'What's the use of keeping a watch on every whale through the season to ensure it's processed within the thirty-three hours the law allows, when the law also allows any whale, however putrid, to go down into the tanks, provided it has been used as a fender?' muttered Gyle as he walked away from the repellent scene.

Then Davison appeared on the flensing-deck, with no law to back him, nor any other authority to support him except that he was Davison, bosun of the ship and the most experienced Shelty whaleman afloat.

'Keep that whale down aft!' he ordered the men operating the winches, who were heaving the stinking carcass through Hell's Gates for final disposal on the forrard plan. Then he addressed the flensers: 'Now just flense that whale again, and strip off all that rotten flesh — you'll have to cut down nearly a foot to reach the burnt part — and heave it all over the side. And if I see another spoonful o' that muck going down the cookers, ye'll all be lacking a job next season, for there's none of you will sail with me!'

When the fetid outer flesh was cut from the whale, Davison showed me what he meant by the 'burnt' part, which he grudgingly, but on sound hygienic principles, permitted to join the oil. It was a strange phenomenon, which I had seen before in the farmyard dung-heap and in the bacteriological laboratory, but never to this degree. The bacterial action in the decaying whale carcass raises heat just as it does in the disintegrating heap of compost or in the culture tube on the bacteriologist's rack. But in the case of the whale the heat is so intense, and so well insulated by the thick blubber from escape by conduction or radiation, that the deeper layers of meat are actually cooked, rendered sterile, and sometimes even charred by the intense activity of millions of billions of heat-producing bacteria. Davison invited me to put my hand deep into the flank muscle of the old fender whale, and I withdrew it with a yelp of pain, for the underlying flesh was blistering hot. Then he offered to share with me a well-done — almost overdone — steak that he cut from the muscles of the back; but this I declined, for I had just seen and smelled the oven that cooked the steak.

'That's why we always speak of a "burnt" whale, and never a rotten one, doctor,' the old whaleman explained. 'And maybe,' he added in his philosophic way, 'if some of the people at home who think we whalemen are a rotten, useless lot were to cut a bit deeper, they would find plenty good clean stuff underneath — though perhaps a bit charred!'

When the last burnt whale was stowed, there began a furious activity on the bridge. Telegraphs clanged, buzzers buzzed, and whistles screeched for half an hour or so. I consulted old Davy on the significance of this outburst.

'It means this, doctor,' he told me — and proceeded to make the only partisan and chauvinistic statement I had heard from him during the whole trip, as he handled his difficult binational, bilingual crew. 'It means we are again a British ship, sailing on a voyage under proper maritime law — instead of a bloody butcher's shop with a squarehead manager, wallowing in the Southern Ocean; and you'll see what I mean in an hour or two!'

I did. I went up on the bridge to see it happen. Mark was busy when I arrived, testing out all his navigational apparatus in preparation for our eight-thousand-mile homeward voyage. Before I arrived, he had smartened up his mates and cadets, and I noticed that they were again taking orders without comment or argument — they were seamen again, and not whalemen any longer. Mark then ordered a lifeboat drill — the first since the whaling had commenced — from which no person aboard was exempt, though some of the gunners, now passengers, had to be assisted from their bunks to the boats. All the boats were inspected, and the emergency rum (stowed in them months before, but long since filched and drunk by cunning old whalemen) was replaced. The morphine kept in the boats against emergencies was also returned. It had been quietly removed by a petty officer and handed to me for safe-keeping early in the voyage because, he explained, his 'crazy lads would try anything when they were bored,' and morphine might do them 'mair harm than the rum.' Then Mark sent word to the chief engineer that, if the water-tight doors were not replaced on the collision bulkheads immediately (they had been removed, and damn the Board of Trade, to make access to the factory decks easier while the whaling was in progress), there would be a log entry in the morning.

After all of which Mark considered the ship fit to sail, so, laying his course for South Georgia, he rang for full ahead.

As soon as he did so, it was as though a telepathic message had been broadcast throughout the ship, for both watches — all hands, in fact — appeared on deck simultaneously. And, to my astonishment, they were all armed with axes, crow-bars, jemmies, and other fearsome weapons, and all had grim, set faces. Davison saw my amazement and reassured me about the ugly scene with a smile. It was no mutiny, but an annual event on every factory ship — the destruction of the 'plan,' or timber platform covering the permanent decks, on which the whales had been hacked and carved throughout the season.

Andra, the mate, appeared in person and gave the order in a loud and solemn shout, like a curfew-crier: 'Pull up the plan!' he cried to the horde of grim armed men who stood waiting. This was the signal that the months of slavery and isolation were over and we were homeward bound. The whalemen set to. Led by Davison wielding the biggest axe I have ever seen, they smashed at the whaling-deck, tore up the blood- and *grax*-sodden timbers, and hurled them overboard. Some of the men worked silently, having no breath for anything but their furious revenge on the platform upon which they had slaved through the hard season. Others emitted savage cries in Norski or Scots or Gaelic as they tore up the planks, while a third group addressed each individual timber with a quiet, cold malevolence as they hove them overside. But all hacked like crazy barbarians destroying

231

some temple of a faith they hated, and in half an hour or so the huge mass of stinking timber was miles astern of us, left to be purified, if that were possible, as flotsam in the icy Southern Ocean.

When the plan was cleared, our ship resumed an appearance that we had forgotten. Our white teak decks, easy and pleasant to walk upon, reappeared from under a mountain of filth, and we could not at first accustom ourselves to them. For days we still walked across them on the spiked heels of our sea-boots, whaleman fashion, expecting to slip in a greasy puddle of *grax* at any moment. Then such strange nautical customs as the telling of each half-hour by bell, and the morning inspection of the ship by master, chief engineer, mate, and surgeon, and the pleasant custom of the officers meeting each Sunday morning for a dram, were all resumed.

The crew, now with plenty of time on their hands, began gathering in a social way again, the Norskis to play their guitars and sing dreary songs about mother, the Shelties to read the Bible and hold their austere religious conventicles, and the mainland Scots for gambling sessions during which large slices of the hard-earned bonus illegally changed hands.

But there was still one ordeal to go through before we became a 'normal' ship again. This was the 'purification' of the ship by ancient methods, and the eradication of every vestige of the whale and everything that might remind the whalemen of the enemy they had fought through the Antarctic summer. This consisted of washing every portion of deck and upper works of the ship, and every small area or object that might have come in contact with a whale, in strong caustic.

The procedure was a dangerous one — I had many men along to see me with caustic burns during the days this nonsense went on, and some who came just in time to save their sight when the contents of Andra's cauldron of corrosion splashed into their eyes. It was also an unnecessary, purely symbolic, and — in my considered medical opinion — entirely useless procedure, for nothing on earth other than total destruction by fire could make a whaling ship bacteriologically sterile at the end of the season. But, when I remonstrated with Andra and Davison, they advised me to shut up. This caustic bath had been given to every whaling ship since the first Phoenician came home towing a dead whale, and would always be given. It had become a sort of semi-religious ritual, and the whalemen dearly loved to celebrate it.

I accepted that, but I became seriously cross at one incident during the ceremony when one of the most valuable things we were bringing home was sacrificed to the mumbo-jumbery. On the tiny deck outside my cabin there had reposed for months three buckets, each with a large notice on the lid: 'Please Do Not Touch' printed in both English and Norwegian. Some crazy whaleman, during the purification ceremony, looked into the buckets and found that they contained bits of whale; they were therefore loathsome and taboo, and over the side they went. They contained the whales' eyes, with muscles attached (something that no learned man has ever examined before), which Davison had carefully dissected out for me during the season, that I might take them home to the Nuffield Medical Research Foundation, which badly wanted them for a purpose I knew about. I cannot help hoping that the whaleman who (jokingly, no doubt) heaved them overboard will some day develop an ocular palsy, from which the line of research being followed on whales' eyes might have saved him!

While the frenzy of cleaning ship went on above, a similar orgy of cleanliness was going on below in the factory. There the job was more difficult, for, though every bit of deck and machinery was hosed down with sea water and the symbolic caustic and then (engineers being more rational in these matters than seamen) run over with live steam or a blow lamp and finally repainted, there were a million crannies where the dank cod-liver-oil smell of stale whale could still hang around, without sunlight and sea wind to finish the job. MacDonald and his boys worked on the problem with the same labour and ingenuity they had put into their work during the season, and within a few days even the Rosedown and Butterworth plants smelled sweet to *our* nostrils. (But how unsuccessful the factory men really were with their 'purification' was seen some six weeks later when the minister of the Seamen's Mission in Liverpool, first visitor to our home-coming ship, stopped at the top of the ladder leading to our spotless repainted factory, with the remark: 'Peugh! What a stench!')

However, by the exacting standards of Andra and MacDonald, and thanks mainly to the unlimited supply of sea water Davison kept pumping into every corner of the ship for days after the caustic ballyhoo had subsided, when we sailed into South Georgia, the whaleman's island, we were a clean ship.

And when we stepped ashore on the island — the first solid land we had felt beneath our feet for five months — though we probably stank to high heaven, we felt clean ourselves.

XIV

SOUTH ATLANTIC SLUM

South Georgia is permanently inhabited and is an important seat of the
whaling industry.

—Whitaker's Almanack

THE year is 1951. The war has been over for five years, but the
British people are still strictly rationed and a large part of the
world is still hungry. The government has just extricated itself
from a fantastically expensive and totally unsuccessful effort to
relieve the world shortage of fats and proteins by developing the
ground-nuts production of East Africa. General Perón is being
as awkward as only an Argentinian can be about the British
colonies in the Southern Ocean, and one of the whalebones of
contention is that place which is probably the greatest single
source of edible oils in the Empire since the failure of the ground-
nuts scheme — the tiny island of South Georgia.

That is the background to the news when we return to the
island, and it seems to us that our little island, though isolated, is
become a pretty important place, worthy of a few headlines in the
bundles of old newspapers awaiting us in our mail. But though
the headlines are all shouting 'Food! Food! Food!', we search
in vain for even a two-line back-page mention of the whaling
fleets or the island on which they are based.

South Georgia was in the news in 1922, when Shackleton died
there. It has scarcely been heard of since, and one can only
speculate as to whether this is due to its alleged remoteness and
inaccessibility, or whether there has, in some quarters, been a
deliberate policy of reticence concerning the island and its
economic importance, in recent years. It was never big news in
hungry post-war Britain, and one wonders why. Ministers of
Food never went dashing out there to take a personal look into

this very important Empire food-basket; itinerant Members of Parliament interested in colonial affairs have never dropped in on the island to examine its administration and capabilities of development; delegations of British trade unions have never been sent out to inquire on the spot into the working conditions of the many hundreds of British seamen and tradesmen whose jobs are tied up with the island; and — most unfortunately perhaps — no British newspaper has, for many years at least, assigned a professional reporter to 'cover' South Georgia.

The result is that the British people probably know no more today about this hugely important island possession than they can learn from *Whitaker's Almanack*. Maybe it is time they did. But if it is to be told them by a private individual who paid but two brief visits to the island, and those several years ago, care must be exercised in the telling. For there may be those who, failing to understand or appreciate the tenor of this book, will be outraged if I allow my composite non-existent whaling characters to describe the island in the colourful way that is the whalemen's wont, who will demand absolute accuracy in my description of the things I saw on the island that appalled me, and who will challenge me if I slip up on any detail and will sue at the drop of a hat.

And so, for the nonce, I shall leave Gyle and Mansell and Mark and Old Burnett and the hundreds of whaling characters whom they represent, to rest a while on board the factory ship, and, with my hat clutched tightly in my hand, I shall take my reader ashore with me to see exactly what I saw of some of the conditions that face the men who work on the island of South Georgia, the Empire's greatest and most lucrative whaling base.

The year, I repeat, is 1951. I am told that improvements have been made since then, and, resisting the impulse to say: 'And high time too!' I will simply acknowledge that much of my description might not apply today, and congratulate whoever it is that has at last realized the necessity, so obvious in 1951, of doing more for the welfare of the whalemen based on the island.

And now let us step ashore again onto the island, this time to examine it as the 'important seat of the whaling industry,' but thankful that we are going to put our feet on solid ground again, after months at sea.

The solid ground is a disappointment. We do not go into any dock nor alongside any wharf, but tie up to a vessel grounded in the mud at the head of an offal-filled bay. It does not take a seaman to guess that this ship cannot be far off her half century, but I note from the ensign drooping from her stern that she is still in commission. The man who shows me the way across her canted junk-littered decks informs me that she is a very famous ship, for it was aboard her, some time before I was born, that the notorious Dr. Crippen was arrested, the first criminal, history states, to be apprehended through the agency of wireless telegraphy.

I clamber down an insecure gangway, and set foot on the main jetty. The thought occurs to me that this jetty of Britain's greatest whaling base is a structure of which the poorest fishing port of Scotland would be ashamed. There is a narrow gauge railtrack, such as one finds in coal-mines, leading up from the jetty in amongst the huddled jumble of factory buildings, oil tanks, and tin sheds of which this permanent British settlement seems to consist. There is no road, footpath, or other track for the passage of men that I can see, so I step gingerly from sleeper to sleeper on this rickety railtrack which must have carried many millions of pounds' worth of material over many years, and must have carried as much food and other necessaries into the hungry post-war British housewife's shopping basket as any track of its size in the world. But I am careful not to miss my step on the sleepers, for if I do so I shall not land on the solid earth my ship-weary legs are craving, but more probably into a knee-deep pool of grey sludge, the composition of which I would not dare to describe to my reader in case his lunch or supper should be imminent.

This, I remind myself, is the main thoroughfare through Britain's greatest whaling station. This is the main artery of one

of the most important modern industries. I bethink me of Robert
Burns's couplet:

> Your poor narrow footpath of a street,
> Where twa wheel-barrows tremble when they meet,

. . . and I try to think what Burns would have made of a main
thoroughfare which *one* wheel-barrow would not dare to face.

But Burns, like everybody else who walks up that 'street' for
the first time, would have been more concerned with the smell
than with the road-making. I am accustomed to the smell of a
factory ship, and it would take the pen of a Burns to describe
that, but the smell of this shore station is incredible even to a far-
travelled doctor whose olfactory education has not been neglected. One cannot, of course, lay blame for this, for whaling is a
stinking business, but one feels that a little ingenuity and expense might do something to relieve the filth and stink, and it
should not be an insuperable problem of sanitary engineering to
remove, or at least render innocuous, some of the unbelievable
amount of decaying organic matter that collects in and around a
whaling station, not for days, as on a factory ship, but for weeks,
months, years, and — in the case of this long-established station
— decades.

At last I find one fairly well-coagulated rod of mud, and step-
ping off the bogie-track I take a look round. I see one house
which, at a pinch, might be spared condemnation by a con-
scientious borough surveyor of a dilapidated suburb, but I can
see nothing else which I, as a doctor, would pass as a fit permanent residence for human beings, even in an equable climate.
However, I think my standards are probably too high, based as
they are on many years' experience of British Army billets and
bivouacs in peace and war; and I remind myself that this highly
productive island has only been a British colony since the days of
Captain Cook, and the chief British settlement on it has only been
inhabited for several decades, and may be temporary to the extent
that it might have to pack up before the end of this century.

So I give a quizzical nod to the Union Jack flying over the one presentable habitation I can see, and pass on to try to find out where and how the whalemen live.

It is difficult. In the first place, the friendly bogie-line I am following suddenly grovels into a rusty shed, and I can only proceed by wading through a morass of grey sludge, noticing as I do so that strings of bubbles come up where my sea-boots disturb it. Being of a scientific disposition, I stir up one puddle with one of the many old bits of iron lying around, and set a match to the huge glug of bubbles that emerges. It ignites, and burns with a ghostly blue flame. I don't need to ask a chemist what that means!

The second difficulty is finding my way, even though the whaling port is only a few acres in area. I stop a workman, whom, by the length of his beard, I judge to be nearing the end of the compulsory eighteen months' residence in the South laid down by the whaling companies. I ask him to direct me to the things that interest me most in this important seat of the whaling industry: to the social centre, or bar, or canteen, or whatever, where the whalemen spend the dreary winter evenings during the six months that no ship comes near the island; to the library; to the cinema; to the barracks or cantonments, presumably outside the stink of the whaling station, where the men sleep; to any gardens or recreation grounds or places not directly concerned with the business of making money out of whale oil that there might be in this important British whaling station; *and* to any church, chapel, or place set aside to non-commercial, never mind spiritual, observances in this Christian community.

The bearded one plods off down an alleyway even sludgier than the one in which I am standing, and as he disappears round the corner of a rusty tin hut he says nothing, but I can hear his laughter long after he has dived into his 'doss' at the end of the hut and is telling the two whalemen who share it with him about the nut who has come down this trip expecting to find something civilized on South Georgia.

I go on unguided. I find the library. The reading matter provided for the whalemen cut off for eighteen months from all newspapers, magazines, and normal day-to-day reading, amounts, I am proudly told by those who claim to have supplied it, to nearly *1800* volumes! And this library of one of the Empire's most important outposts is added to, they tell me, by no fewer than 150 volumes every year. (I glance round as I write at the very modest and insufficient library of about 2000 volumes that I have myself collected since I returned to Scotland and think of the more widely reading men whom I met on South Georgia.) And when I consider the munificent annual contribution of what does not even approximate to one volume per man in the South, the imp in me cannot help visualizing the scene — hypothetical, I hasten to add — in which each whaleman is handed his volume with the words: 'Now there's your book! Get down to South Georgia for eighteen months and read it!' And, of course, though I hesitate to say this of Britain's greatest whaling station, rather more than half the books are written in Norwegian.

There is a cinema. It is financed mainly by the whalemen out of their own pockets, so one should not perhaps criticize it too harshly; but it is rather a pathetic gesture of defiance on their part, signifying that even in their isolation they are not bereft of the major amusement of civilization. I examine the cinema, again judging it against my rather high standards, and find it rather inferior to the worst NAAFI 'gaff' I ever inspected in the temporary camp of a British regiment. I am told that there are no fewer than seventeen films on the island at this time, so I attend the performance of the most recent to arrive. I find myself viewing a newsreel of events that occurred months before I left the U.K., and then yawning through an unedifying film I saw some two years before at a second-rate (but rather cleaner) Arab cinema in an out-of-the-way Middle East town.

I leave the pathetic little 'Kino' and seek the bar or club-room or social centre or whatnot of the hundreds of men working on the station. I do not find it. It does not exist. I am somewhat astonished, but of course my standards are high. I know that in the Scottish Highlands, for example, where many industrial camps are being set up not two months but only two hours from civilization, a club-room or social centre for the isolated workers is the first thing the Welfare Officer of the firm concerned demands, and gets. I ask where I will find the Welfare Officer of the whaling station, and I am answered by another bearded chuckle.

I ask about church, or chapel, or any institution provided by government, or industrial interests, or missionary enterprise, directed to some higher purpose than the production of more whale oil. And to this question the bearded one does not reply with laughter. For, like the majority of the whalemen on the island, be they Shelty or Scowegian or reckless hard-swearing mainland Scots, he is a man on whose life, for better or worse, religion has made a deep and ineradicable impression.

He tells me that not only is there no place in this long-established whaling station set aside for any spiritual — or, on a lesser plane, for any cultural or morally advancing enterprises — but he knows of no meeting ever called for any higher purpose than to make whoopee or to discuss matters concerning production and money, certainly since he came to the island eighteen months ago, and, from what he hears, since the whaling station was founded. There is, however, a church with an organ near the Argentinian whaling station at Grytviken.

But the total absence of public works; the apparent complete lack of government interest in this permanent and, financially and nutritionally, important British base; the cultural and educational neglect of the most (unnecessarily) isolated British community in the world; the collapse — for it once did exist — of any spiritual aid or moral betterment that any church of any denomination might have given to the island . . . I become almost incoherent when I begin to list the wrongs I see patched on the bottom of this 'important seat of the whaling industry.'

So let me wade a few yards farther through the main street of the British whaling industry until I come to the one place in a sordid and neglected British colony which I feel privileged and qualified to criticize without fear of refutation — the 'hospital.'

The 'hospital' I visit caters for all sick and injured men from two shore stations, one a large factory and the other an engineering and ship-repair yard, and for the crews manning the small ships operating from the shore station. But it is also the only place to which the seriously ill and injured from two large whaling fleets, each of about sixteen vessels, can be evacuated during the whaling season. Since accidents are frequent and severe in the whaling business, and since there is no provision for evacuating casualties from the island except to hospitals in the U.K. or Norway, thousands of miles away and often many months later, I expect to find something really outstanding in the way of pocket hospitals, for surely the sick, if they are denied removal, deserve the highest standard of medical and nursing aid.

Again, my standards are too high, and I am disappointed. The very 'hospital' itself is difficult to find, for it is tucked away right in the middle of the stench and sludge of the whaling station, and is scarcely distinguishable from the grimy sheds and factory buildings all round it. Inside, things are better. Some attempt has been made by obviously devoted people to turn two or three small rooms which surely were never designed for medical purposes, into some semblance of wards, sideroom, and dispensary-cum-operating-theatre.

There are several patients lying around, and it does not take a doctor to see that the condition of some of them would seem to justify continuous and expert nursing care. Certainly they seem to be getting it, for the whole appearance of the little ward, with its austerely uncomfortable beds, shining brass ash-trays one would not dare to use, and flowers too well disciplined to wilt, suggests that Sister has just swept through on her daily blitz in preparation for Matron's rounds.

But there is no Matron, no Sister, nor any nurse or trained attendant of any kind in this little 'hospital.' The immaculate and well-conducted little ward is the charge of a mess-boy, who, other than the doctor in single-handed medical charge of two whaling stations, is, at this time, the total staff of the 'hospital.' And the mess-boy's whole training in nursing consists of what the doctor has given him on the island.

(I hasten to add that the establishment of this, probably the most isolated British 'hospital' in the world, normally includes a 'diakon' or semi-trained Norwegian male-nurse, in addition to the doctor, but at the time I visit the hospital there is no diakon.)

I meet the single-handed doctor, and find that he at least is a more than adequate factor in the island's inadequate medical organization. Certainly he is a German whose name has not as yet been admitted to the British Medical Register, but (I am told) his employment in territory administered by the Falkland Islands government is quite legitimate, and he is none the worse a doctor because the Medical Council does not accept him. In fact, when I see his work and hear of the appalling difficulties he has faced in trying unaided to maintain a decent standard of medical and surgical care for the isolated whalemen during the long South Georgia winter, I am bound to admit that I know of no duly registered practitioner who could have done as well. And when he, the German, is bitingly critical of the medical arrangements, or lack of them, on this British island, I am silent, for I have already seen enough to know that his criticisms are more than justified.

He shows me round his 'hospital,' and allows me to examine his more seriously ill patients whilst he tells me their histories. There lies in a corner of the 'ward' a patient suspended in an amateurish but ingenious orthopaedic frame constructed by the doctor himself with the help of the station's carpenters. This unfortunate chap was smashed up weeks ago in an accident at his work. He is destined to lie there for weeks to come, until it is economically expedient to evacuate him aboard a slow transport vessel to an orthopaedic hospital at the other end of the earth. There is a man convalescing from an operation for strangulated hernia, a grave surgical emergency with which, anaesthetic and all, the doctor had successfully dealt, aided by his devoted messboy. There was another doctor on the island when this happened, the doctor tells me, over at the Argentinian whaling station of Grytviken, but the weather of South Georgia does not adjust itself to surgical emergencies, and on the many occasions during the winter when the doctor could have done with some help more skilled than that of his mess-boy, he was completely cut off from his Argentinian colleague by gale or ice.

There are two patients in this pathetic little 'hospital' suffering from gross burns, one burned off duty and the other in the course of his work in the factory. Now of all injuries, burns are those that most require a sterile aseptic atmosphere for their successful treatment, and the middle of a whaling station is probably the most septic and infection-raddled environment in which a doctor has ever been expected to treat such lesions; but — although, of course, skin-grafting and delicate plastic surgery such as these patients require is, in the circumstances, outwith the doctor's power — he has, with the elementary apparatus at his disposal, even succeeded in healing some of the burns without very great scarring.

Since I mention the elementary nature of the apparatus and equipment of this 'hospital,' I had better again explain that my standards are high. I have been accustomed during a large part of my life to the scale and quality of apparatus supplied for the medical care of British troops, and since this isolated whaling station 'hospital' is equipped rather less lavishly than the small Field Dressing Stations I have commanded, I am (perhaps) over-critical.

And the year, I repeat again, is 1951, and improvements have been made on the island of South Georgia since I saw it. I hope and trust that some of these improvements have been in connection with medical matters.

Before I finish criticizing this island and get back to my cheerful whaling characters, let me comment on two things: first, the excuses I have heard advanced for conditions on the island in 1951; and secondly, who, if anybody, was to blame for these conditions existing in an old-established British colony right on into the post-war years.

The inaccessibility of the island is the first and most frequent excuse put forward. But how inaccessible is it really? It certainly was a hundred years ago, when sealers and whalers began to use

244

it as a base; but this reputation seems to have been fostered and maintained into the modern age, when nowhere else in the world, at least if it is of similar commercial importance, is regarded as difficult of access all year round, and impossible to approach for nearly six months of the year.

For South Georgia is not in the remote Antarctic as most people imagine. In fact it lies on the same degree of Latitude South that Lancaster lies in Latitude North. It is not nearly as far by sea from the United Kingdom as is, say, Malaya; and its economic importance would seem to justify some sort of regular mail and transport service independent of the whaling companies, were it only three or four times a year. I am told that an air link with the island is not feasible (though I am also told by a Squadron-Leader (Ret.) whom I meet on the island, that its landlocked harbours are perfect bases for Sunderland flying-boats).

But feasible or not, there is a regular commercial air service as far as Montevideo, and a businessman in a hurry can reach the island in about four days— so there seems little justification for taking four months and often longer to evacuate a gravely injured whaleman to a civilized hospital.

There is the excuse that whaling is an impermanent, chancy sort of business, run on a year-to-year basis, and it would therefore be absurd to set up permanent institutions or install government services other than a skeleton administration on an island which, within the next few years, may be abandoned again to the seals and the penguins. Well! . . . That's what they were saying around 1850 when the whaling and sealing companies began to use the island; and no doubt it is the excuse that will still be used during the next century, when, every year, another forty or fifty million pounds' worth of whale products will be gleaned from the Southern Ocean.

An excuse put to me by a responsible person for the appalling state of the main British whaling station on the island is that it is badly sited geographically, because it is built (or bogged down, as one might put it) on the effluent into the sea of the rain and melted snow from a huge catchment area of mountain and glacier. Well! again . . . it has been there for a good many years, and I don't think ground rents or the purchase price of land in South Georgia are exorbitant enough to preclude moving it, or at least building new installations in a more salubrious place, instead of in the same fetid slough.

But it is when we come to examine the question of who is to blame for the unnecessarily grim conditions on South Georgia in 1951 that we meet with the silliest and most unacceptable excuses.

Let us leave the dramatic present of 1951 for the historic past of subsequent years to examine them.

When I came home I was convinced that the whaling people themselves had to share at least equal responsibility with government and administration for what seemed to me, at least from the medical and hygienic point of view, the rotten state of this British colony. Appalled as I was by the neglect of the whalemen in the South, I spent some three months in working out a basic scheme which would give the whalemen a medical and welfare service, of a standard lower certainly than any homeside industrial workers would accept, but the minimum that isolated men in a dangerous occupation might expect a humane modern world to provide for them.

I discussed the project with dozens of whalemen of all ranks, listened to their amendments and, in every case, to their enthusiastic approval. Then I submitted an outline of the scheme to an important whaling company, suggesting that they might set the badly needed ball rolling and start getting other companies, the governments concerned, and perhaps the churches and other benevolent institutions, to co-operate in trying to provide at least a medical service worthy of the important and growing industry.

This, quoted verbatim, is the reply I received to my proposals concerning the proper treatment or disposal of badly injured whalemen:

'With regard to your proposal in attached appendix, we must inform you that we consider this both impracticable and unsuitable for the conditions. Evacuation to the civilized world at any time is economically impossible, and this is accepted by whalers throughout the industry.'

I wonder who else in the modern world would dare to make that statement? Consider the public outcry there would be if we were told that the evacuation to the civilized world of men wounded in Malaya is at any time economically impossible! And in what other dangerous industry would it be 'accepted' that no matter how gravely a man might be injured at his work, no move would be made to evacuate him to a civilized hospital until it was economically convenient, and that he must make do with the rudimentary aid that a single doctor can give him in a sick bay in the middle of the factory where he was injured?

I met the man who put his signature to that astonishing statement.

'Well, look, doc!' he said. 'Were you never in the services during the war? If you were, you must have seen many worse things than you've seen on the whaling!'

To this impertinence I disdained to reply that I had been on active service in three wars, and I had *never* seen a wounded man treated with the casual disregard the whalemen were alleged to 'accept'. I did not point out to him that whaling is not war, but highly remunerative modern industry. Nor did I bother to tell him that in twenty years of medicine, practised mainly in the difficult and dangerous parts of the world, this was the only occasion when the economic excuse was ever put to me for failure to evacuate the gravely ill and injured to civilization.

Now who was to blame? Not the whaling companies entirely, though it is little enough they have done to get together and provide a comprehensive medical and welfare service for their men in the South. The governments concerned have surely some responsibility in the matter, and the British administration of the Falkland Islands Dependencies is the government agency principally concerned. And South Georgia is *not* —let it be for once and ever understood — a barren Antarctic rock, but is, for its size, one of the wealthiest British colonies.

So some blame must surely attach to a government which draws a large revenue from the island in everything from customs dues on all the whale oil that passes through it, to income tax on the whalemen working there, yet only provides postal and telegraphic services in return. Apart from the magistrate himself, the Civil Establishment consists of two customs officers, a constable, the officer-in-charge of the Radio Station, and two operators and four meteorologists whose salaries constitute the only evidence of government expenditure on the island.

Again, the health service is the thing I am best qualified to criticize, and in 1951 it was easy to do so — for there was none. There was no government hospital, no government doctor, no nurse, not even a sanitary inspector, on the island. There was no health service in this British colony to criticize.

There is a final, but gentler, remonstrance to make about this island. There are other parts of the world where government and industry are unable, or fail, to provide adequate bodily and spiritual care for the inhabitants. But in those places the churches, missions, and benevolent societies usually step in to make up the deficiencies. They have not, for many years, set foot on South Georgia. As I have said, there is no priest or pastor or organized religious activity on the island; there is no Seamen's Mission, although there is a greater need for one than in any port I have visited.

In the high latitudes of the North there is that magnificent organization, the Grenfell Society, to which government and industry safely trust the medical care and evacuation, the bodily and spiritual welfare of all those on isolated stations in Labrador and far beyond. There is, alas, no such organization interested in the men isolated in high latitudes in the South. Perhaps there may be some responsible institution somewhere which would cater for the needs of the Southern Ocean whalemen, if it but knew about them.

And perhaps there is somebody who could examine, criticize, and ask questions about the way of life on an isolated British colony, without having to keep his hat clutched tightly in his hand.

XV

THE OTHER SHORE

'What matters it how far we go?'
his scaly friend replied,
'There is another shore, you know,
upon the other side.'

—THE MOCK TURTLE

I MET the whalemen first in a pub. And it was in a pub that I was to bid them farewell.

Our ship was tied up in Liverpool docks, the spoils of our voyage being pumped and heaved ashore, and we had cleaned ourselves of all but the smell of whale, put on uncomfortable clothes, drawn some money — stuff we had not handled for many months — and gone ashore to see civilization and, in our various ways, consort with the civilized world.

Some had hailed taxis and gone straight downtown to look at, to talk to, and — if all went well — to sleep with any accommodating Englishwoman who came up to their by no means undiscriminating standards. Some had dashed to telephone and telegraph to make contact with their own women at home. Some had gone to the restaurants to have at last a meal not smelling of fish and not cooked by a 'Scandahoovian can-opener'; many had gone to the barbers to have removed their beards of eight to eighteen months, and odd they looked with their rosy, baby-soft chins beneath their weathered, leathery brows and noses. And one at least — by name of Gyle — had headed straight for the Turkish baths and had emerged a few hours later, clean, almost inodorous, and dressed — the ultimate incongruity among us — in impeccable evening clothes.

Two of us remained tied to the ship while this process of 'phoenixation,' as Gyle termed it, went on. Davison, the bosun, stayed to see the cargo ashore and ensure that the shoreside crowd did not divert a few thousand pounds' worth of hard-earned oil or by-products from the whalemen's pockets to their own; and I to see my battered, weary casualties of months before safely into the ambulance cars that were at last to take them to comfortable hospital beds long overdue. And, this done, I remained to hang on to the end of the ship's telephone for a trans-atlantic call from the loveliest girl of all.

But the transatlantic operators, with their usual baffled aston-ishment, announced that the weather had beaten them again and I could expect a six-hour delay; and Davy, who knew the habits of the stevedore and reckoned that his cargo was safe until the following morning, suggested around 'opening-time' that the two of us take a turn ashore.

I suggested that we should go and seek our shipmates and see what they were up to, but Davy said there would be no need for that — they would all come to us in time, after they had met with the various disappointments that inevitably awaited them ashore. It appeared that Davy had a cousin, a retired Shelty whaleman, who kept a pub by the Liverpool docks, and Davy was prepared to wager that all our friends, no matter what luck or misfortune they might have met through their first day in civilization, would be in that pub before closing-time. So we went to await them there.

He was right. Many of them had got there before us, and, as we entered the little saloon bar of the cousin's eminently respectable pub, the sound of unmusical but unmistakable whalemen's songs from the public bar told us that some at least of the Whaler Group VIII's and the stokers had not found in Liverpool the glamour and excitement they had dreamed of for many months back, and had returned to the docks to consort with their own kind.

We had not sat long talking to Davy's cousin (a second Davy in every detail) and drinking good Scotch whisky, which tasted queer and insipid after raw plonk, when the door opened and in came a rather inebriated Mark, the man who never drank at sea, on the arm of a very sober and correct Andra. They were rapidly followed by the chief chemist and Old Burnett, the two of them having obviously arranged an armistice between science and engineering until such time as the whaleships took to sea again. And presently Victor, the storeman, arrived, accompanied by a well-dressed businessman whom I barely remembered meeting the previous September, but whom, as soon as he spoke and started shouting down all conversational opposition, I recognized, of course, as Mansell.

Gyle, off to the superb Adelphi Hotel to dine and dance with his wife, was missing, but otherwise we were the same crowd that had been assembling and talking and arguing over hundreds of days and thousands of miles as our whaleship ploughed through, or wallowed in, frozen or tropical seas. The deck now heaved under our feet in uncomfortable stillness instead of in reality, and through the window we heard the honking of car horns and the banging of trucks instead of the whine of winches and the screech of the wind; but otherwise we might have been relaxing, as we had relaxed night after night, in the farthest reaches of the Southern Ocean.

And did we talk of Liverpool, or the homes we would shortly be going to, or the friends we had met, or what had been happening in our personal or national lives while we had been away?

No. We talked of whales and whalemen. We discussed the ships we were now so glad to leave and the voyage we were so thankful was now ended. We found our own gossip about ourselves and our friends much more interesting and entertaining than anything we had heard ashore, and we retold our tales and re-enjoyed our jokes and chattered about catches and barrels and many episodes of our shipboard life.

Then two came in who were welcome and at home in our company. They were Gyle and his wife. Though wined and dined and still dressed for the ball, they had become bored with the elegant conversation of their shoreside friends, and she, as much as he, had preferred to slip away from the glitter of the Adelphi and join us in our dockside pub to talk of whales and whalemen.

'A whaleman's wife she is,' said Gyle as he introduced her, 'so she'd better get used to the company a whaleman keeps.'

Old Burnett, dismal to the last, opened our final theme of conversation before we broke up that night.

'Well, that's another eight months of life wasted' was his comment on our completed voyage. 'And eight months is a long time to take out o' the life of an old man like me. But we'll no' waste two-thirds o' many more years, for another few seasons will see the end of the whaling for ever. The whale owners will have made their pile, and they'll get out before the other sources of animal and vegetable oils steal the market. And the twelve thousand whalemen will be dumped on the beach, and will finish their lives as deck-hands and third engineers on the coastal fishing-boats, and the commander here will go back into the Navy, and the chemist will go and talk his bull to university students instead of to us, and the doctor will go to America and write a book about the queerest characters he ever met outside his loony-bins, and the brief episode of modern steam-whaling will be forgotten by those who took part in it even before the public knows there is such a thing.' Obviously John Haig was by this time getting the better of John Calvin as Old Burnett went on: 'And South Georgia will be deserted again to the seals and the penguins, and the penguins will make a rookery around the grave o' Jack Shackleton and the few hundred whalemen lying there, and——'

'Chief! For Christ sake shut up!' interrupted Gyle. 'The whaling will go on long enough for us to lay *you* in a grave hacked out of the South Georgia ice — which is the only thing that will make you really happy — and my great-grandsons and yours, too, will still be sailing south at the end of this century to put a cluster of daffodils at the foot of the Kvaerner Cooker we're going to put over you as a memorial; so don't apply for a job in the fishing-fleet yet.'

'And by that time' — the chemist took up the fantasy and followed it along his own obsessional lines — 'every whaling expedition will be commanded by a scientist, as the *Discovery II* is today, and twice as many whales will be taken every year, without harming the species, and the seamen will be made to conduct the whaling at long last in a rational way——'

'And I will then be bloody glad to accept a job as mate of a fishing-trawler!' commented Mark, only to be shushed by the now very respectable Andra, who would argue profanely and to the brink of bloodshed with any man afloat, but disapproved most strongly of any disagreement among men ashore and was horrified by the use of the whalemen's favourite adjective before a lady.

But the lady was not horrified. Taking upon herself her husband's role of outside observer and critic of the whalemen, she held the floor of that little room in the whalers' pub for a minute or two and gave us her ideas, not only of the future of the whaling industry, but of the men of all classes, professions, and nationalities who man it.

'Even though there is no money in it and the shoreside businessmen lose interest in whaling, and even if the scientists try to supplant or rationalize the industry and the governments succeed in organizing and controlling it, there will still be men who go and hunt the whale and are not happy doing anything else. Don't ask me why. Maybe it's partly because it's the biggest living thing that ever existed in the universe and therefore offers the greatest incentive to man's hunting instincts. Maybe, partly, it's because the whales live in the strangest, most inaccessible places of the globe and give you natural-born wanderers an excuse for going there after you've been everywhere else. And maybe there's more than just a breath of truth in the explanations the armchair Viennese psychologists and their followers (who would recoil in horror at the smell of a whale) would give of your conduct: that you are all suffering from death wishes and desires to re-enter the womb, which is your beloved warm ship surrounded by the cold, unfriendly ice, and that you are sublimating and rationalizing your unconscious homosexual trends by fleeing the world of women and associating for eight months of the year with nobody but men in what you are pleased to call a spirit of comradeship — and also, of course, that you are all very anxious to

253

prove to yourselves that you are big, tough men, while you are all sissies at heart. . . . But I think the real reason you go a-whaling — at least a reason far more compelling than any of these — and the reason your sons and grandsons after you will go a-whaling, too, long after whaling has ceased to be an economic necessity or even a paying hobby, is that you all have a lot in common with the whale. You are all in sympathy with him, and even, in your more revealing moments in drink and in bed, identify yourselves with him.'

'Now look here!' began Gyle, but she waved him aside and continued:

'No, let me finish. The whale is the misfit and the outcast of the animal species, isn't he? He would not adjust his weight and his stature to make himself an acceptable resident ashore with the lesser beings that frequent the dry land, so the smaller animals ganged up on him and chased him out. And, with a rather pathetic but at the same time rather magnificent gesture, he went his slow, lumbering, colossal way back to the sea. It was the only place left where he could survive, really, but he pretended he was doing it voluntarily because he had no taste for the delights of the land and preferred the sea. And you are all the same — and your grandsons, God help them, will inherit it or acquire it from you. . . . So whaling will go on!'

We were all silent after this accusatory tirade, and looked to Mansell for a reply. Surely the man who had faced a thousand whales, who had weathered endless tearing, blinding Antarctic gales, who had daunted every owner, skipper, gunner, and chief engineer for almost half a century, was not going to be struck silent by a woman's scorn.

It appeared at first that he was. He gazed disconsolately into his drink, and nothing but a few 'wa — wa's' came from him, and a faint muttering that it was probably the cow whales that drove the bulls back into the sea. But suddenly, as we all watched and waited, he slammed back his whisky, shot the cuffs of his silk shirt, gave vent to the loudest and most disconcerting Scandinavian 'U-u-u-rgh!' I have yet heard, grunted, rose to his feet, and in the most courtly manner gave the reply of us all, and of all whalemen through the ages, to the whaleman's wife:

'And so long, madame, as there are women like yourself who will follow and marry no man but the man who seeks the whale — then man *shall* seek the whale.'

'Well — we'd best be getting back to the ship,' said quiet old Davy in his soft Shelty voice, but his cousin came into the room as we were leaving.

'Doctor — you're wanted on the phone. A transatlantic call.'

And I left the whalemen — maybe for ever — maybe for a while . . .

THE END